TRUE WORSHIP

*150 Days of Learning to Worship the
Father in Spirit and Truth*

By BUBBA STAHL, Pastor

August 7, 2015

True Worship
150 Days of Learning to Worship the Father in Spirit and Truth
by Bubba Stahl

Printed in the United States of America.

ISBN 9781498452960

www.xulonpress.com

Table of Contents

Introduction

Becoming a True Worshipper

God created you for a personal relationship with Him and for worship to be your primary characteristic. Worship is the single fruit of knowing God more and more through personal faith in Jesus Christ. There are many expressions and flavors of worship, but worship is the sole result of God's revelation of Himself to you through His Son, Jesus Christ.

King David was the worshiping king of Israel. He united the nation in worshiping God. He was after God's heart, as in pursuing God with a passion. He wrote more of the Bible than anyone and he only wrote one thing, worship songs to God, about God, for God. The psalms that David did not write were written for him. The book of Psalms is his book, the worship book of the Bible. It is the longest book of the Bible and is quoted more in the New Testament than any other Old Testament book.

Every occasion in David's life was an occasion to see the greatness, the power, and the goodness of God. When the lion and the bear threatened his life and the life of the sheep he cared for, David as a young shepherd boy, was filled with courageous rage, fueled by his love for God, and attacked them, and killed them. His passion for God was greater than his fear of physical harm. Later, when King Saul and the army of Israel were overcome with fear by the ranting and raving of Goliath, David was offended that God's Name was being defiled and was filled with contempt for the Philistine champion. Again, David's love for God was greater than his fear of the giant and the armies of the Philistines; attacking Goliath was a worship experience for him. David came against the enemies of God, in the Name of the Lord of hosts, and wrote songs about it.

David worshiped God in all circumstances. When he brought the Ark into Jerusalem, one of his best days, he worshiped God. When David and his men returned to Ziklag and found everything destroyed and all of their families gone (his own men broke down and wept and plotted to kill David), one of his worst days, David worshiped God. Worship was the chief characteristic of his life. Worship was greater than anything else in his life. It defined his life.

The Son of David, the Lord Jesus Christ, based His whole Life on glorifying (worshiping) the Father in Spirit and Truth. He said that the Father was looking for true worshipers. Jesus taught us to pray with the priority of worship. He worshiped the Father on the Mount of Transfiguration as well as the hill called Calvary.

So how can you make this year, a year of worship, the priority of your day, and the chief characteristic of your life? First, know that this is something to pray for, earnestly. Ask the Holy Spirit to teach you and to lead you into worshiping the Father and the Son with His burning passion of love for His word and for Him. Choose to become and desire to become a true worshiper.

Know that if the Holy Spirit is to be your teacher and guide, it will be His Word, the Bible, where you will learn and are shaped as you worship each day. Make time at the beginning of your day (for some this is early in the morning, for others it is late at night) to sit before the Lord, to present yourself before the Lord, and worship Him. This is done with an open Bible, an open ear, a focused mind, a learning spirit, and a loving heart for God.

Begin your time with God each day with a Psalm. This is the worship book of the Bible. There are 150 psalms, one for each day in a five-month cycle. Let that psalm lead you to worship God and to set the thermostat of your time in God's presence. Psalm 119 is the longest chapter in the Bible and is in its entirety a song of worship to God for His word. It is divided up into twenty-two, eight-verse sections. Each day, supplement the psalm for the day with a section from Psalm 119. Stay with that eight-verse section for one week before going on to the next section.

Praying through the Psalms will take 150 days, or twenty-one weeks. Supplementing one section of Psalm 119 with the Psalm for the day will take twenty-two weeks. Take one or more verses from that section of Psalm 119, put it in your heart for the day by memorizing it, and pray it throughout the day. In doing so you will stay in the atmosphere of worship and prayer throughout your day. Let that verse or verses be the last thing you meditate upon as you go to sleep and the first thing you set your mind on when you awake.

Included in the psalm for the day is a reading from Proverbs, the gospels, and the New Testament letters. In following this plan, you will read the entire New Testament during the next 150 days. Number the gospel and New Testament letters readings each day to correspond to the Psalm for the day. In doing this, you will be able to continue following Jesus with the account of His life and ministry, as well as continually learning from the apostles doctrine in the New Testament letters to the churches as you pray through the Psalms during future five-month readings.

Once you have completed the first 150-day cycle of praying the Psalms with the Proverb and New Testament readings, start over and add the reading marked as 2nd along with the New Testament readings. After the second 150-day cycle start over with the reading marked as 3rd. It is recommended that you always read in the gospels to be constantly following the life of Jesus. After completing the 4th reading and the 4th 150-day cycle through the Psalms you will have read the New Testament four times, prayed the Psalms four times, the book of Proverbs four times, and the Old Testament once; all in a 20-month period of time. Your whole Bible will have been marked with readings corresponding to the Psalms and you can start over.

This method of numbering the Proverbs, the New Testament, and Old Testament readings with the Psalms is almost impossible with the Bible on your phone or electronic device. You will need to use a Bible, with pages, and a cover. I suggest that you purchase a new Bible as you begin this daily time with God.

May God bless you as you begin to learn to worship the Father in spirit and truth and become a true worshiper.

Dedication Page

This book is dedicated to the pastors in Budaka, and Mayuge, Uganda. They were the first to hear the teachings in this book during pastors conferences held in their areas in January, 2015.

All of the royalties from the sale of this book will be given to Salt Block Ministries for mission work in Uganda and around the world. Visit us at www.saltblock.org.

> *"But the hour is coming and is now hear, when the true worshipers will worship the Father in spirit and truth, for the Father is seeking such people to worship him. God is spirit and those who worship him must worship him in spirit and truth."* John 4:23 – 24.

Acknowledgements

I would like to thank the ladies who edited the early drafts of this book; Margaret Stelly, RoseAnn Smith, and Amy Kitchens.

I would also like to thank the members of the seven churches where I have been privileged to serve as pastor for the past thirty-two years; Calvary Baptist Church in Rotan, Texas; New Prospect Baptist Church in Nemo, Texas; First Baptist Church in Breckenridge, Texas; Parkway Baptist Church in College Station, Texas; First Baptist Church in Boerne, Texas; First Baptist Church in Corpus Christi, Texas; and the First Baptist Church in Kingsland, Texas. These wonderful people encouraged me to read, study, pray, preach, and love God's Word.

God called me to preach on August 7, 1982. Within a few weeks we had moved from El Indio, Texas to Abilene and I had enrolled in Hardin-Simmons University. Within a few months I was called to be the pastor of Calvary Baptist Church in Rotan, Texas.

The summer of 1983 I was with our students at Youth Camp at the Big Country Baptist Assembly. Charles Culpepper was the Bible teacher that summer. He taught the adults while the students were in their Bible studies. He taught on the abundant life of Christ as life, the exchanged Life, the Grace-Life. It goes by several names, but the teaching rang true with me. I sat under Charles that week and learned of Major Ian Thomas and the Torch Bearers. I learned of Watchman Nee, Oswald Chambers, and other exchanged life teachers. Most of all, I learned that I was crucified with Christ and that it was not my life but His living in me, with me, through me, and as me before the Father and the watching world around me (Galatians 2:20). I would like to thank Charles Culpepper for putting me on the right trail of the Apostles Doctrine early in my ministry.

It has served me well and I have found that others have been liberated from the mud-pits of religion and legalism when they hear and receive the life-giving truth of Christ in you, the hope of glory.

I would like to thank my beautiful wife, Beth, for her encouragement, support, and partnership in ministry, and for her patience during the first nine months of 2015 while I wrote this book. Her sacrificial heart reveals God's love and the reality of Jesus Christ on a continual basis.

Most of all, I would like to thank God; the Father, the Son, and the Holy Spirit, for the calling, inspiration, revelation, and strength to write something for Him. I know in my heart that the Father is pleased. To Him be all the glory.

> *"Not to us, O LORD, not to us, but to your name give glory, for the sake of your steadfast love and your faithfulness!"* Psalm 115:1

Endorsement

I've treasured every interaction that I've had with Bubba. He always brings an encouraging word and a message of hope. I have every confidence that this book will, like its author, be a breath of fresh air.

— Max Lucado, pastor and bestselling author

How To Use This Book

The purpose of this book is to encourage and instruct you to worship the Father in spirit and truth. Jesus said, *"...for the Father is seeking such people to worship him. God is spirit, and those who worship him must worship him in spirit and truth."* John 4:23 – 24.[1] This book is primarily a workbook to guide you in learning to become a true worshiper, according to God's word.

The book of Psalms is the worship book of the Bible. Prayer is worship, therefore worship is prayer. This book will teach you to begin your personal worship time with the Father in His word beginning with a psalm, followed by readings from the New Testament and the Old Testament. God's word will shape and flavor your prayers, which pleases the Father. This is what it means to worship the Father in spirit and truth.

There are 150 psalms. When you pray one a day, you will pray through the Psalms in 150 days, in five months. Both Jews and Christians have worshiped privately and corporately with the Psalms using this method for thousands of years. This book is arranged to instruct and encourage you in this age-old practice.

This book also presents a Bible reading method for those who would like to try a new one, or for those who would like to begin one. Once again, it is arranged around the Psalms, reading and then praying a psalm each day corresponding to the day of the month. It includes a reading from the book of Proverbs, dividing Proverbs up into 150 readings. Also the gospels and Acts are divided into 150 readings, as well as the letters to the churches into 150 readings. The readings are given with each day's devotional thought.

Psalm 119 is the longest psalm and the longest chapter in the Bible. There are twenty-two prayer sections to this amazing chapter, one for each of the twenty-one weeks of praying through the Psalms. One section can supplement the psalm for the day. Staying with that particular section for seven days can be a primer for your prayer time.

One way to use this book is to read and pray the Psalm for the day along with the reading from Proverbs, the reading from the gospels and Acts, and the reading from the letters to the churches. This allows God to speak to you first in your personal prayer time. Begin your response, your prayer, with the prayer section from Psalm 119 for the week. Number the readings for Proverbs, the gospels/Acts, and the letters to the churches to correspond to the Psalm for the day with the first 150-day reading of Psalms. In doing this, you will have the New Testament marked for future readings to correspond with the Psalms. You will also have read the New Testament over a five-month period, as well as the Psalms and Proverbs, and you will have prayed Psalm 119. Continue this method of numbering with the Old Testament readings.

I recommend including the gospel/Acts readings each time as you read the Old Testament selections. You will already have them marked. One of the principles of interpretation is to understand the Old Testament through the lens of the Life of Jesus. He fulfilled the Law and the Prophets. You understand the partial in light of the fullness of Christ. In doing this, you will be following Jesus in the gospels everyday.

The devotional thought for the day is a supplement to reading and praying the Scriptures. Read and pray the Bible first. If you have time, read the devotional thought. If not, don't worry; you will be back on that page in five months. The most important and powerful thing to read is God's word. Always begin in God's word, not with the devotional thought. If you miss your prayer time for particular day, don't try to make it up the next day.

Stay with the psalm and reading that corresponds to the day of the month. When you miss a meal, you don't eat double the next meal. Marking your Bible to correspond to the Psalm for the day is key.

This book is a workbook to teach you and to guide you in a life-long method of personal prayer and worship time with God. God's word will shape your prayers if you ask Him to and allow His word to become your words to Him in prayerful worship. This is what it means to worship the Father in spirit and truth.

January 1

Read and pray Psalm 1, Proverbs 1:1 – 7, Matthew 1, Romans 1:1 – 17, Psalm 119:1 – 8.
2nd time praying through the Psalms; Genesis 1 – 2.
3rd time praying through the Psalms; Isaiah 1 – 2.
4th time praying through the Psalms; Joshua 1 – 2.

Worship With Purpose

Purpose means destination. Maybe you have heard about the conversation that a family had as they were driving down the highway. The child said to the father, "Daddy, when will we be there?" The father replied, "Be where, son? Where we are going? We are not going anywhere particular, son, but we are making good time."

There are many people today who live that way, with no particular destination in mind. There are many Christians today who do not know where they are going when it comes to worship; they worship but without a destination. Or worse, they do, but it is not where the Bible teaches worship should go.

When Jesus taught on true worship, new covenant worship, it was to a class of one; the Samaritan woman at Jacob's well (John 4:19 – 26). Her question about the right place of worship was legitimate. There was a great debate between the Jews and the Samaritans about worship in that day. The so called "worship wars" have been around much longer than recent times.

The Samaritans lived in the heart of the Promised Land. Sychar was less than a mile from the place where Abraham built the first altar in the Promised Land (Genesis 12:6-7). It was the first place of worship. It was the second "purchased" plot of ground of the Promised Land (Genesis 23, the first; Genesis 33:18 – 20, the second), and Jacob worshiped there, at Shechem. Moses told the elders of Israel that when they crossed over into the Promised Land they were to build an altar on Mount Ebal and were to write on the stones the whole law. Half of the people were to stand on top of Mt. Ebal and the other half on Mt. Gerizim, and they were to declare the blessings and the curses of the law. Sychar was in between these two mountains. It was one of the earliest places of worship for Israel in the Promised Land. The Samaritans claimed it as the place of true worship.

The Jews claimed that Jerusalem was the only true place of worship. The worship leader of the Jews, king David, had united the twelve tribes with worship, according to God's word, at Jerusalem. He had purchased the place of worship, the threshing floor of Araunah, which became the building site for the Temple. It was the same site that Abraham had offered up Isaac hundreds of years earlier (Genesis 22). The Samaritans were part of the "split" that occurred following the death of king Solomon (1 Kings 12). The tribes of Benjamin and Judah who had survived the Exile, returned to Jerusalem and had rebuilt the Temple on the same site as Solomon's Temple. It had to be the true place of worship. And so the argument went on and on.

Jesus told the woman of Sychar that the time had come when neither place was the right place. Jesus introduced a new place when He said, *"...true worshipers will worship the Father in spirit and truth, for the Father is seeking such people to worship him. God is spirit, and those who worship him must worship him in spirit and truth."* John 4:23-24.

So, where is that place? Jesus answered the question in John 4:25-26, *"The woman said to him, 'I know that Messiah is coming (he who is called the Christ). When he comes, he will tell us all things.' Jesus said to her, 'I who speak to you am he.'"* With that answer, Jesus teaches the first and most important truth for those who desire to learn true worship; He gives the purpose of true worship by revealing the destination of true worship.

In those verses Jesus reveals Himself to this woman as the true Messiah, the Christ. Jesus Christ is the place, purpose, and destination of true worship. The Samaritan woman left her water jar and ran into the city as the first evangelist in John's gospel. The whole town came out to meet Jesus and declared Him the Savior of the world. Jesus stayed with them an additional two days, according to 4:39-43. Can you imagine attending that two-day discipleship conference?

Here is the point: The revelation of Jesus Christ is the place and destination of true worship. It begins and ends in Christ. Jesus reveals Himself to those who are worshiping the Father in spirit and in truth. He is the purpose of worship. He is also the leader and teacher of true worship. He is also the object of true worship, for He and the Father are one. Hallelujah.

If you desire to know Christ more and more, know that there is only one way; learn to worship the Father in spirit and truth, because the place, purpose, and destination of true worship is the revelation of Jesus Christ of Himself to true worshipers, those who worship the Father in spirit and truth. So what does "in spirit and truth" mean? That, my friend, is the question you will find the answer to as you allow God's word to shape your time with Him. Pray Psalm 119:1 – 8. Memorize 119:1 and form it into a prayer for your day.

January 2

Read and pray Psalm 2, Proverbs 1:8 – 15, Matthew 2, Romans 1:18 – 32, Psalm 119:1 – 8.
2nd Genesis 3 – 4.
3rd Isaiah 3 – 4.
4th Joshua 3 – 4.

God's Order for Worship

When you use the word "worship" you may think of the order of worship in a worship service. Or you may think of the music of the worship service. Both of these are helpful but only if you keep them in their place as servants to help in worship. Both have been made into the focus of worship, which is idolatry.

Jesus told the woman of Sychar at Jacob's well, *"God is spirit, and those who worship him must worship him in spirit and truth."* John 4:24. This is God's order for worship. But what does that mean? There is actually a word in Romans 12:1-2 for an order of worship, *"...to present your bodies as a living sacrifice, holy and acceptable to God, which is your spiritual worship."* The phrase "spiritual worship," is the Greek word *latreuo*[2], which literally means "rules for worship," or the worship guide. We get our English word "liturgy" from this word. It is used in several places in the New Testament.

In Hebrews 9:1 it is used to describe the rules for Old Testament worship, *"Now even the first covenant had regulations for worship..."* The phrase "regulations for worship," is the word *latreuo*. Also in Hebrews 12:28, *"Therefore let us be grateful for receiving a kingdom that cannot be shaken, and thus let us offer to God acceptable worship, with reverence and awe, for our God is a consuming fire."* In this verse, the word *latreuo,* is simply translated "worship" with the understanding that this is something we offer to God. It is the activity of giving God something.

Now, back to Romans 12:1-2. In this passage, this word is translated different ways depending upon which translation you have. It may say "reasonable service," or "spiritual worship," or "rational service." It is the word *latreuo.* So what does it mean? One thing is for sure, Romans 12:1-2 defines it for us. *"Therefore, brethren, I appeal to you by the mercies of God, to present your bodies as a living sacrifice, holy and acceptable to God, which is your spiritual worship. Do not be conformed to this world, but be transformed by the renewal of your mind, that by testing you may discern what is the good and acceptable and perfect will of God."*

Know this, as you sit down with your open Bible each day for your personal time of worship, you are presenting yourself before God as a living sacrifice in Christ, who makes you holy and acceptable to the Father. This is what it means to worship the Father in spirit and truth.

January 3

Read and pray Psalm 3, Proverbs 1:16 – 19, Matthew 3, Romans 2, Psalm 119:1 – 8.
2nd Genesis 5 – 6.
3rd Isaiah 5 – 6.
4th Joshua 5 – 6.

The Foundation of Worship

Jesus fulfilled the Old Covenant and established the New Covenant in Himself. The foundation of the New Covenant is the new relationship with the Father through faith in Christ. The foundational expression of that new relationship is true worship. In John 4:19-26, Jesus lays the foundation of true worship.

Builders know that the foundation of a building is the most important part, for if the foundation is off, the whole building will be faulty regardless of how well it is built. Everything rests upon the foundation. Jesus ended the Sermon on the Mount with the story of two builders, one who built upon a true foundation, and the other who built upon a false foundation. You remember the outcome (Matthew 7:24-27).

As in the parable, it is hearing and doing the words of Jesus that assures you of the true foundation for worship. Jesus said we must worship the Father. The word "must" is the same word He used in His conversation with Nicodemus in John 3:3 when He said, *"You must be born from above."* It is also the same word He spoke to His parents when they found him in the Temple with the teachers and Jesus said, *"Did you not know that I must be about my Father's business?"* Luke 2:41-51. And again in John 4:4, the same word is used when Jesus told His disciples that they must go through Samaria.

You must get this right, worshiping the Father. It is foundational. God created you to worship Him and through faith in Christ you have been recreated. The new creation has begun in you with new life in Christ. And the foundation of the new creation is true worship. It is the first activity of the new birth and it is the essence of the Father's business, which is why Jesus had to go through Samaria. It is also something to learn from Christ, according to His Word.

Pray, "Lord Jesus, teach me to become a true worshiper of the Father and what it means to worship the Father in spirit and truth. I must learn this. I deeply desire to learn this. Nothing else will be right until I understand this and do it. Here I am, in Your class, Worship 101. Teach me, Lord, Your servant is listening." AMEN.

Memorize some more of Psalm 119:1 – 8 and add it to this prayer today.

January 4

Read and pray Psalm 4, Proverbs 1:20 – 23, Matthew 4, and Romans 3, Psalm 119:1 – 8.
2nd Genesis 7 – 8.
3rd Isaiah 7 – 8.
4th Joshua 7 – 8.

Worship is a Response to God

In Romans 12:1-2, you find clear instructions on worshiping the Father in spirit and truth. The first word, in most translations, gives the most light, and is often overlooked. It is the word "Therefore." The little Greek word *dia* is translated "therefore." This word underlines one of the important principles of interpretation, which is to know the context. The word *dia,* means "in the light of what has just been said, here is what you are to do." Whenever you read the word "therefore" get ready for instructions from God for a response on your part to what He has just said.

One of the ways of God is that He always gives instructions with His gifts. Every gift comes with His instructions. The gift, or grace, of His word, and the revelation of spiritual truth from His word, comes with instructions. These instructions are invitations to join Him in the creative work of His word in your life.

God does not threaten in order to manipulate, He invites. He does not offer something that He cannot produce, He invites with a promise of what He will do. Faith believes that God can provide what He has promised. Faith is the response to the invitation of God. The invitation of God, the revelation of Himself in His word, has the faith for responding in it for the one who will receive it.

God invites you to worship Him in spirit and truth. These two words, "spirit and truth" best summarize what Romans 1 – 11 reveals about God. Everything that God has said about Himself in these eleven chapters invites you to worship Him in spirit and truth. In the light of the overwhelming brilliance of the multi-faceted mercies of God, you are invited into the presence of the God and Father in the Name of the Lord Jesus Christ. Hallelujah.

January 5

Read and pray Psalm 5, Proverbs 1:24 – 33, Matthew 5, Romans 4, Psalm 119:1 – 8.
2nd Genesis 9 – 10.
3rd Isaiah 9 – 10.
4th Joshua 9 – 10.

Full or Empty Worship

In Matthew 15:7 – 9, Jesus rebuked the scribes and Pharisees for their hypocrisy and called their worship empty and vain. He said, quoting Isaiah 29:13, *"These people honor me with their lips, but their heart is far from me. In vain do they worship me, teaching as doctrines the commandments of men."*

According to Jesus, you can go through the sounds and motions of worship, but not be worshiping. The difference between full and empty worship is huge to God, and should be to you if you desire to worship the Father in spirit and truth. This is who the Father is seeking to worship Him.

The two verses in Romans 12:1 – 2 are a gold mine of spiritual truth and instruction on full worship. There is a phrase that connects verse one to verse two that is instructive. In between the instruction about presenting your body and your mind is the phrase, *"...which is your spiritual worship."* The two words "spiritual worship" in Greek are *logikos latreia.* We get our English word "logic" from the first one and our word "liturgy" from the second. Some translators will translate this phrase *"...which is your reasonable worship."*

The Greeks viewed logic and reason as truth. It was mathematical in its form and function for arriving at conclusions. They considered it to be true, genuine, and real. This word *logikos* is the Greek word for logic, built upon the word *logos*, which also means "true or full word." The word *latreia*, means the order and activity of worship. Again, our English word "liturgy" is from this word. A liturgy is the order and act of worship in churches today.

In this phrase in Romans 12:1, *"...which is your logikos latreia,"* you understand that Paul is describing true and full worship. This is what you desire to learn. This is what Jesus was talking about with the woman of Sychar in John 4. This is full worship; true, real, and genuine. Today, ask the Holy Spirit to teach you what it means to worship the Father in spirit and truth. Memorize and meditate on more verses from Psalm 119:1 – 8 with that prayer.

January 6

Read and pray Psalm 6, Proverbs 2:1 – 10, Matthew 6, Romans 5:1 – 11, Psalm 119:1 – 8.
2nd Genesis 11 – 12.
3rd Isaiah 11 – 12.
4th Joshua 11 – 12.

Faith Pleases the Father

Romans 12:1 – 2 begins with the word "Therefore," which means in the light of what has just been said, here is what you are now to do. "Therefore" introduces obedience from what has just been said. This is the definition of faith, which is why you find the phrase "the obedience of faith" at the beginning and end of Romans (1:5, 16:26).

Obedience is the fruit of the word that God has just spoken. It proves that the word has been received into the good soil of the heart. The Hebrew language had a word for this kind of "hearing," the kind that produced the fruit of obedience. It is the word *shemah*, and is translated as "hear" in the Old Testament. But it is also translated as "obey." For the Hebrews, hearing was inseparable from obeying; first you hear, then you obey. The two are one. This is called being faithful. It is also one of the ways of God; first He says it, then He does it. This is why faithfulness pleases God; He sees Himself in it, and God is fully pleased in Himself.

True worship is full of faith only when it is the result of the revelation of God, which is why worship based upon man's rules and word is empty. Man's rules and word may be good and pleasing to man, but it is man's, and not God's. Worshipers may be very sincere and obedient to man's rules and word and still have nothing that pleases the Father because their worship is void of His word.

When you begin to see (this is a revelation) that the obedience that pleases the Father does not come from you, but rather from His word, your whole focus and purpose changes from man-centered (with you or others as the focus), to God-centered (with Christ as the focus). When this happens, you have taken the first step toward pleasing the Father, because He is totally Christ-centered. This fills worship with God. And, this is what it means to worship the Father in spirit and truth.

January 7

Read and pray Psalm 7, Proverbs 2:11 – 19, Matthew 7, Romans 5:12 – 21, Psalm 119:1 – 8.
2nd Genesis 13 – 14.
3rd Isaiah 13 – 14.
4th Joshua 13 – 14.

Questions and Anger For Worship

The Q&A in the discussion of true worship has to do with "questions and anger," rather than "questions and answers." In many of the Psalms, David would present his questions and anger to the Lord because he could not find any answers. If you are to be honest with God, and you should since He knows your true heart anyway, you will sometimes come before Him with unanswered questions and even with anger because of the situation that you are in. God's word gives guidance through those troubling times.

David would go before God with *"Why, O LORD, do you stand far away? Why do you hide yourself in times of trouble?"* Have you ever been there? We all have. This is how David began his time of worship with God in Psalm 10. Other times he began with *"How long, O LORD? Will you forget me forever?"* If you have never lived in Psalm 13 for a season, the question may seem strange, but in the frustrating times of those seasons in life, that question may be all you can bring to God. So is that still worship? How do you worship God with Q&A like that? Know this, not only can you, but you must.

One reason you must learn to worship with Q&A is that others are not able to answer questions like that, and they sure can't handle your anger. The danger of those seasons in life is that you turn to others for answers with your anger. This never ends well. Or you will suppress the anger in order to just "live with the questions," telling yourself to "just get over it." This becomes the pressure cooker for depression. You cannot manage the anger of others any more than you can manage your own. But God can and does, if you will present yourself to Him, Q&A and all. This is what it means to worship the Father in spirit and truth. This is what being a true worshiper looks like.

During those seasons, present yourself to the Lord, Q&A and all, and worship, even if all you have are big questions and anger. Give it to Him by giving yourself to Him. God can handle it, because He knows you and loves you. Together, you and God can work through those troubling times.

Our problem is that we give up on God, get tired of waiting, and cave to the temptation to take matters into our own hands. But by giving yourself to God, Q&A and all, you are trusting that He will handle you, and lead you to see that He is greater than the big questions and much greater than your anger. Give it all to Jesus! He can take it, in fact, He did, on the cross. Once you get there, you are on the holy ground of worshiping the Father in spirit and truth.

Today, if you are covered up with Q&A, let David teach you how to worship with it. He learned and so can you. If you are not there today, you probably know someone who is. Pray for them. Be there for them, but don't attempt to answer their questions and for sure do not receive their anger. Encourage them that they can trust God, especially with Q&A. Pray Psalm 119:1 – 8 one more time. Tomorrow you will begin the next section, Psalm 119:9 – 16.

January 8

Read and pray Psalm 8, Proverbs 2:20 – 22, Matthew 8, Romans 6, Psalm 119:9 – 16.
2nd Genesis 15 – 16.
3rd Isaiah 15 – 16.
4th Joshua 15 – 16.

True Worship and Sacrifice

From the very beginning, sacrifice, the giving of innocent life in the place of the guilty, has been the main element in worship. In Genesis 3:21, the Bible states that God made garments of animal skins for Adam and Eve. God provided the first sacrifice. Cain and Abel worshiped God through sacrifice (one was full with faith, the other was empty without faith). Noah and Abram built altars and worshiped with sacrifice. God gave Moses specific instructions concerning worship, all centered upon sacrifice, the giving of innocent life in the place of the guilty. But why worship through sacrifice?

All of the Old Testament instructions concerning sacrifice were fulfilled in the Lord Jesus Christ, the Lamb of God who takes away the sin of the world. The Father could see the Son in the shadows of the Old Testament sacrifices, and it pleased Him. Sacrifice reveals the heart of God. He is love.

When the Lord Jesus poured out His holy life on the cross to pay the penalty for your sins and mine, it pleased the Father (Isaiah 53:10) because it fully revealed the heart and love of the Father toward you and me. The Father rewarded His Son by raising Him from the dead and giving eternal life with Himself, revealing the heart and love of the Father toward the Son.

This life is yours through faith in Christ, if you are willing to believe that in Christ you can die to sin and be rewarded, now, with eternal life with God. This is sacrifice, and it is the true worship that the Father is seeking today.

The Father sees Himself in the sacrifice of His Son, and through faith, your faith in Him, it pleases Him. The reward is an intimate, personal, and eternal relationship with Him. Today, thank the Father for sending His Son to die your death and to give His life to you. This is a confession of truth, which pleases the Father when He hears it from your heart. This is what it means to worship the Father in spirit and truth. Memorize Psalm 119:9 and pray it throughout this day.

January 9

Read and pray Psalm 9, Proverbs 3:1 – 4, Matthew 9, Romans 7, Psalm 119:9 – 16.
2ⁿᵈ Genesis 17 – 18.
3ʳᵈ Isaiah 17 – 18.
4ᵗʰ Joshua 17 – 18.

What is a Living Sacrifice?

God is pleased with sacrifice only when it is according to His word. Many different religions practice sacrifice as worship, but like Cain's sacrifice, they are empty because they lack what God is looking for; His word.

But Romans 12:1 – 2 states that God is pleased with a holy, acceptable, and living sacrifice. He rewards it with the revelation of His good, pleasing, and perfect will. And so, what is the living sacrifice that is pleasing to God?

The key word is "living" and comes from the Greek word *zoe*, which means something that has life in it. In this case, it is a sacrifice that has life in it; holy and acceptable life. In John 6:51, Jesus called Himself *the living bread*, referring to the holy life in His body, which He would give for the life of the world. Taken out of context, the phrase "living bread" would have the meaning of bread that had weevils in it or something else alive.

The living sacrifice that God is looking for is the life of His Son, Jesus Christ, living in my body. This is the holy and pleasing (acceptable) life that abides in you who have been born from above. It is the life of God, the Holy Spirit.

But a sacrifice is something that is given to God in death. God's word does not instruct you to present Christ in you as a sacrifice, but rather your body as the sacrifice, which has the life of Christ. Your mind and your body have sin in it (Romans 7:17 – 20), even though the penalty for your sins has been paid in full by Jesus Christ and His death on the cross, the power of sin is still active in you. This is the conflict between the Spirit and the flesh that Paul so often describes (Galatians 5:16 – 26). Paul gives instructions for overcoming the power of sin in you in Romans 6. In 12:1 – 2 he gives instructions for true worship as you present your body under the search light of the Holy Spirit to reveal sin to turn away from (gift of repentance) by seeing it for the deadly, destructive, deceiving thing that it is. This is an act of true worship.

Ask the Holy Spirit to reveal to you lies that you have believed and sin that you have accepted and tolerated. Sacrifice it as you see Jesus on the cross paying the penalty of it. Let this be a daily act of worship. God is pleased with this because He sees His Son in it, and the great sacrifice He paid to remove it as far as the east is from the west. Hallelujah.

January 10

Read and pray Psalm 10, Proverbs 3:5 – 12, Matthew 10, Romans 8:1 – 11, Psalm 119:9 – 16.
2ⁿᵈ Genesis 19 – 20.
3ʳᵈ Isaiah 19 – 20.
4ᵗʰ Joshua 19 – 20.

Repentant-Worship

When you hear the word "repentance" what do you think of? Some may think of someone with drooped shoulders, a downward look, tears of regret and sorrow. Sadness is often associated with repentance. But the Greek word *metanoia* does not have the element of sorrow. It means to change your mind and direction. If anything, there is the note of joy in it for having discovered a better way. Repentance is a gift from God when He reveals to you His thoughts and ways (which are not our ways and thoughts; Isaiah 55:8 – 9).

We bring in the element of sorrow because when God reveals His thoughts and ways to you, you feel regret and sorrow for having sinned and grieved the Holy Spirit. But until God reveals His thoughts and ways to you, you will do nothing but sin. When He does, there is presented to you a choice, good and evil. The gift of repentance is that choice. When received by faith, God's ways are chosen, and His good and pleasing and perfect will is known for what it is; good and pleasing and perfect. When rejected, His good and pleasing and perfect will is rejected and never known or experienced. Wrong choice.

Repentant-worship is receiving the revelation of God in His presence and the gift of His thoughts and ways (the gift of repentance), and then with joy, forsaking your old thoughts and ways and joining God in His. There may be tears, but they will be tears of joy.

Jesus told a parable in Matthew 13:44 about a man who discovered treasure in a field, and for joy went and sold all that he had, and bought that field. There was no remorse or regret in having sold all that he had. There was joy because he had discovered something greater than all that he had.

When God reveals Himself to you, His thoughts and ways, it is a gift, the gift of repentance; and new thoughts, His thoughts and new ways, His ways, are offered to you. When you receive His revelation, you receive the gift of repentance. Giving thanks for this gift is worship. It is true worship. Memorize and meditate on more of Psalm 119:9 – 16 for today's prayer and worship.

January 11

Read and pray Psalm 11, Proverbs 3:13 – 18, Matthew 11, Romans 8:12 – 39, Psalm 119:9 – 16.
2nd Genesis 21 – 22.
3rd Isaiah 21 – 22.
4th Joshua 21 – 22.

Model For True Worship; Communion

When Jesus gave His disciples what we call the Lord's Supper, or Communion, He was giving them a new model for worship, just as He did with the model prayer. The old covenant had a prescribed way to worship, which Jesus fulfilled. The new covenant likewise has a new way to worship, which Jesus modeled and taught his followers in the upper room on that Passover Eve.

It was out of the Passover meal that Jesus formed the new pattern. The Passover was the first corporate worship experience the nation of Israel was given. Before it, individuals worshiped God with sacrifice, but now God was creating a nation for Himself, from which all the nations of the earth would be blessed. Their first activity as a nation of God and for God was worship, according to His word. Jesus, the promised off-spring of Abraham, Isaac, and Jacob, was now on the scene and the new covenant was now inaugurated.

With the new covenant established, a new worship was also begun, in line with old, but new. Like the old, it would be based on the ground of redemption through sacrifice. The old was established with the blood of a lamb which believers applied to their door posts, according to God's word. The sacrificial death and flesh (the lamb was eaten) of that lamb liberated the believers from the bondage of slavery and led them out of Egypt, and into the Promised Land.

The new covenant worship is also based upon the blood of the Lamb, the Lamb of God, which takes away the sins of the world. It is by His blood that we are set free from the penalty of our sins and the power of sin. But we do not leave a land; we leave a bloodline, the bloodline of Adam, to a new humanity, to Christ Jesus, the last Adam (1 Corinthians 15:45). And like the old, you too must eat the Lamb; you receive Jesus Christ. His life becomes your new life, and you are born from above, like Him. It is in Him that you now walk toward the Promised Land, your resurrection body.

Like the old, all of this is by faith in what God has said. The slaves in Egypt heard the word of God, believed, and obeyed. The slaves of sin hear the gospel, believe, and receive Christ. The old covenant worship was by faith in what God had said and the new covenant worship is by faith in what Christ has done. God the Son has given His followers the foundation upon which all new covenant worship rests. It rests upon Him and His death and resurrection from the dead. Your response, the first act of worship, is to believe.

January 12

Read and pray Psalm 12, Proverbs 3:19 – 26, Matthew 12:1 – 21, Romans 9, Psalm 119:9 – 16.
2nd Genesis 23 – 24.
3rd Isaiah 23 – 24.
4th Joshua 23 – 24.

True Worship and Communion; Part 2

There are five accounts in the New Testament of the Lord's Supper in the upper room; Matthew 26, Mark 14, Luke 22, John 13-17, and the earliest, 1 Corinthians 11. All five give you a model for becoming a true worshiper of the Father in spirit and in truth.

When Jesus took the bread and wine of the Passover celebration and created the foundation of true worship, He defined true worship as a faithful and sacrificial response to the word and work of God; to the revelation of Himself in Christ. Response is a key word because worship begins with God's activity, his work, which always follows His word. First He says it, then He does it. This is one of the ways of God. He is faithful to His own word, always. He defines faithful. He is faithful. He speaks, then does what He said. In creation, He said, *"Let there be light...,"* then He did it, *"...and there was light."*

God's word and work reveal His nature and character. As Jesus stood before His disciples in the upper room with the pieces of the Passover meal on the table, He spoke the New Creation into being with the bread and the wine, then went out and did it. By His sacrifice on the cross, Jesus paid in full the penalty for your sins and opened the way back into perfect fellowship and communion with the Father. This is true worship.

True worship is a faithful and sacrificial response to His words and work of salvation in the new creation. True worship celebrates who Christ is according to what He has said and done. He is faithful and mighty to save.

Trusting Christ is a sacrifice because he calls you away from the world, the flesh, and the devil. As you trust Him, you turn away from the world, just as the Israelites did from Egypt, in order to follow Him. This turning-trust is your first act of worship and is based upon His faithful sacrifice for you. The result of this true worship is communion with God, which is fellowship in Christ. Hallelujah.

January 13

Read and pray Psalm 13, Proverbs 3:27 – 35, Matthew 12:22 – 50, Romans 10, Psalm 119:9 – 16.
2nd Genesis 25 – 26.
3rd Isaiah 25 – 26.
4th Judges 1 – 2.

True Worship and Communion; Part 3

Worship is the faithful and sacrificial response to the gracious revelation of God in Christ. Jesus fulfilled worship, and so it is only in Him that you truly worship. He is the complete revelation of the Father, in Spirit, and Truth.

When you turn away from the world, the flesh, and the devil with the trusting-turn, because of God's revelation, you have begun your walk of worship towards knowing Jesus Christ in order to worship Him. Like the wise men in Matthew 2:2, you can also truly say, "I am here to worship Him." But like the wise men, you also are on a learning curve. They needed more information. They came to Jerusalem, but did not find the newborn King. When worship is your purpose for being here, you are in a constant state of learning; learning more and more about the one you worship, the Lord Jesus Christ. Unfortunately, many have dropped out of the school of worship in order to pursue other amusements that appeal more to the flesh.

Back to the upper room. When Jesus took the bread and the wine and created the new model for worship, He was teaching. John's account brings this out with clarity. John devoted a fourth of his account of the gospel to the upper room teaching on the Holy Spirit and worship. It was around the table, with the pieces of the Passover, the bread and the wine, that Jesus gave new meaning to worship. The upper room had become their classroom.

Some of you may recoil by the next statement, but consider this: true worship is about you and what you are receiving from the Lord in the way of knowledge. I use the word "knowledge" in the Hebrew definition of the word *yadah,* which means an intimate, interactive, creative relationship. In the Old Testament, when you "knew" something or someone, you and it, or they, were personally involved with each other and something new was the result. *"Adam knew his wife, Eve, and she gave birth to a son…,"* Genesis 4:25.

If you are not learning and knowing Jesus Christ more and more, you are not yet to the place of worship. He is that place, and in Him you learn and something new is created in your life, HIS LIFE! And His life gives the Father great pleasure. This is true worship. Declare this truth to the Father in prayer: Jesus Christ gave His life for me in order to live His life in me, with me, through me, as me, before the Father and the watching world around me.

One more day of praying Psalm 119:9 – 16. Memorize and meditate on more of it today.

January 14

Read and pray Psalm 14, Proverbs 4:1 – 9, Matthew 13, Romans 11, Psalm 119:9 – 16.
2nd Genesis 27 – 28.
3rd Isaiah 27 – 28.
4th Judges 3 – 4.

True Worship and Communion; Part 4

In the upper room, on the night that Jesus was betrayed, with the pieces of the Passover meal on the table, Jesus created a new model for worship for the new covenant in Himself. In the Old Testament, God gave the nation of Israel the model for worship in Exodus 19-20 after He had delivered them out of the bondage of slavery in Egypt on their way to the Promised Land. The old covenant worship was based upon sacrifice conducted by Aaron, the high priest, and his sons. The nation of Israel had to first learn the model, and then do it in order to come before God and worship. In the upper room Jesus taught his disciples the new model for the new covenant, fulfilling the old. First they needed to learn it, and then they would do it. But what would they be doing once they learned it?

The Apostle Paul gives one of the clearest presentations of this new form of worship for the followers of Christ in Romans 6. In that chapter he states that we must first "know" something (6:3-11). Paul uses four different Greek words for "know" in that passage, each one with a greater depth of knowledge (6:3, 6, 9, 11). In other words, as you begin to study and explore the death, burial, and resurrection of Christ, you begin to understand with greater and greater depth that you died with Him, were buried with Him, and rose with Him. His sacrifice was for you but not without you.

This mind-blowing truth sets you freer and freer from the power of sin as you daily present yourself before God just as the Old Testament worshipers would present the prescribed sacrifices to the high priest at the altar before the Tabernacle and later the Temple.

The word "present" is the Greek word, ***paristemi,*** and was used to describe the position of a servant, standing beside his/her master, ready to serve. This position was at the right elbow of the master, just behind the master, ready to hear the next command in order to quickly obey. It was also used in the Greek translation of the Old Testament of worshipers standing before God with their sacrifices.

Paul uses this word "present" five times in Romans 6 (verses 13, 16, 19, and again in 12:1) to describe the position of one who has learned to worship according to God's word. This is what a true worshiper does each day after learning the new model to worship the Father in spirit and in truth. As a living sacrifice (12:1-2) in Christ, you stand before the Father in Christ, as His servant, ready to obey His word. Jesus taught this in the upper room in John 13-16, and then did it Himself in His prayer in John 17, and work of salvation in John 18-20.

Summary: The new worship model is found in Christ, the once-for-all sacrifice for you (but not without you). Faith immerses you in this truth and you rise to worship the Father in the spirit and in this truth by first learning it, studying it, and then doing it by presenting yourself in Christ before the Father daily. Each day, and throughout the day, becomes an experience of worshiping the Father in spirit and in truth.

Spend some time today in Romans 6 and 12:1-2 asking the Holy Spirit to teach you what Jesus meant when he said, *"...the hour is now here when true worshipers will worship the Father in spirit and in truth, for the Father is seeking such people to worship him."* John 4:23

January 15

Read and pray Psalm 15, Proverbs 4:10 – 12, Matthew 14, Romans 12, Psalm 119:17 – 24.
2nd Genesis 29 – 30.
3rd Isaiah 29 – 30.
4th Judges 5 – 6.

What Pleases the Father?

The foundation of sacrifice in the Old Testament and the New is the seriousness of sin and the solution of God for it, which is sacrifice. The first sacrifice in the Bible was by God on behalf of Adam and Eve. In Genesis 3:21, it states that God provided for Adam and Eve animal skins for clothing. Innocent animals died at the hand of God to cover the shame and sin of Adam and Eve. With this sacrifice, Adam and Eve learned God's solution for sin. They in turn taught their sons this practice. Sacrifice pleases God because it was His will and creation. But not all sacrifice pleases Him.

In Genesis 4:1-7, Cain and Abel brought their sacrifices before the Lord. Both grain and livestock sacrifices were legitimate sacrifices, but in Genesis 4:4-5 it says that God had regard for Abel's sacrifice but had no regard for Cain's.

The Hebrew word for "had regard" means to gaze upon and look at something with amazement, joy, and pleasure. When that word carries a negative prefix (no regard) it means blindness. Somehow Cain knew that something was missing from his sacrifice, that God was blind to it. God spoke to Cain about it, giving him instruction how to correct it, but Cain refused to follow God's instruction (had no regard for what God said), and took matters into his own hands, and we know the rest of the story.

So what was it that pleased the Father with Abel's sacrifice but was missing from Cain's? The answer is found in Hebrews 11:4-6. Abel sacrificed by faith in what God said, believing that this was something that God desired according to his instructions. Cain just sacrificed; same activity, but totally different motive, purpose, and outcome. God could see Abel's faith in his sacrifice but could not see any faith in Cain's. Hebrews 11:6 states it clearly, a verse you may have memorized, *"And without faith it is impossible to please him, for whoever would draw near to God must believe that he exists and that he rewards those who seek him."*

This is the same thing that God is seeking to see today. Sacrifice and worship are still inseparable, but not just any sacrifice. The sacrifice that the Father is looking for is the kind that pleases Him, and there is only one kind that pleases Him, the sacrifice by faith in Him, faith in what He has said and done through Christ Jesus, His Son. This faith pleases him because He sees Himself in it; His word in your life, His creation in a person. Jesus Christ in you, with you, living His life through you, as you, before the Father, and the watching world around you.

When Jesus told the woman at the well that the hour had come for true worship to be in Him, in spirit and in truth, and that this was what the Father was seeking, she believed Him and became a true worshiper. And as a result, she became obedient from her heart. This is true worship.

January 16

Read and pray Psalm 16, Proverbs 4:13 – 19, Matthew 15, Romans 13, Psalm 119:17 – 24.
2nd Genesis 31 – 32.
3rd Isaiah 31 – 32.
4th Judges 7 – 8.

Light From Servant Thoughts

Servant-thoughts inform good, acceptable, and perfect choices according to the word of God. They originate from the Holy Spirit who lives in you, with you, through you, as you, before the Father and the watching world around you. They are on fire with God's glory and reveal the life of the Lord Jesus Christ.

As the Spirit of Christ (who lives in you, with you, through you...) speaks, according to the word of God, these fiery thoughts give birth to faith for choosing the good, acceptable, and perfect choice of God. The knowledge of good and evil is clearly seen (experienced) and the good, acceptable, and perfect will of God is known and chosen.

Your will becomes God's will, through faith born from God's word, and you know Christ more and more from His life living in you, with you, through you, as you, before the Father and the watching world around you. The gift of the light of these fiery-servant-thoughts guides your steps. This is called wisdom in the Bible. Desire it, but know where it comes from and how you receive it. Servant-thoughts, on fire with God's word and glory, from and for Christ, will serve you today.

Memorize a verse or two from Psalm 119:17 – 24 and pray it throughout the day. Servant-thoughts are birthed from God's word in your heart and head.

January 17

Read and pray Psalm 17, Proverbs 4:20 – 23, Matthew 16, Romans 14, Psalm 119:17 – 24.
2nd Genesis 33 – 34.
3rd Isaiah 33 – 34.
4th Judges 9 – 10.

The Desire of Servant-Thoughts

The Lord woke me up one night and said as clear as a bell, "Your servant-thoughts earnestly desire to serve you today." Servant-thoughts? Didn't know I had any servant-thoughts. The Lord said, "Yes, you do. Many. They belong to Me and you, and they earnestly desire to serve you. They can't wait until you get up." For the next two hours I dreamed and prayed about these servant-thoughts.

In my dream Jesus said that one of the desires of our (His/mine) servant-thoughts is to inform of the good, acceptable, and perfect choices during the day; and that these servant-thoughts earnestly desire to inform of the truth of that good choice. They stand ready and eager to serve. God said, "They have been transformed. They are faithful thoughts because I AM faithful. Listen to our faithful-servant-thoughts today."

Servant-thoughts are like passageways from your new heart, where the Holy Spirit dwells, to your old mind, will, and emotions. One of the startling experiences that a new believer has after being saved is that he has a new heart, but the same old sinful mind and thoughts, still makes the same sinful choices, and still has bad feelings. What's the deal?

When you ask Christ to save you, He gives you a new and perfect heart. All your sins are forgiven; past sins, present sins, future sins. You still sin, but not from your heart. Your thoughts, choices, and feelings are in the process of being saved. You grow in the grace and the knowledge of the Lord Jesus Christ. As you grow spiritually, your mind, will, and emotions are transformed and you are being saved.

Servant-thoughts are essential in the communication from your heart, from the Holy Spirit and the new you, to your mind, which is being transformed. The gift of light (some call it inspiration) is carried by your servant-thoughts and delivered to your mind. Your mind receives this gift by faith, which is also delivered by your servant-thoughts, and your mind gets transformed more and more.

Today, thank God for your servant-thoughts. Strengthen them by memorizing some more of Psalm 119:17 – 24 and praying it throughout the day. Praise the Lord for servant-thoughts!

January 18

Read and pray Psalm 18, Proverbs 4:24 – 27, Matthew 17, Romans 15:1 – 13, Psalm 119:17 – 24.
2nd Genesis 35 – 36.
3rd Isaiah 35 – 36.
4th Judges 11 – 12.

Servant-Thoughts are Fighters

The Lord said, "Your servant-thoughts earnestly desire to serve you today." Servant-thoughts originate from the Holy Spirit who lives in you, with you, through you, as you, before the Father and the watching world around you. The Bible says that you have the mind of Christ, 1 Corinthians 2:16, if you have His Spirit. Servant-thoughts accomplish many functions for you, the new you, the born-again you. One of those activities is to fight. Servant-thoughts are fighters. An old World War II veteran, receiving a metal for bravery, was quoted as saying, "We didn't survive by digging in; we survived by fighting."

The Bible teaches that a child of God through faith in Christ has peace with God, and conflict with the world, the flesh, and the devil. The frontline of spiritual warfare is in your head, where you think, choose, and feel. It is there that your fighting servant-thoughts wage war against the flesh (unaided human ability, aka pride), by destroying strongholds of the flesh, by the annihilation of arguments (lies you have previously believed), and every lofty (prideful) opinion that attempts to raise its ugly head against the knowledge of God.

These spiritual fighters take captive every enemy thought and carry out the penalty of disobedience on it, which is death (2 Corinthians 10:3-6). Your servant-thoughts are killers of the flesh that dwells in you. There is no prison for the flesh, only the hill called Calvary, (Romans 6:3-11 and Galatians 2:20).

Your servant-thoughts are armed to the hilt, full battle-rattle. Today, trust your fighting servant-thoughts. They are eager to fight and win for you today. Memorizing Scripture arms your servant-thoughts with the sword of the Spirit, which is the word of God. Work on Psalm 119:17 – 24 to keep the sword of the Spirit sharp for servant-thoughts today.

January 19

Read and pray Psalm 19, Proverbs 5:1 – 6, Matthew 18, Romans 15:14 –
33, Psalm 119:17 – 24.
2nd Genesis 37 – 38.
3rd Isaiah 37 – 38.
4th Judges 13 – 14.

Servant-Thoughts Always Win

Servant-thoughts are fighters. They wage war against the flesh according to God's word. These spiritually minded thoughts are set on the mind of the Spirit and are determined to give direction for wise choices; to discern between good and evil.

These servant-thoughts have a simple and particular strategy for advancing and destroying the strongholds of the world, the flesh, and the devil in your life. They "stand." In Romans 6 this word is used five times (twice in 6:13, once in 6:16, then twice in 6:19), being translated with the word "present." *"Do not present your members to sin as instruments for unrighteousness, but present yourselves to God as those who have been brought from death to life, and your members to God as instruments for righteousness."* Romans 6:13. The Greek word is *paraistimi*, and literally means to stand beside.

In the Greek world, *paraistimi* was the position of a bondservant in relation to his/her master. The bondservant would stand beside, slightly behind the master's elbow. At this position, they could easily hear the desire of their master and quickly carry out that command.

In Romans 6, in most translations, it is translated "present," as in the one to whom you present yourself to (to stand beside) in order to obey. According to Romans 6:12 – 23, you will obey the one you present yourself to each day. This same word is used again in Romans 12:1-2 describing how you are to present your bodies and minds as living sacrifices to God.

In Ephesians 6:10 – 19 you learn about the armor of God that He has provided for you "…to stand against the schemes of the devil…" This is the same word that is used in Romans 6:12 – 23 and 12:1 – 2. This teaches a very important truth about spiritual warfare. You stand strong in the Lord against the lies of the world, the flesh, and the devil by standing beside Christ in the humble and obedient position of a bondservant.

Servant-thoughts access the weapons of truth, salvation, righteousness, the gospel of peace, faith, the word of God, and Spirit-prayer, to kill the power of the lie of sin in you so that you can walk in the Spirit, by the Spirit, in order to enjoy the power of Christ today. Praise God for your fighting servant-thoughts. They always win.

January 20

Read and pray Psalm 20, Proverbs 5:7 – 14, Matthew 19, Romans 16, Psalm 119:17 – 24.
2nd Genesis 39 – 40.
3rd Isaiah 39 – 40.
4th Judges 15 – 16.

Worship is a Mind-Set

Worship is your faithful and sacrificial response to the revelation of God, of Himself in Christ, and it pleases the Father. It all begins with God and what He reveals of Himself to you. This pleases Him when you trust Him with what He reveals to you. This is worship; you trusting what God reveals of Himself.

Jesus lived His life this way, in a daily worship-walk of faith. He said in John 8:28-29 that He always did what pleased the Father; always. Every thought and activity was an offering of worship to the Father because His ear was exclusively tuned to the voice of the Father, the word of God.

The Apostle Paul said in Romans 8:5-8 that the mind that is set on the Spirit is a mind of life and peace. But the mind that is set on the flesh is a life and mind of death, and is hostile to God for it does not submit to God's law, indeed it cannot, and can never please the Father.

The daily choice belongs to you. Which direction will you choose to walk, in Spirit and Truth, or in the world, flesh, and devil? The choice is an informed choice based upon what is revealed, either by God, or by the world, the flesh, and the devil. Make no mistake, the world, the flesh, and the devil also reveals. The difference is this: God reveals truth while the world, the flesh, and the devil reveal lies. The lie appears to be right, but never is. Once revealed, you choose which one you will set your mind on and study, or you will choose which one to reject. The mind can only "set" on one or the other, not both. To attempt to entertain both is to believe the lie that you can.

When the Chinese began building the Great China Wall (around 200 BC) it was to protect their country from the invading hordes from the north. They built a wall, which ended up being 13,000+ miles long, 20-30 feet wide, 30-50 feet high, and yet their enemies were still getting through. By chance they discovered the problem; the gatekeepers were being bribed.

The world, flesh, and devil are constantly attempting to bribe the gatekeeper of your life, which is your mind, with a lie. The only solution is to keep your mind set on the Spirit and the truth; in other words, set your heart and mind on the Lord Jesus Christ and in God's word. One of the best ways to do this is to begin your day (for some this is late at night, for others early in the mornings) in God's word and in prayer. Presenting yourself before God in his word and in prayer, feeds your mind the truth. This is the best guard against the lie. Taking a verse from your daily worship-study with you (memory work) in order to meditate on it, fuels the worship engine of your heart throughout the day, and keeps your mind set on Christ. Everything you do will please the Father.

No matter what field God has called you to work in, whether it is school, home, business, medicine, law, construction, technology, or church, the mind that is set on Christ in spirit and truth will produce the fruit that pleases the Father. Regardless of the field, the mind that is set on the world, the flesh, or the devil will produce nothing but thorny weeds of death. Choose wisely at the beginning of each day.

January 21

Read and pray Psalm 21, Proverbs 5:15 – 17, Matthew 20, 1 Corinthians 1:1 – 17, Psalm 119:17 – 24.
2nd Genesis 41 – 42.
3rd Isaiah 41 – 42.
4th Judges 17 – 18.

Worship as Desire

God created you in His image. You are a trinity; spirit, soul, and body; three that are one. Sin fractured and destroyed the union, not only with God, but also with yourself and everyone around you. Through faith in Christ, you are born from above, given new life in Christ and with Christ, *"…the old has passed away, behold, and the new has come."* 2 Corinthians 5:17. Through faith in Jesus Christ you are born again, born from above, with a new heart in Christ. He now lives in you, with you, through you, as you, before the Father and the watching world around you.

Your new life in Christ is the new creation in the midst of the old, literally, in the midst of your old mind and body. And your mind is being transformed by the renewing of your mind; you are being redeemed; and you live in hope of the resurrection and a new body, *"…reserved in heaven for you who are kept by the power of God, through faith, for a salvation ready to be revealed in the last day."* 1 Peter 1:5.

The process of salvation that you are now experiencing is the process of being made whole; the union of spirit, soul, and body, from the inside out. Communion is the dominant desire of your new life and identity in Christ. Joined together with Christ and in Christ, fellowship with the Father is your constant experience and joy. Communion is not only your dominant desire, it is at the same time your constant and fulfilling contentment. The desires that God has given you, He fulfills, according to His word.

Your spirit desires communion and growth. Your soul (mind, will, and emotions) desires knowledge and peace. Your body desires food and growth (to be fruitful and to multiply). God's word gives clear instructions, direction, and gifts for these God-given desires. Receiving and trusting His instructions, direction, and gifts results in contentment and joy; the union of desire and contentment with Him. This is what it means to seek the Lord, to desire Him and the fulfillment (contentment from union) that only He gives.

True worship is fueled by desire, the hunger for communion and the indescribable joy of contentment that is only found in Christ, with Christ, through faith in Him. Today, ask God for a stronger and stronger desire and hunger for Him. This is the will of the Father. Feed upon His word and be satisfied in Christ. Your servant-thoughts earnestly desire to teach you and to be fruitful and multiply.

Spend one more day with Psalm 119:17 – 24, praying and meditating on the requests, the confessions, and the promises of that prayer.

January 22

Read and pray Psalm 22, Proverbs 5:18 – 20, Matthew 21, 1 Corinthians 1:18 – 31, Psalm 119:25 – 32.
2nd Genesis 43 – 44.
3rd Isaiah 43 – 44.
4th Judges 19 – 20.

The Enemy of Worship

The enemy of worship is the world, the flesh, and the devil. Paul talks about each of these in Ephesians 2:1 – 3 by describing the dead life of sin, following the course of the world, and the devil. The devil is described as working in the sons of disobedience through the passions (desires) of the flesh and of the mind.

"And you were dead in the trespasses and sins in which you once walked, following the course of this world, following the prince of the power of the air, the spirit that is now at work in the sons of disobedience, among whom we all once lived in the passions of our flesh, carrying out the desires of the body and the mind, and were by nature children of wrath, like the rest of mankind." This is the strategy of Satan. He works from the outside in with a lie through the desires of the body and the mind, with the heart as his target.

God works from the inside out, with the truth, and with the world as His target. He works by the Holy Spirit, through the Son, working in you, with you, through you, as you, before the Father and the watching world around you, for His glory and for your joy. AMEN.

In Genesis 3:1 – 6, you find the strategy of Satan to work from the outside in with the lie, first by casting doubt on the provision of God by questioning all that God had provided, *"Did God really say you shall not eat of any tree in the garden?"* He did not even mention the tree of the knowledge of good and evil. Eve did. The first temptation was that God could not be trusted to satisfy their appetites, according to His word. This was the first lie. The second lie was that they needed to satisfy their own appetites. The third lie was that they could provide for themselves without any consequences or regard for what God had said. They could establish their own authority and no longer be under the authority of God's word.

Under their own authority, rather than God's, their own physical, mental, and spiritual desires took over, *"...the woman saw that the tree was good for food...a delight to the eyes, and that the tree was desirable to make one wise…"* But notice the direction, from the outside in. The tree appealed to her physical appetite for food (body). It was beautiful and peaceful, pleasing to the eye (soul), and there was a hunger for what it appeared to give if it was consumed; wisdom (spiritual).

The devil's strategy has not changed and neither has God's. Beware of being led by your appetites rather than what God has said. Know what God has said. Trust what God has said. He is good, all the time, and all the time, God is good. He has promised to fully satisfy and fulfill your deepest longings with Himself, according to His word. This is what worshiping the Father in spirit and truth looks like.

Today, worship the Father in spirit and truth by asking for a new and deeper hunger for what He has said. Then, eat and be satisfied. Begin by memorizing the first line of Psalm 119:25. Pray it throughout the day for yourself and for someone you know.

January 23

Read and pray Psalm 23, Proverbs 5:21 – 23, Matthew 22, 1 Corinthians 2, Psalm 119:25 – 32.
2nd Genesis 45 – 46.
3rd Isaiah 45 – 46.
4th Ruth 1 – 4.

Worship and God's Word

Psalm 119 is the longest chapter in the Bible with 176 verses. It is the longest prayer in the Bible with all but the first three verses addressed directly to God. Psalm 119 is a prayer to God for His word and with His word. It has twenty-two, eight-verse sections corresponding to the letters of the Hebrew alphabet. You have been taking one of those eight-verse sections a week for the past four weeks, memorizing and praying one verse from it for the day. As you continue this practice, God's word will begin to shape your prayers according to His word. Think of that section each morning as priming the pump of prayer for the day.

One of the things that you will learn from this exercise is that this long prayer has relatively few requests. You will also learn that the majority of those requests ask for instruction, *"...teach me your statutes...teach me your precepts."* This request is repeated over and over in this prayer.

Another thing you quickly notice is that the majority of the requests to learn from God's word are tied to praising God. Here are a few examples: *"I will praise you with an upright heart, when I learn your righteous rules."* 119:7. *"Blessed are you, O LORD; teach me your statutes."* 119:12. *"The earth, O LORD, is full of your steadfast love; teach me your statutes."* 119:64.

From this you learn that worshiping the Father puts you on an eternal learning curve from His word. This is because God's word reveals who God is and worship is a faithful and sacrificial response to God as He reveals Himself in Christ from His word. The more you worship Him in spirit and truth, the more you learn of Him, and the more you know Him. This leads to more and more worship of Him.

Psalm 119 will teach you to pray, if you desire to learn to pray, by teaching you to worship the Father by asking Him to give you understanding and insight into His word. This is what it means to worship the Father in spirit and truth. Work on some more of Psalm 119:25 – 32 in order to meditate on it today.

January 24

Read and pray Psalm 24, Proverbs 6:1 – 5, Matthew 23, 1 Corinthians 3, Psalm 119:25 – 32.
2nd Genesis 47 – 48.
3rd Isaiah 47 – 48.
4th 1 Samuel 1 – 2.

Worship and the Wisdom of God

The phrase, *the fear of the Lord,* is used throughout the Bible to describe worshiping God. To fear the Lord does not mean to be afraid of Him, but rather to have great respect and honor for Him. It is to know God as God, as the one who is greater than anything in the natural universe, because He created all there is, according to His word. It is also to know that His power is eternal. It understands, from His word, that God is holy. You *fear the Lord* as a response to the revelation of God, of Himself in Christ, according to His Word.

Proverbs 9:10 states, *"The fear of the LORD is the beginning of wisdom…"* The word "beginning" in Hebrew is *techilaw*, which means the first thing or the entrance. The first step in receiving and entering into the wisdom of God is to learn to worship Him, to fear the Lord, to know Him from His Self-disclosure, according to His word. As you trust what God has said concerning Himself, you fear, or respect/honor Him as God. This is the beginning of wisdom, which is essential in worshiping the Father in spirit and truth. Wisdom pleases the Father. It is how you worship Him.

The Hebrew language has several words for wisdom, each with a particular aspect and meaning. The first time the word is used in the Bible is in Genesis 3:6. In that verse it states that Eve *"…saw that the tree was good for food, and that it was a delight to the eyes, and that the tree was to be desired to make one wise…"* The tree of the knowledge of good and evil was her counterpart in the Garden (more on that later), and its fruit was not to be eaten. The consequence would be death, according to God's word.

Satan had already planted his three-fold lie that they would not really die if they ate of the fruit of the tree and that God knew that if they did eat, their eyes would be opened, like God, and they would know good and evil. She decided to follow the lie, according to Satan's word, rather than the truth, according to God's word, in order to get wisdom. She was deceived into believing that eating the fruit would be the beginning of wisdom, rather than fearing the Lord. Adam and Eve decided to get wisdom on their own rather than receive it according to God's word as the fruit of worship.

The Apostle John defines loving the things of the world in 1 John 2:16 as *"...the desires of the flesh and the desires of the eyes and the pride of life..."* He warns in that passage of having the love (worship) of the world rather than the love of the Father. This statement directly corresponds to Genesis 3:6. The pride of life is the desire for wisdom without worshiping God.

Today, respond to the invitation of the Father from His word to fear Him in awe and wonder because of His goodness, His greatness, His wisdom and love. The fruit of true worship is wisdom.

January 25

Read and pray Psalm 25, Proverbs 6: 6 – 11, Matthew 24:1 – 31, 1 Corinthians 4, Psalm 119:25 – 32.
2ⁿᵈ Genesis 49 – 50.
3ʳᵈ Isaiah 49 – 50.
4ᵗʰ 1 Samuel 3 – 4.

Worshiping With *Sakal* Wisdom

The Hebrew language has many different words that are translated as "wisdom." The first one mentioned in the Bible is the word *sakal.* It is first seen in Genesis 3:6 as something that Eve was led to believe the tree would give her, *"...and a tree desirable to make one wise."* The word, *sakal*, means to have the ability to process information so that a right decision can be reached and the right action taken. It includes not only the right understanding and right choice, but also the right action. For that reason it is one of the most comprehensive words for wisdom. It is a triune word; right understanding, right choice, right action.

The meaning of understanding, choice, and action is seen in its use in Deuteronomy 29:9, *"Therefore keep the words of this covenant and do them, that you may prosper in all that you do."* In that verse, the word "prosper" is the Hebrew word *sakal.* Prosperity in the Bible is not the accumulation of stuff, but rather having *sakal*, keeping God's word and doing it.

In Joshua 1:7 – 8 this word is translated as having "good success." The command given to Joshua from God was to be careful to do all that was written in the Law, and to meditate on it. The result would be *sakal*; he would have good success. Another word for *sakal* is obedience, because in the Old Testament, obedience means hearing and doing God's word.

In 1 Samuel 17 you read the story of how David killed Goliath. In chapter eighteen they started singing songs about David (he became a rock star overnight, no pun intended) and at the same time, king Saul started throwing spears at him out of jealousy. In that chapter, three times, it says that David "behaved wisely," which is the word *sakal.* Praise and criticism have caused many to lose focus and direction, but the gift of *sakal* kept David focused upon the Lord.

Two of the most telling uses are found in Isaiah 52:13 and Jeremiah 23:5. In both of those passages, God's chosen Messiah, the son of David, is described as having *sakal.* In fact, this is the first thing that God says about the Christ, His Servant; He behaves wisely, with the right understanding, which leads to the right choice, which leads to the right action. This glorifies the Father, every time.

In one of David's worship songs, Psalm 14:2, *sakal* is defined; *"The LORD looks down from heaven on the children of man to see if there are any who understand, who seek after God."* The word, *sakal,* is translated "understand" in that verse. God is searching for those who seek after Him. And those who are searching for Him are those who have *sakal.* This is what it means to worship the Father in spirit and truth. These are the ones the Father is seeking to worship Him.

The Father is searching for those who will bring to Him the fruit of obedience from the Vine (John 15:1 – 8) in faithful and sacrificial worship. Today, as you abide in the Vine, ask the Father to give you the gift of *sakal* so that you can worship with it. Pray Psalm 119: 25 – 32.

January 26

Read and pray Psalm 26, Proverbs 6:12 – 19, Matthew 24:32 – 51, 1 Corinthians 5, Psalm 119:25 – 32.
2nd Exodus 1 – 2.
3rd Isaiah 51 – 53.
4th 1 Samuel 5 – 6.

Sakal; Knowing and Doing God's Will, God's Way

The Hebrew word *sakal* is used in the Old Testament to describe hearing and doing God's will from God's word for every occasion in life. In most places it is translated with the phrase "behave wisely."

Romans 12:2 states that God's will is good, pleasing, and perfect. And so, to hear and do God's will from God's word will enable you to present your life as a good, pleasing, and perfect offering and fragrance to the Father; to worship the Father in spirit and truth.

But how can you know for sure what is the good, pleasing, and perfect will of God? This is a question that many ask, but the problem is that it is the wrong question to ask. God desires you to know Him, to seek Him, more than anything else there is; more than something about Him, like His will. There are only two kinds of knowing; knowing about something or someone, and knowing of something or someone. The two kinds of knowing are very different.

When you know about something, you handle the information; you manage it for when you need to use it. But knowing of someone is a relationship. You don't manage (manipulate) a relationship. You don't use a person in a relationship. Of course, we know that people do, but this is not the way God created us to relate with Him or others. It is certainly not the way He desires to relate with you.

In a personal relationship with the Father, through faith in the Son, the Holy Spirit imparts Himself to you so that you can know Him, love Him, desire Him, and enjoy Him in life. God does this by speaking into your life, from the inside out, where He lives in you, with you, through you, and as you. This is worshiping the Father in spirit and truth.

Sakal, behaving wisely, is His life, from His word, which He has spoken in you. It is the good, pleasing, and perfect will of God, which is the result of knowing Him in a good, pleasing, and perfect relationship.

And *sakal,* the will of God and the desire and power to do it, is only given in a personal relationship with the Father, through faith in the Son, and by the Holy Spirit. Apart from Him you can do nothing, or worse, you will try to do something in your power, under your own control, in order to know about His will. This was what Adam and Eve were tempted to do, which they did. We are all very aware of and all too familiar with the outcome.

Sakal is desiring to know God, according to His word. Today, seek the Lord with all your heart. Don't worry about knowing and doing His will. God is the only One who can do His will. Desire to know Him, in His word, for it is only in that relationship that His desires will become yours. This is His good, pleasing, and perfect will.

January 27

Read and pray Psalm 27, Proverbs 6:20 – 26, Matthew 25:1 – 30, 1 Corinthians 6, Psalm 119:25 – 32.
2ⁿᵈ Exodus 3 – 4.
3ʳᵈ Isaiah 54.
4ᵗʰ 1 Samuel 7 – 8.

God's Word and Sakal Wisdom

One of the main words in the Old Testament for wisdom is **sakal**. The source of **sakal** is the heart of God expressed with the word of God. When the living and creative word of God is trusted from your life in Christ, it grows and produces fruit. Behaving wisely, **sakal**, is the fruit of God's word.

But the world, the flesh, and the devil are also speaking; loudly. In Genesis 4:7, God spoke to Cain to change the direction he was headed, and said, *"...sin is crouching at the door. Its desire is for you, but you must rule over it."* The sin that God was speaking about was the sin that was in Cain's heart to kill Abel, his brother. It was in his heart ready to spring into action and come out. Since Cain rejected God's word (as seen by his actions in Genesis 4:8), the sin God warned him of was simply waiting for an occasion, which presented itself in 4:8. Cain's jealousy turned to anger, which lashed out in violence, and killed Abel.

Jesus spoke of this in the Sermon on the Mount (Matthew 5 – 7), where He taught that the source of your actions is your heart and mind; conceived in the heart, developed in the mind, birthed and carried out with the body. Jesus taught the need for a new heart. Through faith in Jesus Christ you receive a new heart, a new life, His life, fully pleasing to the Father.

But you still have your same old sinful mind, will, emotions, and body. And like Cain, sin is crouching at the door, waiting and ready for an occasion to come out, and its desire is for you. Romans 6 – 8 outline how to overcome the power of sin and its relentless knocking at the door to come out.

When you receive Jesus Christ you are saved (past tense, completed action) from the penalty of your sins (plural; as in all of them), and by the Holy Spirit living in you, you are now being saved (present tense, ongoing action) from the power of sin (singular, as in the lie of sin). And one day, hallelujah, you will be saved (future tense, completed action) from the presence of sin, when you receive the resurrection body; reserved and being guarded in heaven for you (1 Peter 1:3 – 5).

Choosing to listen to the Holy Spirit, who lives in you, with you, through you, as you, before the Father and the watching world around you, rather than to the lie of the world, the flesh, and the devil, will create in you the right response to whatever is going on around you.

You have no choice over what happens to you, but you do have a choice as to what happens in you. When you choose to trust what God has said, He creates *sakal*, which is the right response to whatever is happening to you at the time. The right response is an expression of the heart of God, the life of Jesus, and brings pleasing glory to the Father.

This is what worshiping the Father in spirit and truth looks like in everyday living. And it comes from the new heart, through faith and servant thoughts, and spiritual discipline over the body. As the body learns, and it will, a new habit is formed, just as the old ones were with sin. The old dies and the new reigns with Christ.

Today, listen to what God has said, trust what God has said, your servant thoughts are eager to serve you to carry out *sakal*, so that you will behave wisely in every situation of the day.

January 28

Read and pray Psalm 28, Proverbs 6:27 – 35, Matthew 25:31 – 46, 1 Corinthians 7, Psalm 119:25 – 32.
2nd Exodus 5 – 6.
3rd Isaiah 55 – 56.
4th 1 Samuel 9 – 10.

Wisdom From a Listening Heart

In 1 Kings 3:9 you read of Solomon's request for wisdom. God had spoken to him and said, *"…ask me for what I will give you."* Solomon's prayer in 1 Kings 3:6 – 9 is a study of prayer. Before his request, Solomon reviews with God all that God had done leading up to putting him on the throne of his father, David.

When he finally got to his request, he asked for a *leb shomeah*, a listening heart, for the purpose of leading God's people with *bayin*, with discernment between good and evil. Discernment between good and evil is the meaning of the little word *bayin*. Do you remember the name of the tree in the midst of the Garden of Eden along side of the tree of life? See Genesis 2:9 for help.

But Solomon did not ask for *bayin*, he asked for a *leb shomeah*, a listening heart, so that he could govern with *bayin*, with discernment between good and evil. A listening heart tuned to receive God's word, produces the fruit of *bayin*. The purpose of *bayin* is to see clearly good from evil, in order to know and do the good, pleasing, and perfect will of God; to worship the Father in spirit and truth.

The root of the word *bayin* means to cut and separate. This is something that only God can do and has been doing from the very beginning. In creation God did a lot of separating; He separated light from darkness, He separated the waters above from the waters below, and He separated the land from the sea, by gathering. When God delivered the nation of Israel from Pharaoh and his army, He cut the Red Sea, and Israel walked through the sea on dry land. Only God can cut and separate water.

God separates good from evil, and He does it with His word; *bayin* is the result. One of the confessions in Psalm 119:104 is, *"Through your precepts I get understanding: therefore I hate every false way."* The word *bayin* is translated "understanding." The purpose of *bayin* is to clearly see the difference between good and evil; to choose the good way and to reject the false way.

Today, ask God for a listening heart tuned to His word for the purpose of having **bayin**. Spend time in the Father's presence listening to Him from His word. Let Him know that according to His word, through faith in Christ, you will also be given **bayin**, the understanding between good and evil, in order to choose the good, the pleasing, the perfect will of God, and to hate the evil false ways of the world, the flesh, and the devil. Thank God for the gift of His word, His Spirit, and His Son. Spend one more day with Psalm 119:25 – 32.

January 29

Read and pray Psalm 29, Proverbs 7:1 – 5, Matthew 26:1 – 35, 1 Corinthians 8, Psalm 119:33 – 40.
2nd Exodus 7 – 8.
3rd Isaiah 57 – 58.
4th 1 Samuel 11 – 12.

Taught By the Bible and Led by the Spirit

The old hymn, *I Am Resolved,* has the line *"…taught by the Bible, led by the Spirit, we'll walk the heavenly way."*[3] Being resolved to be taught by the Bible and led by the Spirit is one of the ways of God. His word will change and shape your will to resolve such a thing. This is also at the heart of the meaning of one of the Hebrew words for wisdom, the word *bayin.*

Yesterday, you learned that *bayin* is from a root word meaning to cut, to separate. It developed into the word for understanding in the sense of knowing good from evil. In the context of Solomon's prayer in 1 Kings 3:6 – 9 you also learn that it is necessary for leading others in a life that pleases the Father; the good, pleasing, and perfect will of God.

The word *bayin* is used 169 times in the Old Testament, over three times more than any other Hebrew word for wisdom (and there are many). Every time it is used, it is in the context of leadership.

For example, the first place this word shows up in the Old Testament is in Genesis 41:33 describing Joseph as he led Egypt to prepare for the seven years of plenty followed by the seven years of famine. Another example is of the Levites in 2 Chronicles 34 – 35, during the days of Josiah, and how they possessed *bayin* to lead and teach Judah in worship with the songs and instruments of David. God gives *bayin* from His word to reveal His will to give direction to your life so that you will choose the good, pleasing, and perfect will of God, and then, to lead others to do the same.

Your will is the decision-maker of your life. It makes a decision, informed by your mind, to be carried out by your body. It is powerful. Have you ever heard the term "will-power?" Once set it is hard to change. It will overrule the mind and the body in leading, which is why it is so important that it be set right in discerning good from evil.

When you submit your will to the leadership of the Holy Spirit, He will lead you from God's word, and you will begin walking in the Spirit, by the Spirit, to carry out the good, pleasing, and perfect will of God.

Your will is then in possession of, and is possessed by *bayin,* and you are worshiping the Father in spirit and truth.

Today, begin praying Psalm 119:33 – 40. Memorize the first line and meditate on what you are asking God for from that request.

January 30

Read and pray Psalm 30, Proverbs 7:6 – 9, Matthew 26:36 – 75, 1 Corinthians 9, Psalm 119:33 – 40.
2nd Exodus 9 – 10.
3rd Isaiah 59 – 60.
4th 1 Samuel 13 – 14.

Talents From God Are For God

Sometimes you will hear the phrase "naturally gifted and talented" to describe someone who excels in a particular ability. The abilities in these individuals come natural for them. They seem to flow and also appear effortless in accomplishments.

The Bible has a word for these talents. It is the Hebrew word *hokmah.* It is used to describe people who have special ability from God. The first place this word is used is in Exodus with the construction of the Tabernacle in the wilderness. In Exodus 31:1 it states, *"The LORD said to Moses, 'See, I have called by name Bezalel…and I have filled him with the Spirit of God, with ability…and all craftsmanship…'"* The word "ability" is the Hebrew word *hokmah.* This is the first place in the Bible that someone is described as being filled with the Holy Spirit and it is in the context of being equipped to do a task. The ability to do that task is called *hokmah.*

This word is used in conjunction with the other words for wisdom because, like the other words, *hokmah* is from God's word and for God's purposes. One of the ways of God is that He gives what is needed before it is needed. And God gives *hokmah* from His word to equip and empower with His ability for the task at hand. Wisdom from God knows that the abilities you have are from God and for God. When exercised, you worship the Father in spirit and truth.

In the New Testament we call these abilities spiritual gifts. They are abilities and talents from God and for God. God's word gives directions on how, what, where, and when these spiritual abilities are to be engaged. They are empowered by the Holy Spirit and carry out and accomplish His good, pleasing, and perfect will. And it pleases the Father because the task is from Him, for Him, and done by Him through faith in His Son, the Lord Jesus Christ. He sees Himself in it and is pleased. He gets the glory and you get the joy.

Work on the second line of Psalm 119:33 – 40, and pray it throughout the day. The word "understanding" in verse 34 is the word you learned yesterday, *bayin*.

January 31

Read and pray Psalm 31, Proverbs 7:10 – 15, Matthew 27:1 – 26, 1 Corinthians 10, Psalm 119:33 – 40.
2ⁿᵈ Exodus 11 – 12.
3ʳᵈ Isaiah 61 – 62.
4ᵗʰ 1 Samuel 15 – 16.

Wisdom and Spiritual Warfare

"Your commandment makes me wiser than my enemies, for it is ever with me." Psalm 119:98. The word "wiser" is the Hebrew word *hokmah*, which has the meaning of a special skill and/or ability. This verse teaches that God's word equips you for spiritual warfare with *hokmah*.

It also teaches that the front line of spiritual warfare is in your mind. Wisdom overcomes the enemies of God. If you remember, it was wisdom that was the bait for the first temptation (Genesis 3:1 – 6). Through faith in Jesus you have the mind of Christ and the wisdom of God, which enables you to overcome temptation and to defeat the world, the flesh, and the devil.

The wisdom of God enables you to see the clear difference between good and evil, the difference between the truth and the lie. When you choose the good, pleasing, and perfect will of God (the truth) in the light of His wisdom, the enemies of God flee from the light in weakness and defeat. Each step you take in the victorious light of God's wisdom reveals more and more lies that you have believed and weakens the power of sin in you life.

You fight with victory rather than for it. Christ has already defeated the world, the flesh, and the devil. The Lamb, having been slain, is standing, and He has conquered (Revelation 5:5 – 6). The truth of God's word sets you free. This is what it means to worship the Father in spirit and truth.

The ability to walk in His victorious light and power is what *hokmah* enables you to do. The light of *hokmah* reveals to you that the prison doors of sin are not only opened, but are gone. You have the ability to walk out and never look back.

Today, thank God for His word and *hokmah*, the spiritual ability He has given to you in Christ. Memorize and meditate on the third line of Psalm 119:33 – 40, understanding that "the path" in that verse is the Way, the Truth, and the Life.

February 1

Read and pray Psalm 31 and the same readings from yesterday in order to stay with the proper numbering of days; February 1, Psalm 31.

A Word From The Word

When Jesus was being tempted in the wilderness to turn stones into bread, He said, *"...Man shall not live by bread alone, but by every word that comes from the mouth of God."* Matthew 4:4. Jesus was given wise ability, with a word from Deuteronomy 8:3, to see through the lie of the tempter. He knew the verse and the context of that verse.

The children of Israel had been wandering in the wilderness for forty years. Just before they entered into the Promised Land, Moses reviewed the Law for them. The passage that Jesus quoted was from that scene. He had just spent forty days in the wilderness, fasting in preparation to begin His ministry. As Satan tempted Him to become a "bread messiah," Jesus answered with the truth of the deepest hunger of man, which is a word from God for daily living. Jesus came as God's Messiah, revealing and fulfilling the word of the Father.

When Jesus taught His disciples to pray, He included the need that we have for food with the request, *"...and give us this day, our daily bread..."* Matthew 6:11. Daily bread is needed to satisfy the hunger of the body, but a daily word from God is needed to satisfy the greater hunger of the soul; the hunger and thirst for righteousness. When that hunger is satisfied you are worshiping the Father in spirit and truth.

The Greeks had two words for "word." The first one is the word *rhemah*, which is a single spoken word. This is the word used in Matthew 4:4 in the phrase *"...but by every word..."* And then, the word *logos*, which is a collection of words that form a single meaning. John began his gospel using this word, *"In the beginning was the Logos, and the Logos was with God, and the Logos was God."* John 1:1. He described Jesus as the full revelation of everything God has said and will ever say, because Jesus fulfilled and revealed the word of God. He is the *Logos* of the Father.

You could say that *logos* is a collection of many *rhemah* that form a single meaning. Jesus was given a *rhemah* from God's word for the *hokmah* (wise ability) needed to combat the lie of Satan; a single word from the word of God.

In Ephesians 6:10 – 18, Paul gave instructions to believers on how to stand against the schemes of the devil with the mighty armor of God.

One of the weapons, the only offensive one, is *"...the sword of the Spirit, which is the word of God, praying at all times in the Spirit..."* The word used is *rhemah*; a powerful, single, word from the word of God. This is your memory verse for the day. Don't leave home without it.

Today, memorize and pray Psalm 119:36. Pray this word before you are tempted, when you are tempted, and after you are tempted. The experience will turn into a worship service, worshiping the Father in spirit and truth. If God said it, He will do it, if you will pray it.

February 2

Read and pray Psalm 32, Proverbs 7:16 – 20, Matthew 27:27 – 66, 1 Corinthians 11, Psalm 119:33 – 40.

2nd Exodus 13 – 14.

3rd Isaiah 63 – 64.

4th 1 Samuel 17 – 18.

Wisdom and Spiritual Disciplines

Proverbs 1:2 – 3 concentrates several Hebrew words for wisdom in two verses, *"To know (yadah) wisdom (hokmah) and instruction (musar), to understand (bayin) words of insight (bayin), to receive instruction (musar) in wise dealing (sakal)..."* You have learned that *hokmah* is wise ability or skill, and that *bayin* is discernment to know between good and evil, and that *sakal* is to behave wisely. The word today is *musar*, which is translated "instruction," in the verses above.

This word is from a root word that means to bind, as in to learn something to the extent that you are bound to it until it becomes a part of you. It came to be understood as a word for the discipline of education.

Wisdom is something you are instructed in from God's word. It is something you are bound to and it becomes a part of you. It is from God; the fruit of His word. Understanding the root and use of the word *musar* gives meaning to the purpose of spiritual disciplines. Many books have been written on spiritual disciplines. Biographers always point out the practice of spiritual disciplines in the lives of great Christians.

Spiritual disciplines teach by repetition behavior that reflects the wisdom of God from His word.[4] This is the meaning of the word *musar*; the discipline of instructions in the wisdom of God from His word. The wisdom of God from His word pleases the Father because He sees Himself in it. Learning this instruction is worshiping the Father in spirit and truth. This is foundational and definitive in our lives.

Today, determine to receive instruction (*musar*) in wisdom (*sakal*). Ask God, the Holy Spirit, to be your instructor. Meditate upon a word from God's word by memorizing Psalm 119:37. Pray it throughout the day.

February 3

Read and pray Psalm 33, Proverbs 7:21 – 27, Matthew 28, 1 Corinthians 12, Psalm 119:33 – 40.
2nd Exodus 15.
3rd Isaiah 65 – 66.
4th 1 Samuel 19 – 20.

Knowing the Father in True Worship

Jesus told the woman of Sychar at Jacob's well that the Samaritans did not know who they worshiped, John 4:22. The same can happen to you. The Hebrew word for "know" is *yadah*, which is the knowledge that results from a personal, interactive, and intimate relationship. It is used exclusively of persons and what they share in a personal relationship. This is not knowledge about someone, but rather the knowledge of someone.

The first place you find this word is in Genesis 2:9, *"The tree of life was in the midst of the garden, and the tree of the yadah of good and evil."* God told Adam he was not to eat of the tree of the knowledge of good and evil. The consequences would be death. In Genesis 3:5, Satan told Eve, *"...you will not really die. For God knows that when you eat of it your eyes will be opened, and you will be like God, knowing good and evil."* This word, *yadah*, is used twice in that verse.

Adam and Eve knew God personally, interacting with Him in an intimate relationship of love and adoration. They knew Him as their creator, provider, protector, and companion. The lie from Satan was that they did not really know God, that He could not really be trusted, and that He did not really trust them either. It also called into question the goodness of the tree that God created and placed right beside the tree of life in the midst of the garden.

The lie attacked the very heart of their lives with God, of their knowledge of Him, with false knowledge about the tree, themselves, and about God. It made the knowledge about God more attractive than the knowledge of Him. This was not the purpose of the tree of the knowledge of good and evil, which was right beside the tree of life, in the midst of the garden. More on that later.

As they entertained this false knowledge, it took over their senses and dulled their appetite for true knowledge, the knowledge of, which is *yadah*, and we all know, too well, the rest of the story.

True worship is from the truth of knowing *(yadah)* the Father through faith in Jesus Christ. The desire to know Him more and more is true worship. To substitute knowledge about Him for knowledge of Him is to substitute religion about God for the relationship with God. When this happens, you have fallen prey to the schemes of the world, the flesh, and the devil.

Today, pray for more and more *yadah* of God, with God, from God.

February 4

Read and pray Psalm 34, Proverbs 8:1 – 5, Mark 1:1 – 20, 1 Corinthians 13, Psalm 119:33 – 40.

2nd Exodus 16.

3rd Jeremiah 1.

4th 1 Samuel 21 – 22.

The Knowledge of Good and Evil

The phrase, the knowledge of good and evil, is found several places in the Bible. Looking at the context of the places it is found gives meaning to it, and to the meaning of this mysterious tree in the midst of the garden in Genesis 2:9. The tree of the knowledge of good and evil was beside the tree of life in the midst of the garden. God told Adam to eat of the trees of the garden, *"...but of the tree of the knowledge of good and evil you shall not eat, for in the day that you eat of it you shall surely die."* Genesis 2:17.

This tree, like all of the trees of the garden, was pleasing to the sight; it was just not good for food. It had another purpose. Its place in the garden lends to understanding the purpose. It was at the very center of Eden right beside the tree of life and its appearance was dazzling and spectacular. The Garden of Eden was the worship center of the earth and of all of creation. Here Adam and Eve knew and walked with God. The entire water source for the earth flowed from the garden. A garden grows. The worship center of the earth was to grow and eventually encompass the whole earth. The earth was created to be the center of creation; the worship center of the entire material universe.

Adam worshiped God by working the garden and keeping it. The Hebrew word translated "work" in that verse means to serve and is used several times in the Old Testament for "worship." Adam served and worshiped God by keeping the garden.

The Hebrew word translated "keep" is one of the main words in the Old Testament. The word *shamar* means to value and to see the great worth of something. It is closely related to worship in that regard. It means to watch and guard because of the great worth and value of a thing. It means to study with keen observation. After Cain killed Abel, and God asked him where his brother was; Cain's sarcastic answer revealed his guilt, *"Am I my brother's keeper?"* Genesis 4:9. The word there is *shamar*.

The point is this: the tree of the knowledge of good and evil was to be recognized as having supreme worth, standing right beside the tree of life, at the very heart of the worship center. But for Adam and Eve, the knowledge of good and evil would come from another source. Spend one more day with Psalm 119:33 – 40 as your prayer for the day.

February 5

Read and pray Psalm 35, Proverbs 8:6 – 11, Mark 1:21 – 45, 1 Corinthians 14, Psalm 119:41 – 48.
2nd Exodus 17.
3rd Jeremiah 2.
4th 1 Samuel 23 – 24.

Wisdom and the Knowledge of Good and Evil

One of the terms for wisdom in the Old Testament is the phrase, *leb shomeah*, which means "a listening heart." It is found in king Solomon's prayer in 1 Kings 3:6 – 9. A listening heart is one that is tuned to receive God's word.

Our world is filled with all kinds of messages, like sound waves, and your heart can be tuned to receive the ones you choose, similar to a dial on a radio. What your heart is set on is what you will receive and hear. Solomon asked God for a heart that would be set on Him and His word; a *leb shomeah*.

Solomon somehow knew that the result of a listening heart would be the knowledge of good and evil. God loves prayer requests with results that are according to His word. These are called requests with purpose. You recognize them with the phrase "so that" or "in order to."

Solomon's request had purpose, *"Give your servant a listening heart to govern your people, that I may discern between good and evil."* 1 Kings 3:9. The word "discern" is the Hebrew word *bayin* and means to cut and separate. A heart that is tuned to God's word results in the ability to cut and separate good from evil. This is called the knowledge of good and evil.

If you remember, the Hebrew word for "knowledge" is *yadah,* which means the personal, interactive, intimate experience with someone, of someone. With a listening heart tuned to God's word, for the purpose of discerning good and evil, a person chooses to know in a personal, interactive, intimate experience the good without the evil. Knowing good in a personal, interactive, and intimate experience with it gives a person the knowledge about evil without the personal, interactive, and intimate experience of evil. This was God's plan from the very beginning. This is the way that Jesus knew about sin, without the personal, interactive, and intimate experience of it.

In seeing and knowing God from the revelation of Himself in Christ from His word, the goodness of God is experienced with the joy of having chosen wisely to reject the evil. This choice glorifies God because it is the fruit of His word. God sees Himself in that wise choice and is thrilled at His own goodness. This is what the Lord Jesus Christ expressed in every situation and event of His life on earth. It brought the Father great pleasure. This is how to worship the Father in spirit and truth.

Today, pray the first line of Psalm 119:41 – 48 by memorizing it now. Take it with you and pray it throughout your day.

February 6

Read and pray Psalm 36, Proverbs 8:12 – 21, Mark 2, 1 Corinthians 15:1 – 34, Psalm 119:41 – 48.
2nd Exodus 18.
3rd Jeremiah 3.
4th 1 Samuel 25 – 26.

The Knowledge of Good and Evil in the New Testament

You will find the phrase, "good and evil," in Hebrews 5:14, *"But solid food is for the mature, for those who have their powers of discernment trained by constant practice to distinguish good from evil."*

The context of that verse speaks of the solid food of the word of God as compared to the milk of the word. The writer of Hebrews compares a little child who is unskilled in the word of righteousness and only feeds on milk, to a mature believer who is strengthened on the solid food of the word, and is trained through spiritual development to distinguish good from evil.

The Greek word *diakrisis*, translated "distinguish," means to cut and separate. Its companion is the Hebrew word *bayin*. It means to clearly see and make a true and right judgment call. This wisdom is the result of spiritual growth and development, which comes through the constant training of spiritual disciplines. The Greek word *gumnadzo*, is translated "trained." We get our English word "gymnasium" from this Greek word.

Faithful study and obedience to God's word and the development of a lifestyle of spiritual disciplines leads to spiritual growth and maturity. The mature are recognized by their hunger for God's word, their life of obedience, spiritual exercising, and their ability to distinguish between good and evil.

In John 4:34, Jesus said, *"My food is to do the will of him who sent me and to accomplish his work."* Desiring God's will and choosing it to be done on earth as it is in heaven is the mark of the spiritually mature. This statement by Jesus is in the context of His teaching on true worship.

The knowledge of good and evil is one of the main characteristics of a mature believer. Armed with this wisdom, the mature follower of Christ desires the will of God, chooses it, and then carries it out in joyful obedience. This fruit grows and develops from the inside, out. It is not something you pick and eat (Genesis 2:17).

Today, eat this word from Hebrews 5:14 by reading it, studying it, hearing it, meditating on it, receiving it, and praying it. Then join God in doing it.

February 7

Read and pray Psalm 37, Proverbs 8:22 – 31, Mark 3, 1 Corinthians 15:35 – 58, Psalm 119:41 – 48.
2nd Exodus 19.
3rd Jeremiah 4.
4th 1 Samuel 27 – 28.

The Wisdom of the Bride

In Romans 16:19, Paul compliments the church at Rome, then challenges them with a vision. He said, *"For your obedience is known to all, so that I rejoice over you, but I want you to be wise as to what is good, and innocent as to what is evil."*

This church brought great joy to the apostle because of their obedience. For Paul, this meant that they were together in unity, teaching and learning sound doctrine, and missionary work. He challenged them with a vision of growth, *"...but I want you to be wise as to what is good, and innocent as to what is evil."* This phrase reaches back to creation and the tree in the midst of the Garden of Eden, beside the tree of life.

A vision statement is a picture of a person, place, or thing. It is a preferred state of being; it is directional. A mission statement is the activity of that vision, or the activity that leads to that vision. The New Testament presents the vision of the church as the Bride of Christ (Ephesians 5:25 – 33, Revelation 21:1 – 2). In the verse above you can see that the Bride has wisdom as one of her main features. She is adorned with wisdom; the wisdom of the Father, through faith in the Son, and by the Holy Spirit.

The wisdom of the Bride is not the wisdom of the world, the flesh, or the devil. It is the wisdom of God. It is good, and there is only one who is good; God (Mark 10:18). The Greek word for good is *agatha,* and is used throughout the Bible to describe one of the attributes of God. God is *agatha,* all the time. Jesus uses this word in Matthew 7:17 to describe how a good tree bears good fruit.

Being wise with the goodness of God is also described as being innocent as to what is evil. The word "innocent" is the Greek word *akeraious.* It means not having any experience or knowledge of something destructive or defiling. In other words, the Bride has no knowledge of evil. She is pure. Her goodness is her beauty; it is the wisdom of God, from the word of God, through faith in the Lord Jesus Christ, her Head, and eternal Husband.

The Church was chosen before the foundations of the world and she was beside her Husband in the midst of the garden in Genesis 2:9 as a vision for Adam and Eve of what was to come; the tree of life and the tree of the knowledge of good and evil.

Meditate on that vision today and how it relates to worshiping the Father in spirit and truth.

February 8

Read and pray Psalm 38, Proverbs 8:32 – 36, Mark 4, 1 Corinthians 16, Psalm 119:41 – 48.
2nd Exodus 20.
3rd Jeremiah 5.
4th 1 Samuel 29 – 31.

The Purpose of the Tree of the Knowledge of Good and Evil

The tree of the knowledge of good and evil was not for food, because God said, *"You may surely eat of every tree of the garden, but of the tree of the knowledge of good and evil you shall not eat, for in the day that you eat of it you shall surely die."* Genesis 2:16 – 17. The fruit of the tree of the knowledge of good and evil was not for food; it had a different purpose.

In Genesis 2:8 – 17, the Garden of Eden is described as the place on earth where Adam and Eve would live. It states that God planted the garden Himself. It was His garden. It says God made every tree of the garden pleasing to the eyes and good for food. The Hebrew word for "pleasing" is *chamad,* which means desirable. It will be used again in Genesis 3:6 when Eve sees that the tree was *"...desirable to make one wise."* This was not the purpose God had for it.

The other feature of the garden was the river springing up and branching off in four directions as the water source for the whole earth. Before the flood, before it rained, the earth was watered by big rivers branching off and becoming smaller and smaller rather than the other way around, the way it is now. It was similar to the way God created the circulatory system of the body. The garden was the literal heart of the earth, the worship center of creation. Life flowed from the garden, giving life to the whole earth.

And then, the main feature of the garden, next to Adam and Eve of course, was the two trees in the midst of the garden. They were given names before the animals. They were called the tree of life and the tree of the knowledge of good and evil. And the one mentioned above in 2:16 – 17 was given a different purpose than for food, and like all the other trees, it was desirable, pleasing to the eyes. So what was the purpose of the tree of the knowledge of good and evil? It was for worship. It was the heart of the heart.

There are two companion passages with Genesis 2:8 – 17; John 15:1 – 11, and Revelation 22:1 – 5. John 15 is red-letter describing the

Father as the Gardener, Jesus as the Vine, and believers as the branches, bearing fruit. But the fruit of the Vine has one purpose, it is all for the Gardener and His glory, 15:8. Revelation 22 is the final chapter of the Bible describing the center of the New Creation with the river of life flowing from the throne of God and of the Lamb and through the middle of the street of the city (the Bride of Revelation 21:9 – 27), bearing fruit with healing leaves. Beautiful.

All three of these companion passages are describing what it means to worship the Father in spirit and truth. The fruit of the tree of the knowledge of good and evil was the first fruits of the garden, a tithe of the garden, reserved for God, to worship Him, produced by the Bride beside and abiding in her glorious Husband, her Head, the Lord Jesus Christ and the redemption He brought to pass in the fullness of time; the tree of life. This is once again seen as the heart of the New Creation with the only exception being that the tree of the knowledge of good and evil is now given a new name, the city, the New Jerusalem, the Bride of the Lamb.

Today, take a few minutes to read again Genesis 2:8 – 17, John 15:1 – 11, and Revelation 22:1 – 5 and meditate on the beauty of what it means to worship the Father in spirit and truth, in Christ, as a member of the Bride of Christ.

February 9

Read and pray Psalm 39, Proverbs 9:1 – 12, Mark 5, 2 Corinthians 1, Psalm 119:41 – 48.
2nd Exodus 21.
3rd Jeremiah 6.
4th 2 Samuel 1- 2.

King David and the Psalms of Worship

The last verse of the book of Judges ends with, *"Everyone did what was right in his own eyes."* Judges 21:25. This statement underscores the problems that Israel had at the time of the judges. King Saul, Israel's first king, followed in that same spirit of rebellion and disobedience. Finally, in 1 Samuel 15, God rejected Saul as king because of his rebellion and his faithlessness, and told Samuel that He had found a man after His own heart (1 Samuel 13:14), and had provided for Himself a king among the sons of Jesse of Bethlehem (1 Samuel 16:1 – 13).

David was a shepherd boy, keeping his father's sheep around Bethlehem. They brought David to Samuel and God said to Samuel, *"Arise, anoint him, for this is he."* 1 Samuel 16:12. In the next verse it states that the Spirit of the LORD (all caps means the covenant Name of God given to Moses at the burning bush) came upon David mightily from that time forward.

Saul was tormented from being rejected by God and David was sent for because it says that he was "skillful" with the harp (Hebrew *yadah*) and had understanding (Hebrew *bayin*). These two words, *yadah* and *bayin* are associated with the word and wisdom of God.

When David sang his songs of worship with Saul, it says that the king was refreshed. The Hebrew word for "refreshed" is *ravach,* and literally means to breath deeply. David's worship of God was soothing to Saul and brought him temporary relief. True worship clears the atmosphere around the person who is focused upon the true and living God. It is like a sea of glass (Revelation 4:6).

The book of Psalms is the longest book in the Bible and is known as the worship book of the Bible. Most of the psalms were written by David, with others written for him. David is a model for becoming a true worshiper of the Father because his heart was set on pursuing and knowing God. Regardless of the situation he found himself in, and David got himself in some serious situations, he could find and focus upon the Lord.

82

This is what it means to be a person after the heart of God, worshiping the Father in spirit and truth.

Keep in mind the psalm that you began your time of worship with today. What did it say about God? Focus on the Lord today and the attribute that was highlighted in that psalm for you today. Pray it back to the Father throughout the day and you may just notice that people around you will begin to breath more deeply.

February 10

Read and pray Psalm 40, Proverbs 9:13 – 18, Mark 6:1 – 29, 2 Corinthians 2, Psalm 119:41 – 48.
2nd Exodus 22.
3rd Jeremiah 7.
4th 2 Samuel 3 – 4.

David and the Attitude of Worship

Some will say that you must prepare for worship by getting into the proper frame of mind. Others will talk about a particular song that gets them into the right mood for worship. We are more like king Saul than David when we get in that condition.

David had an attitude conducive to worship. He did not have to get ready to worship; he stayed ready. David did not require a special setting or a certain melody or a favorite place or group of people before he could worship. David worshiped God with his life, in every situation of his life. For David, every occasion was a good occasion to worship the Lord. David was addicted to the LORD. He had an attitude that kept him in a worship setting. This is a discipline; it is something to learn.

In 1 Samuel 17 you read how David picked up five smooth stones as he approached Goliath, getting close enough to him so that Goliath could hear what was about to happen to him. In that familiar story you can pick up five smooth statements of truth by which to learn and develop an attitude of worship.

The first smooth truth is called knowing who is in charge. In 1 Samuel 17:8 you read the words of Goliath as he shouted from the valley Elah to the army of Israel, *"Why have you come out to draw up for battle? Am I not a Philistine, and are you not servants of Saul?"* When David arrived on the scene and heard Goliath, he said in 17:26, *"...who is this uncircumcised Philistine that he should defy the armies of the living God?"* David knew that the armies of Israel were not Saul's servants; they were servants of the living God. The armies of Israel had forgotten this because Saul had forgotten it. But David knew.

He knew the stories of how Abraham attacked five great kings and their armies with only 318 men and rescued his nephew, Lot (Genesis 14). David knew the stories of Moses, a shepherd with a staff in his hand, who stood eye-to-eye with Pharaoh, the most powerful man on earth with chariots and armies at his command. He knew the stories of Joshua and how he led an army of former slaves who had grown up wandering around the wilderness of the Sinai Peninsula, to defeat the giants of the land who lived in walled-up cities.

When you, like David, know the one who is in charge, according to His word, you develop an attitude called humility. Humility is an attitude that knows and lives in the strength of another, in David's case, in the strength of the living God.

David saw himself as the servant of the LORD. He was under God's authority and spoke with His authority. Humble people come across as arrogant to those who are not under the same authority because they view themselves and the situation from an entirely different perspective. Humility changes every situation from "Oh no; what in the world am I going to do?" to "Oh boy; now lets see what God is about to do!" This is the attitude of one who worships the Father in spirit and truth.

Today, know that God is in charge, according to His word. This one truth will change your whole view of the situation, transforming it into a worship experience because you are being transformed into a true worshiper with a humble attitude.

February 11

Read and pray Psalm 41, Proverbs 10:1 – 5, Mark 6:30 – 56, 2 Corinthians 3, Psalm 119:41 – 48.
2nd Exodus 23.
3rd Jeremiah 8.
4th 2 Samuel 5 – 6.

A Second Smooth Truth For Worship

Worship is not something you do as much as something you become. Your life can become a *"living sacrifice, holy and acceptable to God... discerning the good, pleasing, and perfect will of God."* Romans 12:2. This is something you first desire, then learn, and then become. David will teach you from God's word.

The second smooth truth to pick up from the story in 1 Samuel 17 is seen when David was taken before king Saul in 17:31 – 37. Saul reminded David that he was just a boy and that Goliath had been a warrior since he was a boy. This is one of the hindrances of worship; focusing on the circumstances, limitations, and conditions rather than upon the character of God. Saul was an expert on seeing and knowing (*yadah*) circumstances, limitations, and conditions, which was why he was so fearful all the time. David knew (*yadah*) God and God's word. He focused upon the Lord, not upon circumstances.

The second smooth truth to pick up is David's reply to Saul. It is found in 17:34 – 37. David told Saul what he did when the lion or bear came to kill, steal, and destroy the sheep he was charged to keep. David said he went after them, attacked them, and killed them, all in the Name of the LORD. It was a worship experience for David to protect the sheep from lions and bears, for he saw himself as a servant of God and saw the sheep as God's sheep, not his. He knew his actions of protecting the sheep pleased God, and that God would do what only God can do, if he would do what God wanted him to do, which was to work and keep the sheep (Genesis 2:15).

David's statement in 1 Samuel 17:37 is the second smooth truth. *"The LORD who delivered me from the paw of the lion and from the paw of the bear will deliver me from the hand of this Philistine and he will be like the (dead) lion and bear for he has defied the armies of the living God."*

This statement is a confession of faith and confidence in the truth of God and His promises to Abraham, Isaac, and Jacob. The Promised

Land had been given to the patriarchs and their descendants. There was no room for Philistines in the Promised Land (nor is there today). This was according to God's word. David knew God's word and believed Him and so he could speak with authority and could act with the same authority and confidence. David knew God and knew that the battle was the LORD's, and that he was the weapon of God in that fight.

Knowing God through faith in Jesus Christ and declaring God's word in particular situations becomes a worship experience because it pleases the Father when we know Him and trust Him in every situation. Knowing His word concerning your life, His promises, His desire for you, and the power and authority in His Son, is a mighty weapon against the world, the flesh, and the devil, which are like the lion, the bear, and the Philistine. This is a powerful smooth truth for worshiping the Father in spirit and truth.

Today, focus your attention on knowing God, according to His word, on learning from Him more and more of your new identity and new responsibility in the new life you have in Christ. Confess the truth of who God is, what His promises are, who you are in Him and Him in you. Spend one more day praying Psalm 119:41 – 48.

February 12

Read and pray Psalm 42, Proverbs 10:6 – 9, Mark 7, 2 Corinthians 4, Psalm 119:49 – 56.
2nd Exodus 24,
3rd Jeremiah 9.
4th 2 Samuel 7 – 8.

The Third Smooth Truth For Worship

Much can be learned from David about becoming a true worshiper. He was the worship leader of Israel from the time he was just a boy. Becoming a true worshiper, one who worships the Father in spirit and truth, is a learning experience. And learning is personal. There are no substitutes for learning. Only you can learn. No one can learn for you.

The third smooth truth from the story of David and Goliath, found in 1 Samuel 17:38 – 39, which teaches the simple truth of worship from personal experience and learning. As young David stood before the king, Saul tried to put his armor and weapons on David for the fight with Goliath. When Saul put his armor on David it says, *"And he tried in vain to go, for he had not tested them."* The phrase "tried to go" is the Hebrew word *ya-al,* and means to try to please another without success.

David allowed Saul to dress him in his armor, but David knew that it was Saul's armor, not his. David knew what God had given him, and he had developed the skill (*hokmah*) of how to use it for God's glory. He would defeat Goliath with what God had given him, not with what Saul had to offer.

When you present yourself before the Father as a true worshiper, you come before Him as yourself, dressed in what He has given you, and nothing else. You can learn from others, but others cannot worship for you, or like you. Worship is personal. Worship is unique in that regard. The Father is pleased when you worship Him with who you are in Him, and with what He has given to you in and through His Son, the Lord Jesus Christ.

This is the third smooth truth for worship; knowing who you are in Christ and presenting yourself to the Father with what He has given to you in Christ. This is your true self and this is what it means to worship the Father in spirit and truth.

Today, think about a song God blessed you with in the past. Maybe the message of it ministered to you at a time of need or maybe it was simply one that God gave you for Him. Think about the meaning of the words and phrases of the song and give them to the Father, from you, the true you, and worship the Father in spirit and truth. Memorize the first line of Psalm 119:49 – 56, and make it your prayer for the day.

February 13

Read and pray Psalm 43, Proverbs 10:10 – 16, Mark 8, 2 Corinthians 5, Psalm 119:49 – 56.
2nd Exodus 25.
3rd Jeremiah 10.
4th 2 Samuel 9 – 10.

The Fourth Smooth Truth For Worship

When young David faced Goliath in 1 Samuel 17, he had five smooth stones, his shepherd's staff, a leather strap called a sling, and the faith and knowledge that he was on the side of the living God, the God of Israel.

Goliath had come against God. He did not know that, but David did. And David knew God and he knew the promises of God for Israel. Armed with that knowledge and the skill he learned from keeping sheep safe from predators, he was confident in defeating Goliath and the Philistine army.

In 1 Samuel 17:41 – 47 you hear the conversation that David had with Goliath before the fight. Some might call this trash talk, but for David it was truth talk. Goliath was amused that David would come out to fight him without weapons. He cursed David by his gods and said that he was about to give David's little scrawny body to the birds and the beasts of the field. David answered that he was about to give the whole army of the Philistines to the birds and wild beasts, right after he killed and decapitated Goliath.

The next thing David said is the fourth smooth truth for learning to worship the Father in spirit and truth. He said in 1 Samuel 17:45, *"You come to me with sword and with a spear and with a javelin, but I come to you in the name of the LORD of hosts, the God of the armies of Israel, whom you have defied. This day the LORD will deliver you into my hand..."* David said what he said and did what he did in the name of the LORD. When you become a true worshiper, worshiping the Father in spirit and truth, you do everything in the name of the Lord Jesus Christ.

The apostle Paul said it like this in Colossians 3:17, *"And whatever you do, in word or deed, do everything in the name of the Lord Jesus, giving thanks to God the Father through him."* But what does it mean to do what you do in the name of the Lord Jesus Christ, giving thanks to the Father through Him? It is more than just saying the words, "In the name of Jesus..." You must learn what those words mean if you are to worship the Father in spirit and truth. More than that, you must learn what that Name means.

Living in the name of the Lord Jesus means that His life (His character, strength, and desires) is your life (your character, strength, and desires). Christ is your life, Colossians 3:4. When you live before the Father in the name of the Lord Jesus Christ, you are a fragrant aroma to God, a pleasing sacrifice, and the Father can see His Son in you, with you, living through you, as you, and it brings Him glory. You get the joy, and He gets the glory.

When David said those words to Goliath, he wanted to make sure Goliath knew who he was fighting. It wasn't David he was fighting; it was the God of David, and of Israel that he was fighting. And God always wins the battle.

Today, thank God for your life in Christ. Work on line two of Psalm 119:49 – 56 and pray it throughout the day. Think about one of the promises of God and pray it as your hope today, in the Name of the Lord Jesus Christ.

February 14

Read and pray Psalm 44, Proverbs 10:17 – 25, Mark 9:1 – 29, 2 Corinthians 6, Psalm 119:49 – 56.
2nd Exodus 26.
3rd Jeremiah 11.
4th 2 Samuel 11 – 12.

The Fifth Smooth Truth For Worship

David had the last word in the "truth talk" with Goliath in 1 Samuel 17:47. It was literally the last word that Goliath heard before the last thing that he saw, which was the rock from David's sling. What David said in 1 Samuel 17:47 is one of the foundational truths for worshiping the Father in spirit and truth. He said, *"…that all this assembly may know that the LORD saves not with sword and spear. For the battle is the LORD's, and he will give you into our hands."*

Young David was teaching both armies that day, as well as king Saul, that there is a greater purpose in battle than victory for "our side." The greater purpose is the revelation and glory of the living God. Each of the five smooth truths from this story shares this in common. Together they glorify and reveal who God is, and His desire to be known and trusted.

Quick review: The first truth is from 1 Samuel 17:26 stating there is only one true and living God and David saw himself as the humble servant of the LORD, not as a servant of king Saul. David's confidence flowed from living in the strength of His Master. The second truth is from 17:37; God protects His shepherds when they fight for His sheep. The third truth is from 17:39; God is a Person and worship is personal. There are no substitutes for serving and worshiping God. The fourth truth is from 17:45; God's Name is His character and strength. And the fifth sums up the other four; this is all about God being glorified and known as Savior, not with man's strength, weapons, or tools, but in His Name and power alone. The purpose, the destination of worship, is God and God alone being glorified and known.

As you learn to become a true worshiper, the Father will be glorified and known more and more as the loving, forgiving, saving, almighty God that He is. As you worship the Father in spirit and truth, the Lord Jesus Christ is lifted up more and more. It was the Lamb, having been slain, standing, that John saw in the midst of the throne in Revelation 5:5 – 8, and among the four living creatures and the twenty-four elders.

Today, commit yourself to become a true worshiper of the Father, in spirit and truth. Confess to God your earnest desire to learn the meaning of worshiping the Father in spirit and truth. Know and embrace the revelation, purpose, and the glory of the Father in the Lord Jesus Christ, the Lamb of God who was slain and rose again on the third day.

February 15

Read and pray Psalm 45, Proverbs 10:26 – 32, Mark 9:30 – 50, 2 Corinthians 7, Psalm 119:49 – 56.

2nd Exodus 27.

3rd Jeremiah 12.

4th 2 Samuel 13 – 14.

Worshiping the Father Can Be Harmful to Your Flesh

David became an instant hero and close friend of Jonathan, king Saul's son, and also an instant target for Saul's spear-throwing jealousy. Saul personally tried to kill David three times (1 Samuel 18:11, 19:10). For the next ten years, David was on the run, hiding in the caves of the wilderness of Judea. During those years in the wilderness, David wrote many of the psalms that will help you today to worship the Father in spirit and truth.

The message of the "wilderness psalms" is that God is an oasis in the desert of difficult times. He is a safe place. Like David, you too will be pursued by an enemy seeking to kill, steal, and destroy you, simply because you are becoming a true worshiper of the Father in spirit and truth. David wrote in Psalm 61:2 – 3, *"Lead me to the rock that is higher than I, for you have been my refuge, a strong tower against the enemy."* God will lead you to the higher ground of worshiping Him in spirit and truth, according to His word.

The world, the flesh, and the devil are the enemies of true worship because true worship is characterized by the abandonment of self-worship. This is why David prayed, *"Lead me to the rock that is higher than I..."* Until you ask God to lead you to the *higher rock*, you will stay stuck in the mud of self-worship. The higher ground of true worship lifts you above the lies of self-worth, self-love, and self-seeking. True worship sees from the word the surpassing worth of the Father and His desire for you to know Him and His love for you in Christ.

In the wilderness psalms, you learn from David how to seek the Lord with all your heart in the midst of harsh and threatening circumstances. In seeking Him, you worship Him, for in seeking Him you abandon self for Someone greater. This overcomes the world, is harmful to the flesh, defeats the enemy, and pleases the Father.

Today, memorize and pray this prayer, *"Father, lead me to the Rock that is higher than I, for You have been my refuge, a strong tower against the enemy!"*

February 16

Read and pray Psalm 46, Proverbs 11:1 – 5, Mark 10:1 – 31, 2 Corinthian 8, Psalm 119:49 – 56.
2nd Exodus 28.
3rd Jeremiah 13.
4th 2 Samuel 15 – 16.

True Worship is Asking, Seeking, Knocking

One of the stark contrasts between Saul and David was their obedience. David was obedient to God and Saul was obedient to his own fears. In 1 Samuel 15:22, God told Saul through the prophet Samuel, *"Has the LORD as great delight in burnt offerings and sacrifices, as in obeying the voice of the LORD? Behold, to obey is better than sacrifice, and to listen than the fat of rams."* At that point, God had rejected Saul as king. This was not the first time Saul had deliberately disobeyed. But it was the last. God did not speak to Saul again.

David on the other hand was constantly asking God before he made his plans. His desire was to know and do God's will, not his own. The phrase, *"And David inquired of the LORD,"* is repeated several times throughout the chapters covering his life. He sought the Lord with all of his heart, which is what it means to pray.

The Hebrew word for "inquire" is *sha-al*, which means to ask, beg, inquire, search, or dig. It is used to describe prayer, which is worship, especially in the book of Psalms. This word combines asking, seeking, and knocking into one word, *sha-al*. It is obedience. God invites us to ask Him. When we do, it pleases the Father for it expresses trust in Him. This is why Jesus instructed us to *"ask and never stop asking, seek and never stop seeking, knock and never stop knocking...,"* Matthew 7:7. This is what it means to worship the Father in spirit and truth.

David wrote in Psalm 27:4, *"One thing I asked of the LORD, that will I seek after: that I may dwell in the house of the LORD all the days of my life, to gaze upon the beauty of the LORD and to inquire in his temple."* In this one request, David knew that all of his requests would be answered for he would be seeking after what God desired to give him. He knew that God's will would be done on earth as it is in heaven. This is what it means to worship the Father in spirit and truth.

Today, memorize some more lines from Psalm 119:49 – 56 so that you can meditate and pray them throughout the day.

February 17

Read and pray Psalm 47, Proverbs 11:6 – 11, Mark 10:32 – 52, 2 Corinthian 9, Psalm 119:49 – 56.

2nd Exodus 29.

3rd Jeremiah 14.

4th 2 Samuel 17 – 18.

The Oil and Water of Worship and Unforgiveness

King Saul would not give up pursuing David. It says in 1 Samuel 23:14, *"And Saul sought him every day, but God did not give him into his hand."* Two times in these chapters, God gave Saul into David's hand, but David would not touch *"...the LORD's anointed."* (1 Samuel 24:6, 26:11). It also states that David would return to live in *"the stronghold."*

The word "stronghold" is the interesting word *matsad* in Hebrew. It means a strong fortification, but the root word is a verb, which means to hunt, to chase, to pursue. This word is mentioned twice in these chapters, which describe how Saul was chasing David to kill him, and how David refused to hunt Saul. This is instructive.

We know from the Psalms that David had a heart that hunted God. The Lord Himself described David as a man *after* His own heart. David wrote in Psalm 42:1, *"As the deer pants for flowing streams, so pants my soul for you, O God."* It would have been easy for David to rid himself of the relentless fury of Saul and yet David had a different passion. His desire to know and pursue God was stronger than anything else in his life. Having a strong and passionate pursuit that becomes a fortification in your life can go either way; like that of Saul or like that of David.

Choosing to chase God everyday is to deny yourself of chasing everything else. One of the things we chase after is to "get even" with those who have hurt us, or have hurt those we love. This is called unforgiveness. If you are going to pursue the Father with a passion, to worship Him in spirit and truth, you must rid yourself of unforgiveness.

Some might say, "I can forgive, but I can't forget." It is impossible to forget an event in your life, especially if it carries strong emotion and pain. David knew that feeling all too well. What you can do is to release the debt associated with the event by forgiving the person, and asking God to heal you of the pain. When you do, it will not come from you, but from above, through you. When that happens, the memory of the event glorifies the Father, for it was His love that released the debt and His presence that healed the pain. Remembering the event then becomes an act of worship. And David knew that experience very well. This is what it means to worship the Father in spirit and truth.

Living in the stronghold of pursuing the Father and hunting for ways to express His love glorifies Him. Living in the stronghold of getting even, desiring vindication and justice, hunting ways to see "those people" get what is coming to them, ends up in a fortification of sin and separation from God. This is called a no-brainer, because it is not from your brain that you forgive, it is from the new heart that Christ made possible for you through His death on the cross and resurrection from the grave. It will be a sacrifice to forgive those who have hurt you and may still be hunting you. But it was a sacrifice that forgave you. A big one!

Today, decide to live in the stronghold of pursuing the Father in spirit and truth. Make that promise and commitment through faith in Jesus Christ, and He will do it.

February 18

Read and pray Psalm 48, Proverbs 11:12 – 15, Mark 11, 2 Corinthians 10, Psalm 119:49 – 56.
2nd Exodus 30.
3rd Jeremiah 15.
4th 2 Samuel 19 – 20.

Learning to Dance the Hard Way

One of the things that David is known for in the Bible is when he danced before the Lord (2 Samuel 6, 1 Chronicles 13 – 16). The context of 2 Samuel 6:14 and 1 Chronicles 15:29 teaches an important lesson that David learned the hard way.

The Ark of the Covenant had been in a place called Kiriath-jearim, and David wanted to bring it into Jerusalem, the city of God. David loved the presence of the Lord and desired to be near the ark, where God's presence dwelt.

It says in 1 Chronicles 13:1 – 4 that David consulted the commanders of thousands, and the commanders of hundreds, and with every leader about this plan to bring the ark to Jerusalem, and *"All the assembly agreed to do so, for the thing was right in the eyes of all the people."* But David did not consult the LORD.

The next few paragraphs describe the disastrous results of a good idea, but not according to the ways of God. It describes a great crowd, great music, great celebration, brand new equipment, full orchestra, but no Levites. And God's word was very clear about who could handle and move the ark, and David knew God's word, but was not following it.

Right in the middle of the great celebration the oxen that were yoked to the new cart carrying the ark, stumbled. Uzzah, who was driving the cart and was not a Levite, reached out his hand to steady the ark, and it says in 1 Chronicles 13:10, *"And the anger of the LORD was kindled against Uzzah, and he struck him down because he put his hand to the ark, and he died there before God."*

It also says that David was angry with the LORD and was afraid of Him that day. This is the opposite of the phrase, *the fear of the LORD*, which describes great reverence and awe and worship. David wanted to avoid God that day. He thought that the great crowd, great music, great orchestra, new cart, great idea, and unity of the people would impress God. But God is only impressed with His word. And David was not worshiping according to the word of God. The lesson is a compelling contrast with the popularity of the spectacular "worship" settings of American Christianity, which are now being exported into other parts of the world; but are not according to the word of the Lord.

In 1 Chronicles 15:1 – 2, you read how David followed God's word in moving the ark with the Levites rather than with the great parade of people. All Israel gathered in Jerusalem waiting for them and it to arrive. When they arrived in Jerusalem with the ark there was a great celebration, with music, and instruments, and most of all, *"...the Levites carrying the ark of God on their shoulders with the poles, as Moses had commanded according to the word of the LORD."* 1 Chronicles 15:15. And David danced before the LORD with all his might. The great celebration had as much to do with doing things according to the ways of God as it did with bringing the ark to Jerusalem.

Today, meditate on what it means to worship according to the truth of God's word. Of all the different ways that people worship God in the world, with what they have, and with all their might, the real question remains: Is it according to the ways of God, according to the word of God? The Father is pleased when we worship Him in spirit and truth, according to His ways.

February 19

Read and pray Psalm 49, Proverbs 11:16 – 26, Mark 12, 2 Corinthians 11, Psalm 119:57 – 64.
2nd Exodus 31.
3rd Jeremiah 16.
4th 2 Samuel 21 – 22.

Worship With the Sound of Music

David took music and gave to it the highest expression and value, of praise and thanksgiving to God for His steadfast love. In 1 Chronicles 15 – 17 you find the details of musical worship designed by David. This was a new assignment for the Levites who had been assigned by God to lead the nation of Israel in worship. Before David, Israel had only sung to the LORD on a few occasions, but David laced music into the very fabric of their worship.

The first mention of musical instruments in the Bible is found in Genesis 4:21, *"His brother's name was Jubal; he was the father of all those who play the lyre and pipe."* The lyre was a harp of strings, which made the beautiful sound of vibrating cords. The pipe was the musical sound of wind rushing through a horn.

But the context of Genesis 4 records the offspring of Cain and how sin first began to manifest its self-centeredness. Cain and his descendants were determined to live without God and His word. They were the original human high-achievers. The last verse in chapter four introduces the third son of Adam and Eve, Seth, the remnant for God, with these words, *"To Seth also a son was born, and he called his name Enosh. At that time people began to call upon the name of the LORD."* Chapter five records their only achievement; being fruitful and multiplying, which was God's first commandment to man (Genesis 1:28).

But it was God who created the sound of music (no pun intended). In creation, God designed the cords (strings) in the throats of the birds with every note of the musical scale. With the sound of the wind, God gave the blueprint for the first man to learn to whistle. Can you remember when you first learned to whistle? What a great day that was when you learned you had your very own instrument to play any song you wanted.

There are instructions in the book of Psalms for the use of instruments in thanking God and praising Him for His steadfast love. Psalm 150 commands the use of all of the instruments for praising God.

Many of us love Psalm 100 with the command, *"Make a joyful noise to the LORD, all the earth!"* The Hebrew word translated "noise" is the word *rua*, and is related to the word *ruach*, which means breath, or spirit. This word is used throughout the Old Testament for praise and singing. In Job 38:7, Job learns that this was the noise of the stars and of the angels, as God was creating all that there is. And in Joshua 6:5 it was what the LORD told Joshua and the army to sing with the trumpets, with the promise that the walls of Jericho would come crashing down with applause. This was the first time "they brought the house down" with a song.

The point is this: not all music and singing is worship, but it was intended to be. When you chose to give God your song of thanksgiving and praise for His steadfast love, you are letting God know that you have learned the true purpose for the sound of music, the highest purpose. This is what it means to worship the Father in spirit (*ruach*) and truth. The deepest joy and pleasure of music is when you have learned that it pleases the Father as you give it all to Him with thanksgiving and praise.

Today, sing to the Lord a song in worship. Use your vocal cords for their highest purpose; a song of praise to God. Whistle a song to the One who created the capacity to be able to make that noise, knowing that you are worshiping God when you do. Don't let the birds be the only ones who make a joyful noise. You can too. Worship with the sound of music. Put Psalm 119:57 to a tune that you love and sing it to the Lord throughout the day.

February 20

Read and pray Psalm 50, Proverbs 11:27 – 31, Mark 13, 2 Corinthians 12, Psalm 119:57 – 64.
2nd Exodus 32.
3rd Jeremiah 17.
4th 2 Samuel 23 – 24.

Heart-Felt Worship

Jesus said in Matthew 15:7 – 9 that a person could worship with words but no heart. He said, quoting Isaiah 29:13, *"This people honor me with their lips, but their heart is far from me; in vain do they worship me, teaching as doctrines the commandments of men."*

The disconnect of the mouth from the heart is a learned behavior. Around small children you quickly see the open connection of the mouth with the heart. They are naturally and innocently honest and will speak what their heart sees and feels. They must learn from their parents not to say what they know is true. How strange.

Our heavenly Father desires that we unlearn this kind of behavior especially in His presence. Heart-felt worship connects your mind and body with your new heart in Christ, and expresses His life as yours. This pleases the Father because this is what He did through His Son for and to you.

From the Psalms you learn this kind of true worship. David set the standard for this kind of heart-felt worship, and the other psalm-writers followed in his footsteps. He poured his heart out to God in worship because he knew that loving God was the only way to know the love of God. He also knew that God's love was a steadfast love, a sacrificial love, and an out-pouring love. He learned, and so can you, that with God, you got His heart, and that He only wants yours.

An example of this is seen in a very dramatic scene from David's life, found in 1 Chronicles 11:15 – 19. It is a passage describing David's mighty men, his trusted and loyal bodyguards. Their love and devotion to David reminded him of his love and devotion towards God. The telling episode was a time when David's enemies had taken control of Bethlehem, his hometown. David spoke the desire of his heart in 1 Chronicles 11:17 and said, *"Oh, that someone would give me water to drink from the well of Bethlehem that is by the gate!"* The water from that particular well must have had more than a special taste for David.

It was an expression of the deepest desire imaginable. This is what the Father is seeking as He searchers for true worshipers.

The story tells of how three of David's mighty men fought their way through the Philistine garrison at Bethlehem, filled a skin of water from the well by the gate, battled their way out and brought it to David. They must have looked like a buzz saw of swords and knives risking their lives to please their king and leader, David. By the time they presented their gift to David, they must have been quite the sight of fatigue, blood (not all theirs), and their precious gift of water for David. And what a sight the Lord Jesus Christ must have been to the Father as He was lifted up on the cross, presenting Himself to the Father for the deepest desire of the Father's heart, our salvation.

David, overwhelmed with the sight of what he deeply desired, received their gift, and then, poured it out to the Lord in worship. His men had provided him with something of extreme value and worth, giving him the opportunity to express what was in his heart toward the Lord. These mighty men were students that day in the class of what it means to worship the Father in spirit and truth, expressing from the heart the deepest desires of the heart.

As you worship the Father today, in spirit and truth from the Psalms, express to God your deepest desires. Pour out to Him what is in your heart, because in Jesus Christ God did that very thing for you. It pleases the Father when He sees Himself coming from you to Him. This is what it means to worship the Father in spirit and truth.

February 21

Read and pray Psalm 51, Proverbs 12:1 – 4, Mark 14:1 – 31, 2 Corinthians 13, Psalm 119:57 – 64.
2nd Exodus 33.
3rd Jeremiah 18.
4th 1 Kings 1 – 2.

Worshiping With Good Grief

The phrase "good grief" is sometimes used to express frustration or impatience. But when you enter into a time of grief, it is anything but "good," until you discover the good of grief.

Grief means loss. Grief is bitter loss. Bitterness is what remains after everything has been taken away. It is the dregs of life, the bitter pain of emptiness and sorrow. The Hebrew word for "bitter grief" is *maraw,* and is used throughout the Old Testament to describe sorrow and the loss of everything.

In the book of Ruth this is the word that Naomi picked for her new name as she came back to Bethlehem completely destitute (Ruth 1:20). She was a picture of the whole nation of Israel at the end of the period of the judges. So, how could there be any such thing as "good grief" when this experience is the loss of everything? Hold that question for a moment.

In 1 Samuel 30, you find the story of when David and his men returned home to Ziklag only to find that it had been raided by the Amalekites. The Amalekites were the terrorists of the Old Testament. The Amalekites had raided Ziklag while David and his men were away. They took all of their wives, children, and property and then burned everything to the ground.

It says that David and his men became "very *maraw*," (1 Samuel 30:6). This could be described as the worst possible day imaginable in your life. Then, to make matters worse, if that is possible, it says that David's men, in their bitter grief, plotted to stone him to death. They blamed David and David's God. The bitterness of blaming others and God is sometimes the result of horrendous loss and grief.

But in that same verse, 1 Samuel 30:6, there is another word that describes David's response to this situation. It is used in the phrase, *"But David strengthened himself in the LORD his God."* The word is a powerful Hebrew word, *kazak!* An exclamation mark is always associated with this word in defining it. It literally means to have a death hold on someone or something. This is when you are hanging onto the end of your rope, with a big knot on the end. It is used in Judges 13 – 16 describing the strength of Samson.

Here is the point: when David lost everything, his family, his home, his reputation, and was about to lose his life, he grabbed on to God and would not let go. *Kazak!* This is what it means to worship the Father in spirit and truth with good grief.

Now you can turn loose of the question from the third paragraph. Until you get to the place where you can turn loose of the bitter questions in life, and with a greater strength lay hold of God with everything He has in Himself for you, the bitterness of *maraw* will define your life. For some it becomes their identity, flavoring every relationship and everything they do. But with God, your life can have a new definition, new identity, new relationships, and activities.

The strength of *kazak* comes from worshiping God, especially when everything else seems to be gone. It is a heart that is set on the Lord as life and for life, so that when everything else in life has gone south and the wheels have fallen off, there is God holding everything together with His powerful hold on you.

Today, set your heart on the Father, through faith in Jesus Christ His Son, and by the Holy Spirit living in you, with you, through you, as you, there will be an eternal reserve of supernatural strength, *kazak*, the good grief, which glorifies the Father in spirit and truth. Work some more lines from Psalm 119: 57 – 64 and pray them today.

February 22

Read and pray Psalm 52, Proverbs 12:5 – 9, Mark 14:32 – 72, Galatians 1, Psalm 119:57 – 64.
2nd Exodus 34.
3rd Jeremiah 19.
4th 1 Kings 3 – 4.

The Right Way to Worship

One of the key words in the Old Testament for worship is the Hebrew word, *derek*, which is translated "way," or "path." It is used to describe the lifestyle or culture of both the righteous and the wicked. Psalm 1 says that the blessed man is the one who does not *"stand in the way of sinners."* Not only does he not travel in their direction, he does not even go near it. This Psalm ends with the clear instruction, *"The LORD knows the way of the righteous, but the way of the wicked will perish."* Psalm 1:6.

The first place this word is used in the Old Testament is in Genesis 3:24, *"…he placed the cherubim and a flaming sword that turned every way to guard the way to the tree of life."* God had a particular path, His way, to the tree of life. Because of their sinful condition, Adam and Eve would be blocked from knowing that path. In a sense, their steps were no longer straight. Their heart was divided. Their life was fractured. They were unable to walk in the way pleasing to the Lord, in His way.

The cry of the psalmist was to learn the way of the LORD. Psalm 86:11 says, *"Teach me your way, O LORD, that I may walk in your truth; unite my heart to fear your name."* In that simple request you learn that the way of the Lord is a particular direction, that it must be learned from God, that it is learned from His word, and that it has purpose. The purpose of learning the way of the Lord is to live a life of whole-hearted worship.

Jesus said, *"I am the way, the truth, and the life. No one comes to the Father except through me."* John 14:6. When you decide that you desire to learn the ways of God, you begin with Christ and learn of Him. All of the ways of God are seen in the Lord Jesus Christ. Every step He took pleased the Father.

The way to the tree of life is no longer blocked. It was opened with the invitation of Jesus when He said, *"Come to me, all you who labor and are heavy laden, and I will give you rest. Take my yoke and learn of me, for I am gentle and lowly in heart, and you will find rest for your souls. For my yoke is easy and my burden is light."* Matthew 11:28 – 30.

The first step in the journey of becoming a true worshiper who worships the Father in spirit and truth, is the step of following Christ. Learning the ways of God is to learn of Christ and His ways.

Today, learn the prayer of Psalm 86:11. Know what you are asking God for in that prayer and the path of it. Meditate on the destination of that prayer and you will be transformed along the way.

February 23

Read and pray Psalm 53, Proverbs 12:10 – 14, Mark 15:1 – 20, Galatians 2, Psalm 119:57 – 64.
2ⁿᵈ Exodus 35.
3ʳᵈ Jeremiah 20.
4ᵗʰ 1 Kings 5 – 6.

Waiting to Know the Ways of God

Psalm 25 is a song about the ways of God. The Hebrew word *derek*, which is translated "ways," is used several times in this psalm. It is also translated in this psalm with the word "lead." When you decide to follow Jesus, He leads you in the ways of God.

In Psalm 25:4 – 5 you see the connection of learning the ways of God, from the word of God, as you wait upon the Lord. *"Make me to know your ways, O LORD; teach me your paths. Lead me in your truth and teach me, for you are the God of my salvation; for you I wait all the day long."*

In learning this prayer you discover that the ways of God are learned from a personal, intimate, and interactive relationship with God. The word "know" in the first line is the Hebrew word *yadah*. This is not the knowledge about something, it is the knowledge of someone. It is a personal relationship word. This means that you can only know the ways of God within a personal, intimate, and interactive relationship with God. Learning the ways of God is a worship experience.

The request *"Lead me,"* in 25:5 is the Hebrew word *derek*, the same word for "way." God leads in one direction; according to His ways and His word. As you desire to learn the ways of God, from the word of God, and begin moving in His direction, your request for guidance in His will is answered.

Another instructive Hebrew word in this passage is the word for "wait." It is the Hebrew word *kavah*. It is first used in the Old Testament in the creation account in Genesis 1:9, when God "gathered" the waters together to form the seas and the dry land. It also means to join and bind together. It was the word for making rope out of three cords as they are bound (gathered) together into one. This word is used and translated as "wait" in Isaiah 40:31, *"…but they that wait upon the LORD shall renew their strength; they shall mount up with wings like eagles; they shall run and not be weary; they shall walk and not faint."*

Learning the ways of God requires waiting upon the Lord, which means to be gathered and bound together with Him in His word. This requires your time and your attention. This is simple, but not easy. Laziness is the enemy of learning the ways of God. The world, the flesh, and the devil will fight you every step of the way (*derek*). But the reward is eternal. And this is what it means to worship the Father in spirit and truth.

February 24

Read and pray Psalm 54, Proverbs 12:15 – 22, Mark 15:21 – 47, Galatians 3, Psalm 119:57 – 64.
2ⁿᵈ Exodus 36.
3ʳᵈ Jeremiah 21.
4ᵗʰ 1 Kings 7 – 8.

Instructions For Sinners in Worship

Once you have decided to become a true worshiper, one who worships the Father in spirit and truth, you commit yourself to come under the training of the Holy Spirit in the word of God. With that decision comes the understanding that you are not a true worshiper, but have been invited by the true teacher, the Holy Spirit, to receive the right way to worship the Father. This is a humbling experience with the Lord. This is an enlightening experience with God. You will never be the same again, which is one of the ways of God.

In Psalm 25:8 – 9, you read, *"Good and upright is the LORD; therefore he instructs sinners in the way. He leads the humble in what is right, and teaches the humble his way."* One of the ways of God is that He gives instructions to sinners concerning His ways. And God is right in doing this.

The Hebrew word for "sinners" is **katah**, and has the meaning of being on the wrong road and missing the destination. This is also called being lost and not knowing it. It is a humbling experience to learn that you have gone astray and that you are lost and do not know where you are going. Some will not believe and remain full of their own understanding and pride. But God instructs sinners who believe that they are wrong and that He is right, all the time and in every way.

The word for "instructs" is one of the primitive root words in the Hebrew language. It is the word **yarah**. Originally it meant to throw something with a forward motion and with great force. This developed into the idea of an archer shooting a straight arrow with a true bow. It later was used with the understanding of being refreshed with water after near exhaustion.

Used in the context of learning the ways of God it has the meaning of someone who has totally exhausted all of his ways, unable to move in the right direction or make any progress in life at all, when suddenly, like a bolt of lightning, God appears with the truth. With the truth, God gives a new direction, a forward momentum with great power; His power, in the right direction. It is refreshing to learn the ways of God; cool and refreshing like water to a thirsty soul.

This is a humbling experience for sinners as well as an enlightening experience with great joy and refreshment. He instructs sinners in the way. God is good and right in doing this. He sees Himself in the instruction in your life and it pleases Him to do this. This is what it means to worship the Father in spirit and truth. What does Psalm 119:57 – 64 say about "my ways" and God's way?

February 25

Read and pray Psalm 55, Proverbs 12:23 – 28, Mark 16, Galatians 4, Psalm 119:57 – 64.

2nd Exodus 37.

3rd Jeremiah 22.

4th 1 Kings 9 – 10.

Remember When You Worship

One of the most important words in the Old Testament is the word "remember." In Hebrew, it is the word *zakar*, which means to meditate upon, to recall, to confess, to rehearse, to think about, to record. It is used over 300 times in one form or another. Remembering is one of the ways of God.

In Psalm 25:6 – 7, it says, *"Remember your mercy, O LORD, and your steadfast love, for they have been of old. Remember not the sins of my youth or my transgressions; according to your steadfast love, remember me, for the sake of your goodness, O LORD!"* In these two verses you learn why remembering is one of the ways of God. He meditates upon His own goodness. The Lord recalls what He has said and what He has done. He thinks about His own faithfulness and His steadfast love. Remembering is one of His ways. It pleases God to remember.

Our memories are marred with sin. When we think about "the good old days," it is always in the context of having lost something along the way in comparison to the present days. We remember and want to go back. But God remembers Himself with the present and future in mind. He is eternal. God does not lose anything along the way. His memory gives Him joy and glory because He recalls His faithfulness, and He knows He will always be faithful. He looks forward to what He is about to do, according to what He has said He will do.

God desires us to remember what He has said and what He has done. In the Old Testament, God established the feasts of Israel to remember His mighty deeds and to point forward to His promises. The feasts were the foundations of Israel's worship because they pointed to God in their past, so that they could recognize His activity in their present, in order to trust His promises for the future. Remembering gave meaning and purpose to their lives.

When Jesus took the bread and the wine of the Passover in the upper room with His disciples, He said, *"...do this in remembrance of me,"* Luke 22:19. With that word, Jesus gave the full meaning of the Old

Testament feasts as they pointed to Him, as well as giving His disciples the foundation of worship in the new covenant with Him.

When Jesus hung on the cross, the Scripture says that He was crucified between two thieves. One railed at Him saying, *"Are you not the Christ? Save yourself and us!"* But the other rebuked him, saying, *"Do you not fear God, since you are under the same sentence of condemnation? And we indeed justly, for we are receiving the due reward of our deeds; but this man has done nothing wrong. Jesus, remember me when you come into your kingdom."*

At that moment, Jesus must have heard the prayer of Psalm 25:6 – 7 coming from the lips of the thief, and He replied, *"Truly I say to you, today you will be with me in Paradise."* Luke 23:39 – 43.

This man was certainly confessing his own sin and guilt, as well as acknowledging Jesus' innocence. But he was also confessing his faith in Jesus as the coming King. Jesus may not have appeared at that moment as a king, but the man expressed his faith that Jesus one day would reign as King. This brings glory to the Father and this is what it means to worship the Father in spirit and truth.

Today, remember what God has said by meditating on His word. Remember what He has done in your life with gratitude and joy, and recall His promises. God is with you, and Christ is coming again.

February 26

Read and pray Psalm 56, Proverbs 13:1 – 3, Luke 1:1 – 38, Galatians 5, Psalm 119:65 – 72.
2nd Exodus 38.
3rd Jeremiah 23.
4th 1 Kings 11 – 12.

Worshiping on the High Ways

Becoming a true worshiper, one who worships the Father in spirit and truth is a learning experience. God's word is the textbook and the Holy Spirit is your teacher. As God reveals more and more of Himself to you in His Son, Jesus Christ, you know Him more and more. God does this according to His ways. The Bible states clearly that the ways of God are higher than the ways of man (Isaiah 55:9). The ways of God are the high ways.

One of the words for "ways," is the Hebrew word *orak*, which is used many times in the Old Testament and translated as "path," as in a well-trodden road. For example, it is used to describe the caravan routes of the ancient world (Job 6:18), and for the main roads that connected the major cities of the world (Judges 5:6). With that understanding, in the context of the ways of God, you understand that the *orak* of God are the great attributes of His character and nature.

Psalm 25:10 states, *"All of the paths of the LORD are steadfast love and faithfulness, for those who keep his covenant and his testimonies."* These are mammoth truths, highways to travel on with God concerning the revelation of Himself to you, and connecting Himself with you. It says that God's *orak* are all characterized by His choice of loving you and your willingness to see the surpassing value of that choice.

The Hebrew word translated "steadfast love" is the word *hesed*. It is also translated as "mercy," and many times as "loving-kindness." The New Testament word for this is *agape*; God's love. It describes God's willful choice to love and enter into a loving relationship with those who will trust Him. The Hebrew word *emet*, "faithfulness," is a twin to *hesed* simply because God remains faithful to His own choice to love.

God has chosen to love you and He is faithful to His own choice of you. His desire, His will, is for you to choose to love Him and enter into a loving relationship with Him through faith in Jesus Christ. As you do, God reveals more and more of the truth and goodness of His choice of you. It becomes clearer and clearer that this is not about you, but more and more of Him. Hallelujah.

All of the ways of God are seen in God's choice and love for you and His faithfulness to His choice and love for you. This is the major thoroughfare and highway, the *orak* of God, for you to travel on as you learn of Him and become a true worshiper. This is what it means to worship the Father in spirit and truth.

Today, memorize the first line of Psalm 119:65 – 72. Reword that confession into your own words and declare it today to God in your prayer for the day.

February 27

Read and pray Psalm 57, Proverbs 13:4 – 8, Luke 1:39 – 80, Galatians 6, Psalm 119:65 – 72.
2nd Exodus 39.
3rd Jeremiah 24.
4th 1 Kings 13 – 14.

Worship and Walking

When babies learn to walk it is a big deal. They take their first steps and immediately their parents put up barriers to keep them safe. Your steps must also be guided or you will wander away and not even know it. One of the ways of God is that He provides a path for your steps in His word. When you trust His path rather than your own, He rewards you with Himself. He keeps you safe.

Psalm 119 is a tremendous chapter of learning the worship-walk of prayer from God's word. It is a prayer to shape your prayers; a major highway in the direction of becoming a true worshiper. The entire psalm is a prayer. The first three verses are the only part of the chapter that is not a prayer. They are the introduction to the prayer and reveal the outcome of learning and praying this prayer for life.

"Blessed are those whose way is blameless, who walk in the law of the LORD! Blessed are those who keep his testimonies, who seek him with their whole heart, who also do no wrong, but walk in his ways! Psalm 119:1 – 3.

You may ask, how can a person be blameless, keep God's word, and do no wrong? That sounds like perfection and no one is perfect, except God. Exactly. And one of the ways of God is that He gives Himself, which is perfection in His eyes, to those who will trust Him by following His word, by seeking to know Him in His word.

Notice again in the Scripture above that being blameless, keeping God's word, and doing no wrong, is not a performance on your part, but rather a direction you walk. Not everyone can walk, but everyone is moving in a certain direction, seeking after something in life. God has provided a blessed direction if you are willing to trust Him and go His way, after Him.

The word "blameless" in verse one is the Hebrew word, *taw-meem,* which means complete, perfect, whole, in total accord with the truth, in perfect alignment with God. This is a description of the Lord Jesus Christ and the life He lived before the Father and the watching world around Him. Following Christ and walking with Him, pleases the Father, and is in perfect alignment with His word. Jesus is the way, the truth, and the life.

The word "law" is the Hebrew word, *torah*, and means instructions. These are the steps God teaches His children when they are learning to walk. Each step reveals something about God's character. In following His instructions, you learn of Him and know Him more and more. He teaches you of Himself.

The word "keep" in verse two is the Hebrew word, *naw-tsar*, and means to guard closely because of the supreme value of something (its twin is the Hebrew word *shamar*). It has the understanding of watching something carefully and preserving it with great care. Spending time each day in God's word, seeking after Him in it, is what it means to value God's word as the direction you live by and walk in. God has promised His blessing to the one who believes this promise.

The word "do no wrong" in verse three is the Hebrew word *avlah*, which means, wickedness. This word has built in to it the understanding of leading others astray. True wickedness is when it is shared with others, causing them to fall. But the promise of God, for the person who will walk in the pathway of His word, is that they will be blessed and become a blessing for others. They will not cause others to stumble and fall, but will provide help for others to get up and go with them in the blessed way. The path of trusting God from His word is blessed by God and is offered to anyone who is willing to believe and begin moving in that blessed direction.

Today, take another step in learning to pray from Psalm 119. Memorize and meditate on 119:66 and learn of God from the good judgment and knowledge of His commandments.

February 28

Read and pray Psalm 58 and 59 (read Psalm 59 with its readings when February has 29 days, otherwise read both today), Proverbs 13:9 – 14 (mark with #58), Proverbs 13:15 – 19 (mark with #59), Luke 2:1 – 40 (mark with #58), Luke 2:41 – 52 (mark with 59), Ephesians 1 (#58), Ephesians 2 (#59), Psalm 119:65 – 72.

2ⁿᵈ Exodus 40 (#58), Leviticus 1 (#59).

3ʳᵈ Jeremiah 25 (#58), Jeremiah 26 (#59).

4ᵗʰ 1 Kings 15 – 16 (#59), 1 Kings 17 – 18 (#59).

The Ways and Works of God

There is a literary device in the Hebrew language called "an echo." This is when one line "echoes" the same thought of the previous line with different words. This helps interpret the Old Testament. For example, Psalm 145:17 says, *"The LORD is righteous in all his ways and kind in all his works."* In that verse, *righteous* and *kind* are different words, but have the same meaning. They correspond to *his ways* and *his works*, which are also different words, but with the same meaning.

When you learn the ways of God you will also be learning the works of God. To put it another way, God works according to His ways in your life. This particular verse teaches that God is righteous and kind in His ways and works.

The Hebrew word "righteous" is *tsadeek* and is used as an adjective in this verse describing God. It means that God is always right in making people and things right with Him. And He is right in doing this. This verse states that God is like this in all of His ways. As you learn the ways of God you will begin to see that they all line up with this truth: God desires to make people and things right with Himself, according to His truth. And God is right in doing this. He made it right. God is so good.

The echo phrase in this verse says the same thing, but with different words. It states the truth that God is *kind in all his works.* The Hebrew word for "kind" is *haseed*, and is also an adjective. The verb form of this word is *hesed*, which is translated as "loving kindness." This is the covenant love of God and corresponds to the New Testament word *agape*, God's love. You may have heard of the group called *Hasidic Jews.* They derive their name from this Hebrew word, *hesed*. It also has the meaning of faithfulness and holiness.

The point is this: God is right in all of His ways in making you right with Himself, which is a reflection of His faithful covenant-making love expressed toward you in His Son, Jesus Christ. This is also the work that He is doing in your life right now; faithfully making you right with Himself because of His eternal love, which He loves you with. And it pleases Him to be that way.

As you know God more and more by learning His ways more and more, you will experience more and more of His love and joy. This pleases God, which is what it means to worship the Father in spirit and truth.

Today, worship the Father by thanking Him for being righteous in the way that He is faithfully making you right with Himself through Jesus Christ.

March 1

Read and pray Psalm 60 and 61, Proverbs 13:20 – 25 (#60), Proverbs 14:1 – 5 (#61), Luke 3 (#60), Luke 4 (#61), Ephesian 3 (#60), Ephesians 4 (#61), Psalm 119:65 – 72.
2nd Leviticus 2 (#60), Leviticus 3 (#61).
3rd Jeremiah 27 (#60), Jeremiah 28 (#61).
4th 1 Kings 19 – 20 (#60), 1 Kings 21 – 22 (#61).

The Most Quoted Psalm in the New Testament

Psalm 110 is the most quoted psalm in the New Testament, used eight times in all, and it only has seven verses. In Matthew, Mark, and Luke, Jesus quotes it when He asked the religious leaders, only a few days before His death and resurrection, *"What do you think about the Christ? Whose son is he?"* Matthew 22:42, Mark 12:35, Luke 20:41. (other references: Acts 2:34, Hebrews 1:13, 5:5 – 6, 7:17, 21.)

The religious leaders of Israel had been trying to trap Jesus in anything they could find from the very beginning of His ministry. After Jesus rode into Jerusalem on Palm Sunday, they intensified their efforts with a barrage of questions. The Lord handled each question in brilliant fashion, silencing them every time.

Finally, Jesus asked them this question about the Messiah, the Christ. It was an easy answer for them. They quickly said, *"The son of David."* This was based upon the covenant that God made with David, that his son would reign on his throne from Jerusalem, forever (2 Samuel 7). At that point, Jesus introduced one of the songs of David concerning God's Messiah, Psalm 110; *"The LORD said to my Lord, 'Sit at my right hand, until I put your enemies under your feet.'"* Then came the follow-up question from Jesus, *"If then David calls him Lord, how is he his son?"*

The religious leaders knew that Jesus was from the tribe of Judah, David's tribe. They knew that "*son of David*" was one of the favorite names that the crowds called Jesus. They knew that Jesus was a great teacher and were jealous of Him because of the great crowds that followed Him. But when the crowds in Jerusalem on Palm Sunday started attributing to Jesus the title of Son of God with their shouts from Psalm 118, *"Hosanna...Blessed is he who comes in the name of the Lord...,"* it was too much for them.

When Jesus cleaned house in the Temple that day, turning over the money changer's tables and crying out *"My house shall be called a house of prayer for all people, but you have made it a den of thieves,"* they thought He was acting like He owned the place (Which He did! They just didn't know it, yet.).

But they could not argue with Psalm 110. It was God's word. David wrote, in the Spirit, of the divine nature of the Messiah, his son. Everyone knew that David sure wasn't divine. Bathsheba and Nathan the prophet would be the first to vote "no" to that suggestion. But David's greater son, the one that God spoke of in His covenant with David, would be God's Son as well as David's son, the Messiah; our Lord Jesus Christ, fully man, as God intended man to be, and fully God as the eternal Son of God, the Christ, slain before the foundations of the world; in one individual, Jesus Christ.

Jesus is His name, given to Mary and Joseph by the angel before He was born. This is His name as man, just like us, yet without sin. Christ is His name given by the Father; the anointed suffering servant of God, the eternal Son of God. What an amazing truth, the incarnation, God in flesh, Jesus Christ, born in Bethlehem.

Oswald Chambers said, "Christianity is unique in the world's religions not so much with the Fatherhood of God, but rather with the Babyhood of God!"[5] God was born and placed in a feed trough because there was no room in the Inn.

Psalm 110 is the most quoted psalm in the New Testament because of this truth; it points to the true nature of the one-and-only begotten of the Father, our Lord Jesus Christ. It means that His life is the only one that fully pleased the Father. Knowing Christ pleases the Father, which is what it means to worship the Father in spirit and truth.

Today, thank God for the Lord Jesus Christ, your Savior, your Lord, your Master, your King, your constant Companion, and Friend. He is with you, always.

March 2

Read and pray Psalm 62, Proverbs 14:5 – 10, Luke 5, Ephesian 5, Psalm 119:65 – 72.
2ⁿᵈ Leviticus 4.
3ʳᵈ Jeremiah 29.
4ᵗʰ 2 Kings 1 – 2.

Easter and the First Day of the New Creation

In Genesis 1:3 – 5, God created light and separated it from the darkness and there was evening and morning of the first day. The Jews named the days of the week by numbers, one through seven. The first day, we call Sunday, and the seventh day, the Sabbath, we call Saturday. When God created light, He created time by separating light from darkness, the first day. With time, He created the past, the present, and the future.

On Easter Sunday each year we celebrate the first day of the new creation, the day that our Lord was raised from the dead. As part of that celebration, we recognize a new time in the lives of the followers of Christ.

In Him you have a new past with one event in it; the cross. At the cross, Jesus handled all of your past in such a way that brought glory to the Father. He died on the cross, and you died with Him, and the penalty of your sins was paid in full. All of your sins are forgiven. This brought great pleasure to the Father for the way into His presence was opened for "whosoever will" to come.

In Christ you have a new present, life in Him, with Him, by Him, and for Him. When Christ was raised, you were raised with Him to walk in newness of life (new time). This life is His life lived in you, in this world. In this world, you do have tribulation, trials, and troubles, but life in Him, with Him, by Him, and for Him is victorious life over those troubles and trials, and one that brings great pleasure and glory to the Father with joy inexpressible for you. This is because in the new present, the Father is working all things in it for good, just like He did in the first creation. He saw that it was good. The Father sees what He is doing in your life with Him now, and can see Himself in it; and He is pleased with His work. It is good.

In Christ you have a new future, the resurrection. The promise of your new body is guaranteed by the Holy Spirit, who is lives in you, and is preparing you for it right now. This is not something you hope for; it is something you hope in. The new future is as secure as the truth of the resurrection of Jesus from the dead, and the peace that comes from His presence in your heart today. God says that you are seated with Christ in heaven (Ephesians 2:6). One of the ways of God is, first He says it, then He does it, every time. In Christ you have a new past, a new present, and a new future. Don't wait until Easter to celebrate this new reality. Be thankful and celebrate today.

Work on another line from Psalm 119:65 – 72 in order to take it with you today as your prayer throughout the day and worship the Father with it; in spirit and truth.

March 3

Read and pray Psalm 63, Proverbs 14:11 – 16, Luke 6:1 – 19, Ephesians 6, Psalm 119:65 – 72.
2nd Leviticus 5.
3rd Jeremiah 30.
4th 2 Kings 3 – 4.

The Fellowship of the Burning Hearts

Cleopas and his wife were on their way back to Emmaus on the first day of the week, the first Easter Sunday. The account of what happened that day is found in Luke 24:13 – 35. It says that they were discussing together all of the things that had happened that day, when Jesus came along side of them on their journey. They did not recognize Him, and He asked them about the things they were discussing with themselves.

They told Jesus all of the things they knew. You could call them the facts of the gospel; Jesus of Nazareth was a mighty man in word and deed before God and the people; the religious leaders rejected Him, turned Him over to Pilate, and He was crucified. Several ran to the tomb on the third day and saw angels, and some even said that they had seen Him; that Jesus had risen from the dead.

But they were sad about these things. They knew the right information, but they were holding on to their own hopes about other things, hoping that Jesus would be the redeemer of Israel. They believed the testimonies about Jesus, but Jesus called them unbelievers when He said, *"O foolish ones..."* Luke 24:26, because they did not believe all that the prophets had said.

Here is the point: When you refuse to turn loose of your own plans and hopes, and keep trying to manage your own sin and life, or keep trying to manage God, your eyes will be blinded to know the Way, the Truth, and the Life, even if He is walking beside you.

And you will be sad and discouraged because things will not be turning out the way you thought they would, or should. When you listen to testimonies about Jesus and learn information about God, but not listen to God and what He has said in His word, your eyes will stay shut to know Christ. *"But faith comes by hearing, and hearing by the word of God."* Romans 10:17. Faith does not come from hearing testimonies about Jesus, faith comes from hearing God's testimony about Jesus.

At that point in the story, Jesus began to unfold the Scriptures concerning Himself in the Old Testament. What a walking-Bible study they had that first Easter Sunday evening. They arrived at their home and asked Jesus to stay with them. The Bible study had created a hunger for more. The Bible is like that when Jesus is the main course. Jesus stayed with them because they asked Him to stay with them. Have you asked Him to stay with you, because you desire to know more and more of Him from the Bible? You must.

Then something surprising happened. Rather than taking the passive role as a guest in their home, waiting to be served, Jesus took the position and role of the host, not the guest, and took the bread, blessed it, broke it, and gave it to them. He revealed Himself as the Master, not the guest. At that moment their eyes were opened and they knew it was Jesus. And they made a wonderful statement in 24:32, *"Did not our hearts burn within us while he talked with us on the road, while he opened to us the Scriptures?"*

Here is the point: Their eyes were opened by the light from within their hearts of the things from the Scriptures concerning Jesus as the Christ. They were now members of the fellowship of the burning hearts, people who have received the word of God concerning Jesus, the Messiah. These are the things to be talking with one another about, the things concerning Jesus as the Christ from the Bible.

They returned to the upper room and began to share what they learned in the Bible concerning Jesus and how He appeared in their midst. This is a lesson you must learn today. If you want Jesus to show up and reveal Himself, discuss with others the things concerning Christ from the Scriptures. And what wonderful things they are.

Forget about trying to manage your own life and let Jesus be the Master. Listen to what God has to say about His Son, the Lord Jesus Christ, from His word. Allow the testimony of God to light a fire in your heart concerning the things about Jesus. Fuel the fire from within your heart with the Spirit and the word, to open your eyes to see Jesus in your midst.

Today, take that fire with you by memorizing another line from Psalm 119:65 – 72 and praying it throughout the day. This is what it means to worship the Father in spirit and truth.

March 4

Read and pray Psalm 64, Proverbs 14:17 – 25, Luke 6:20 – 49, Philippians 1, Psalm 119:65 – 72.
2nd Leviticus 6.
3rd Jeremiah 31.
4th 2 Kings 5 – 6.

The Seventh Day and Worship

The first thing that was called "holy" in creation was the seventh day, Genesis 2:3. It was also the third thing that God blessed (first blessing was given to the fish and the birds with the command to be fruitful and multiple, 1:22; second blessing given to man with the same command, 1:28).

The seventh day of creation was unique with the third blessing, and then set apart with a characteristic exclusive of God; it was called holy. There would be many other places, people, and things called "holy" by God in the Old Testament, but the seventh day, the first one, was definitive for all the rest.

The seventh day of creation was blessed by God and called holy because God saw that what He had said, He had done, completely and perfectly. *"And on the seventh day God finished his work that he had done, and he rested on the seventh day on the seventh day from all his work that he had done."*

God did not rest because He was tired; He rested because His work was completed. God works by speaking, and all that He had said in creation was accomplished; it was finished, and it was good. God is faithful. What He says, He does, perfectly, every time.

The seventh day revealed God's faithfulness in creation, and it pleased Him. Rest is pleasant. Rest is a slow deep breath. More than that, rest signals completion and a transition to a new beginning. Rest is faithfulness in that what God has said, He will do, and will do again, and again.

God used "seven" in the Old Testament to point to the perfection of His work by His word, His faithfulness; seventh day, seventh month, seventh year, seventh cycle of years, all pointed to His work by His word to reveal that God is faithful. When man joined God in being faithful, he pleased God and was called righteous, holy, and faithful. These are all characteristics of God and are good and please Him.

But the Old Testament also reveals the failure of man to be faithful. Man is seen in the Old Testament as sinful, unfaithful, and disobedient. But in the midst of man's unfaithfulness, God promised One who would come and be perfectly faithful; His Servant, His Son, His Messiah. The Old Testament closed with the promise that Elijah would announce His arrival (Malachi 4:5 – 6, the last two verses of the Old Testament).

The New Testament is the record of the life of rest, the life of faithfulness, the life that is completely and perfectly pleasing to the Father, the life of Jesus Christ, God's only begotten Son. When Jesus was dying on the cross, His last words were *"It is finished!"* John 19:30, and the six days of the new creation were completed; salvation was created by the Father in Christ Jesus.

When you put your faith in the Lord Jesus Christ and the work of salvation that He accomplished by His life, death, and resurrection from the dead, you enter His seventh day, His rest. Joining Christ in His finished work pleases the Father because He sees Himself in you; He sees the faithfulness of His Son. This is what it means to worship the Father in spirit and truth.

Today, rest from trying to please God and see that Christ Jesus did, fully and perfectly. Rest in that truth and receive His life as yours today. Spend one more day praying from Psalm 119:65 – 72. Tomorrow you will begin the next prayer section.

March 5

Read and pray Psalm 65, Proverbs 14:26 – 35, Luke 7:1 – 35, Philippians 2, Psalm 119:73 – 80.
2nd Leviticus 7.
3rd Jeremiah 32.
4th 2 Kings 7 – 8.

Spiritual Adrenaline and Worship

The third and fourth chapters of Hebrews are definitive in understanding faith, the finished work of Christ, and the fulfillment of the seventh day rest. You understand the Old Testament in the light of the New Testament, not the other way around. This is one of the principles of hermeneutics (interpretation of Scripture). The third and fourth chapters of Hebrews give meaning to the seventh-day rest of creation in Genesis 2:2 – 3, and the greater seventh-day rest in Christ.

The message of the book of Hebrews is one of encouragement to believers who were discouraged by the persecution they were enduring. Some were even abandoning their walk with Christ to return to their former faith in Judaism. Others were considering the temptation. Some have never had to face that kind of persecution and so it is hard to identify with the temptation. But in the two chapters mentioned above, the writer reminds us of an important story in Israel's history as it relates to the seventh-day rest. He connects entering and the conquest of the Promised Land with entering the seventh-day rest of God, as well as the battles to face in it.

First, he states that some of those who came out of Egypt did not enter the land because of unbelief. They died in the wilderness, while their children, led by Joshua and Caleb, entered and conquered the Promised Land (3:16 – 19). Then he says that God's promise of entering His rest is still in effect with something much greater than what the nation of Israel received when they entered and took possession of the Promised Land under Joshua (4:1 – 10).

He reminded the believers that David prophesied in Psalm 95 about another day of rest that was coming, *"Today, if you hear his voice, do not harden your hearts."* His point is that there is a greater seventh-day rest of God for the people of God who will receive His word and believe. Then comes the clincher: *"So then, there remains a Sabbath rest for the people of God, for whoever has entered God's rest has also rested from his works as God did from his."* Hebrews 4:9 – 11.

This passage teaches the truth of resting in the Life of Christ, which fully pleased the Father. This defines salvation by faith in Jesus Christ. But in order to rest in peace (RIP) with God through faith in Christ, you must die to the life of trying to please God with your own righteousness and good works. Entering the seventh-day rest of God is to receive the life of Christ, the only life fully pleasing to the Father, believing that He is now your life, and that you are accepted and loved by the Father just as the Son is in Him.

What a relief it is to know that your life pleases the Father. This is what it means to worship the Father in spirit and truth. The seventh day of rest in the Old Testament was the day of worship. Resting in the life of Christ becomes a life of true worship.

The next verse gives some trouble. *"Let us therefore strive to enter that rest so that no one may fall by the same sort of disobedience."* 4:11. The word "strive" is the Greek word, *speodow*, and means to exert intense effort with speed and exhilaration, to be motivated with intense desire. You could call it the Greek concept of adrenaline. We get our English word "speed" from this Greek word.

In the context of Hebrews 3 – 4, this word means that for those who have believed in the finished work of Christ for their salvation, and are resting in His life as theirs to please the Father, there is a new motivation of excitement in living His life; a new battle to fight; new weapons and energy to fight with. In Christ there is a spiritual adrenaline for obedience and good works. The Holy Spirit motivates with spiritual truth and sound doctrine for obedience. No longer are you trying to earn God's favor, but with greater and greater effort, with *speodow,* you are living in it. The grace of God is not opposed to effort; it is opposed to earning. You must still fight. But now, you fight from victory, not for it. The battle has already been won, but the fight is still on.

Today, meditate on the truth that Christ is your life, and that you, the new you, are fully pleasing to the Father in Him, and feel the excitement of spiritual adrenaline. Memorize Psalm 119:73 and begin a new section for the next seven days of praying God's word throughout the day.

March 6

Read and pray Psalm 66, Proverbs 15:1 – 5, Luke 7:36 – 50, Philippians 3, Psalm 119:73 – 80.
2ⁿᵈ Leviticus 8.
3ʳᵈ Jeremiah 33.
4ᵗʰ 2 Kings 9 – 10.

Worship in the Wilderness and the Trail of Graves

God delivered the nation of Israel out of the bondage of Egypt to take them into the land that He promised to Abraham, Isaac, and Jacob. He brought them out in order to take them in. Moses was chosen by God to lead the people even though the people resisted him and God almost every step of the way. A year after they left Egypt, the nation of Israel was camped at the southern border of the Promised Land at a place called Kadesh-barnea, ready to enter and receive the long-awaited promise of God.

Moses sent twelve spies into the Promised Land and for forty days they traveled all the way to the northern tip of their inheritance and back. When they returned, they reported that the land was flowing with milk and honey and brought back a huge cluster of grapes and other fruits. But they also came back with fears and doubts and said, *"However, the people who dwell in the land are strong and the cities are fortified and very large...we saw the descendants of Anak, the Nephilim, there...so we seemed to ourselves like grasshoppers to them."* Numbers 13:28 – 33.

But Joshua and Caleb gave a minority report. They said, *"Let us go up at once and occupy it, for we are well able to overcome it."* But the other ten spies swayed the 600,000 men of Israel with their fear and unbelief. Their disobedient influence led the congregation to begin making plans to stone Moses and to choose for themselves another leader to take them back to Egypt. Never underestimate the influential power of fear, unbelief, and disobedience.

God spoke to Moses and pronounced the verdict: The whole adult population of Israel, except for Joshua and Caleb, would die in the wilderness. They would wander in the wilderness one year for each of the forty days; forty years in the wilderness. Their children would be the ones who would take possession of the Promised Land. Those who voted "no" would get their will done rather than experience God's. When they heard the word, they changed their minds and decided to go against what

God had said and tried to organize an army without Moses or God's directive. They failed miserably.

For the next forty years the nation of Israel wandered in the wilderness of Sinai while Moses, Aaron, Joshua, and Caleb dug graves; 600,000 graves. With every death, unbelief grew weaker until it was purged from the nation. They would have been easy to follow through the wilderness because they left behind a trail of graves, each one declaring the truth that the wages of sin is death. With every funeral, Joshua and Caleb must have preached that the flesh will deceive you, but God can be trusted. His word is true. They must have warned the younger generation with each funeral on the error of taking counsel in your fears and unbelief.

Imagine the graveside service of the final "adult" from that unbelieving generation, when the final shovel of sand was put on the grave. Joshua must have looked at Caleb and shouted, "It is finished! Now, let's go kill some Canaanites, Hittites, Jebusites, and Amorites, and take possession of the Promised Land." Which they did.

We, like Israel, are also in a wilderness experience right now. We have the fire and cloud of the Holy Spirit in God's word to lead us. We have the spiritual bread and the water of Life (the Holy Spirit) from the Rock (Christ) to accompany us. We have the promise of the Father of resurrection before us. And we also are leaving behind us a trail of graves of unbelieving flesh as it dies with every step we take in the Spirit and by the Spirit. And with every grave, faith in Christ grows and pleases the Father more and more.

Your wilderness experience is a worship experience of becoming more and more of a true worshiper as you leave behind your trail of graves. Today, dig another grave as you walk in the Spirit and not in the flesh. Keep working on Psalm 119:73 – 80 and pray more of it today.

March 7

Read and pray Psalm 67, Proverbs 15:6 – 12, Luke 8:1 – 21, Philippians 4, Psalm 119:73 – 80.
2nd Leviticus 9.
3rd Jeremiah 34.
4th 2 Kings 11 – 12.

The Assurance of Worship

A covenant relationship is based upon promises, which are received by faith. Trust gives a covenant relationship the capacity to grow. In a covenant relationship, there is satisfaction in knowing someone, and there is growth in the relationship. In a contract, the relationship is based upon the completion of duties, of work. As long as the work is completed on time and with satisfaction, the relationship remains; but with no growth. The main object in a contract is the project, not a person. God desires to enter into a covenant relationship with you, not a contract.

The covenant relationship God desires with you is within the covenant relationship the Father has with the Son. This was pictured and predicted in the Old Testament in Genesis 15 when God promised Abram that his offspring would outnumber the stars, and the land of Israel to dwell in (15:5 – 7). At the time, Abram was ninety-nine years old, childless, and lived in a tent as an alien in the land; but he trusted that what God said, He would do. God was pleased with Abram because he trusted Him.

In that chapter, Abram asked for assurance, *"O Lord GOD, how am I to know that I shall possess it (the land)?"* God told him to prepare sacrifices for the covenant. In Abram's day, when two parties entered into a covenant relationship, sacrifices were cut in two pieces and the parties involved would walk through the middle of the sacrifices. This bound them together by saying, "May I be torn in two like this sacrifice, if I break this covenant." Sounds gruesome to us, but we can be gruesome in our own ways in tearing apart personal relationships.

Abram obeyed God and prepared the sacrifices and then waited. While he waited, the Bible says that God showed him the future of his offspring, and when they would possess the land. Then Abram watched as *"...a smoking fire pot and a flaming torch passed between these pieces."* The cloud and fire of God entered into a covenant with Himself that day. Abram was included as a witness. His assurance would be found as he trusted what God revealed to him concerning Himself and His own faithfulness. What a worship service that must have been. It pleased God that day to include Abram in what He said He would do because Abram trusted God.

This episode in Abram's life pointed forward to the new covenant in Jesus Christ, when God made an eternal covenant with Himself and included you as a witness. As you see Jesus Christ on the cross, giving His life for you, in order that you might have His, God entered into a covenant with Himself for you, and invited you to watch. He will save you, if you are willing to trust that what He said, He will do. God makes His vow to Himself as you watch, just like Abram did. When you trust God, and the vow His makes to save you through His Son, you enter into the relationship, His relationship and covenant with Himself, for you, and with you.

In your relationship with the Father, through faith in the Son, it is not your faithfulness that gives assurance; it is His. You are a witness at the cross, seeing and trusting that what God said, He did and will do. You are invited into the covenant relationship between the Father and the Lord Jesus Christ, the Son. As you see yourself in that relationship, God is pleased. This is what it means to worship the Father in spirit and truth. Memorize another line from Psalm 119:73 – 80 so that you can meditate on it and pray it today.

March 8

Read and pray Psalm 68, Proverbs 15:13 – 18, Luke 8:22 – 56, Colossians 1, Psalm 119:73 – 80.
2nd Leviticus 10.
3rd Jeremiah 35.
4th 2 Kings 13 – 14.

Faithful Worship

Faith pleases the Father because God is faithful. When He sees faith, it reminds Him of Himself. He sees that it is good because God is good; all the time, and every time, God is good. When you declare that God is faithful you are saying that God can be trusted, that what He says, He will do, because first He says it, then He does it, every time. God works according to His word, without fail. He is faithful.

But what exactly is faith? Where does it come from? What does it mean to be full of faith, and what kind of faith do you want to be full of? In Hebrews 11:1, it says, *"Faith is the substance of things hoped for, the evidence of things unseen."* This verse teaches that faith is a substance. The Greek word translated "substance" is *hoopo-staice*. It is made up of two Greek words, *hoopo*, which means "under," and *staice*, which means "to stand," or "solid structure." Faith is a foundation upon which life rests and is built. It is the unseen strength of life, like the unseen foundation and inner structure of a building, when it rests upon the word of God.

But faith does not have strength in and of itself. Faith in a lie rather than the truth is the exact opposite of strength. It can be deceptive and the source of all kinds of evil when it becomes the foundation for what God has not said. But when it connects with what God has said, and rests upon His word, God goes to work and builds upon it. The strength of faith comes from the truth of God's word.

God's word is an invitation to know Him. God reveals Himself in His word. He reveals what He desires to do. His works declare who He is. Since God is faithful, His word carries the seed of His faith in it. His faith is an invitation for His activity. This is what God is searching for, an invitation to go to work upon His word.

As you hear God's word and receive it as the truth, God's faith in His word becomes the eternal structure and strength in your life. God builds upon His solid rock, the life that is well pleasing to Him, the life that He has already chosen, which is the life of the Lord Jesus Christ. As God builds more and more of Himself in you and with you, more and more of His life is seen and known through you, as you, before Him and the watching world around you. This pleases God. This is what it means to be full of faith. This is what it means to worship the Father in spirit and truth.

March 9

Read and pray Psalm 69, Proverbs 15:19 – 25, Luke 9:1 – 27, Colossians 2, Psalm 119:73 – 80.
2nd Leviticus 11.
3rd Jeremiah 36.
4th 2 Kings 15 – 16.

By Faith You Understand

The eleventh chapter of Hebrews is definitive for the one who is learning to become a true worshiper. It is one of those chapters in the Bible that you return to on a regular basis for insight and understanding into the ways of God.

The third verse reveals why so many struggle with the Bible. It simply says, *"By faith we understand that the universe was created by the word of God, so that what is seen was not made out of things that are visible."*

This verse teaches one of the ways of God. God works by His word. The simplicity of this causes some to stumble. God creates by His word. He speaks, then acts according to what He just said. This is called being faithful. God is faithful to His own word.

When you act according to God's word it is because God's word has created something in you and with you. He creates your faith. It is a personal faith. No one else has your faith. It is as unique as the person, and God creates your faith according to His word. In Romans 10:17 He says, *"Now faith comes by hearing, and hearing by the word of God."* When God speaks into your life, your faith is created in the same way that God spoke into the deep void of Genesis 1:2 and created light.

It is by faith, your faith, that you then begin to see everything else that God is saying and doing, just as it happened in Genesis when God created the universe. Faith gives sight and insight into God's word. One of the ways of God is that you hear by seeing in the light of your faith, and you see by hearing the word of God. God's ways are higher than our ways.

The problem many have is that they want to understand what God says without faith. Impossible. They get discouraged reading the Bible because it does not make any sense, according to their understanding. But understanding God's word is a gift created by God, by faith, your faith that God created, according to His word. And He gives understanding, insight, as you act upon His word more and more. This is called obedience.

Unbelievers have always tried to support their unbelief by their own understanding of the way things appear to them, according to their own understanding. This is possible but not recommended because it denies the work of God in one's life. In the end, the unbeliever is left only with what they have said and done in a life without God, and then, on into eternity. Highly not recommended. Jesus called this the outer darkness where there is weeping and the gnashing of teeth without the light from God's word.

But by faith, which comes from God's word, light is created and understanding is given, and it begins to make sense, spiritual sense. The opposite of weeping and the gnashing of teeth is joy and the jaw-dropping wonder of knowing God.

Today, meditate on Hebrews 11:3 by first memorizing it, then consider all that God has created in your life, not by what you have, but according to His word.

March 10

Read and pray Psalm 70, Proverbs 15:26 – 33, Luke 9:28 – 62, Colossians 3, Psalm 119:73 – 80.
2nd Leviticus 12.
3rd Jeremiah 37.
4th 2 Kings 17 – 18.

By Faith Your Life Works

Faith pleases the Father when it originates from His word. Faith is the expression of God's word when it is from God's word. Faith reveals the Father in and through a life that works according to His word.

In Hebrews 11 you find a list of people whose lives operated by God's word. They heard a word from God and did something based upon it. Actually, God's word did something in them, with them, through them, which worked in the eyes of God.

In man's eyes, it may have seemed a bit strange at the time, like when Noah built the ark. But in the end, it proved to be the right course of action. Or when Abram moved his family to a foreign land far from his home, or when he and Sarah began preparing for their first child, at the age of 90+. Some probably thought they had lost their minds, but in reality, in their hearts and their minds, God's word had been received. His work followed His word and they had a baby shower at the nursing home. God's word previews God's work.

As you study this amazing chapter you will find individuals whose lives worked out a word from God. Their activities vary from sacrificing, to walking, to building, to traveling, to having children, to blessing children, to walking away from successful careers, to fighting enemies, and being homeless. The one thing they all have in common is that they had received a word from God, and that word did a work in them, with them, and through them. And it pleased God. He commended them for the work He did in them, with them, and through them.

The life of faith works in God's eyes because He can see His word at work in the life of the faithful. As Hebrews 11 shows, the life of faith is not easy, but it is simple. It is life according to God's word. You will find in the lives of the faithful great opposition, loneliness, homelessness, as well as great victory, miracles, and blessings as you study these lives. And you will find that God had spoken to each one, which worked in them, with them, and through them, for His glory.

The other characteristic the life of faith has is vision, something greater than this life is clearly seen, welcomed, and spoken. These are the promises of God at work in the life of a person of faith. They live by faith that what God has said, He will do. God is pleased with a life that works like that because that work expresses who He is, since it is based upon His word.

The book of Hebrews begins with these powerful words, *"Long ago, at many times and in many ways, God spoke to our fathers by the prophets, but in these last days he has spoken to us by his son, whom he appointed the heir of all things, through whom also he created the world. He is the radiance of the glory of God and the exact imprint of his nature, and he upholds the universe by the word of his power. After making purification for sins, he sat down at the right hand of the Majesty on high,"* Hebrews 1:1 – 3.

These verses reveal the full and final Word of God, the Lord Jesus Christ. His life fully pleased the Father because every thought, every act, every motive, every intent, every choice, every element of it from start to finish originated from the Father. His life worked and was given for you and to you. When you receive Him, you receive God's word and work as your life, and your life works from God and for God. This is the life that pleases God, and this is what it means to worship the Father in spirit and truth.

March 11

Read and pray Psalm 71, Proverbs 16:1 – 5, Luke 10, Colossians 4, Psalm 119:73 – 80.
2ⁿᵈ Leviticus 13.
3ʳᵈ Jeremiah 38.
4ᵗʰ 2 Kings 19 – 20.

It's How You Finish That Counts

King Asa is a good example of one who started off on the right foot, but ended up on the wrong one. In fact, he ended up with diseased feet to teach an important lesson to those who followed after him (2 Chronicles 14 – 16). The Bible says, *"And Asa did what was good and right in the eyes of the LORD his God...and commanded Judah to seek the LORD, the God of their fathers, and to keep the law and the commandments."* 2 Chronicles 14:2 – 4. Seeking the LORD and keeping His commandments were the standard qualifications for a king. Asa began his rule with that agenda and it pleased God.

These chapters describe how Asa pleased God by seeking Him and trusting Him. When the Ethiopians came against Judah with an army of one million, plus 300 chariots, outnumbering Judah two-to-one, Asa cried out to God, and the LORD defeated his enemies. When Asa's mother, Maacah, set up an idol, he destroyed it, even though she was very powerful. As a result, God blessed Judah with thirty-five years of peace.

After those years of peace, Asa's faith was tested. The army of Israel, under king Baasha, came against Judah and king Asa. Instead of crying out to the LORD and seeking God, Asa turned to Ben-hadad, king of Syria for help. He sent Ben-hadad gold and silver and hired him and the Syria army to come against Israel and king Baasha. Ben-hadad gladly received the money and king Baasha backed off. But God was not pleased. Asa did not turn to Him for help as he had done in the past, but rather went running to Ben-hadad and the help of the Syrians.

God sent the prophet Hanani to Asa to remind him of how God had delivered Judah from her enemies in the past when Asa had turned to the LORD and cried out to Him for deliverance. Then he reminded Asa of this amazing truth, *"For the eyes of the LORD run to and fro throughout the whole earth, to give strong support to those whose heart is blameless toward him."* The phrase "to give strong support" is the Hebrew word *kazak,* and is used throughout the Old Testament to refer to the strength that God gives to those who trust Him. For example, it is used four times in Joshua 1:6 – 18 as God encouraged Joshua after Moses died. God told Joshua that if he would trust Him, as Moses had, He would give him supernatural strength and courage.

The word "blameless" is the Hebrew word *shalem*, and is from the family of words in Hebrew describing the peace of God, wholeness from God, and total devotion to God. The Hebrew word *shalom*, is from this root word, as is *Jeru-salem*, the city of peace. In the context of this verse, it describes a person's heart that is at peace with God, full of faith and devotion to God. In the Father's eyes, this person's heart is blameless.

But Asa did not heed the word from God through the prophet Hanani. Instead of repenting of his sin and turning to God for the strength He promised, Asa got angry with Hanani and had him thrown in prison. His anger consumed him, as anger does, and he inflicted much harm on the people. Asa did not turn to the LORD, but rather turned on the prophet and the people in his sin. God struck Asa with a disease in his feet. Asa started following his anger rather than God's word, and the LORD stopped him in his tracks. Even with this, Asa did not turn to the LORD. The disease ultimately killed him.

The lesson for us is clear: the Father is searching for those who trust Him, according to His word. He gives courage and strength and blessing to those whose hearts are full of faith in Him. But faith must be tested to be proved genuine, as being from the LORD. When Asa's faith was tested, he did not turn to the LORD, but rather to man, and he lost his strength and became afraid. The outcome was disastrous. When faced with a trial, turn to the Father with all of your heart. He is searching for true worshipers, whose hearts are full of faith in Him. He has promised a glorious outcome for them.

Spend one more day with Psalm 119:73 – 80, meditating on what you have learned and prayed from it.

March 12

Read and pray Psalm 72, Proverbs 16:6 – 12, Luke 11:1 – 28, 1 Thessalonians 1, Psalm 119:81 – 88.
2nd Leviticus 14.
3rd Jeremiah 39.
4th 2 Kings 21 – 22.

Changing Your Mind About Worship

God created man with the freedom and ability to change his mind. When your mind is changed you are able to make a new choice, an informed choice, with a new direction to live. The New Testament word for changing your mind is the Greek word, *metanoia,* made up of two words, *meta*, which means to change or transform, and *noia,* which means mind. This word is translated "repent" for that reason. When you repent, you change your mind and go a new direction.

In English, the word, "repent," takes on more of the meaning of regret, remorse, or contrition over a sin. These words are emotional words. But the Greek word *metanoia* gets more at the heart of the meaning of "repentance" by describing a willful decision and a new direction based on better information, with or without emotional influences.

There are two words in the Old Testament for "repent." The first Hebrew word is *nakham,* which has the meaning of being comforted after a loss, or to have compassion, or to feel remorse. This word carries the emotional feeling of repentance. The other Hebrew word is *shoob*, and simply means to turn back, to return. This carries the willful and directional act of repentance. These words give meaning to a necessary element in everyone's life; repentance.

God outlined a specific manner for His people to worship Him in the Old Testament. It was based upon His word, upon substitution and sacrifice. The other nations of the ancient world also worshiped gods with sacrifice, but for a totally different reason. The other nations understood their gods by looking at creation with a strictly sensual view, and with manipulation.

They worshiped the sun, the moon, the seasons, the rain, the reproductive system, and the power they observed in nature. Their sacrifices and worship revolved around bringing something they felt the god needed from them in order to leave them alone, or to reward them with more things. Different gods represented different things that they needed. Some gods controlled the weather and the crops. Other gods represented having children, which equated with being cared for in old age. And some gods represented security from marauding enemies. But none of their gods had any moral basis or direction. They were the gods of increase, the gods of the physical senses. They were called the Baals. These gods were man-centered and revealed the nature of man. They had no element of fellowship with the god and no concept of sin. They are still worshiped today.

When God called His people into His presence, it was with His word, not with some form. He would appear by calling, by inviting. The only thing you can do with a word is to either believe it, or not. God's prescription for worship in the Old Testament was based upon His holy character and man's sinful character. God gave His word to man in order for man to return to Him, to repent. The instructions for worship made this return possible with a substitute to die for the sins of the person. The substitute suffered a horrible death to reveal the horrible result of sin. And the substitute was the innocent one taking the place of the guilty one, revealing the desire of God for fellowship with the guilty. God's desire was for man to return to Him, to repent.

Changing your mind about worship requires changing your mind about God and about His will. It starts with His word for His word reveals His character and will. Changing your mind about worship means to turn away from what you think, and to turn to what God has said. This is what it means to repent. God's word calls you to a new direction, to Him, fellowship with Him. Jesus Christ provided the ultimate substitute and sacrifice for sin so that you could return to the Father and worship Him in spirit and truth, His truth.

Today, turn away from your will and way of thinking, and turn back to God's will, according to His word. Allow God's word to shape your prayers and to change you. This is called a lifestyle of repentance, of continually having your mind changed from your will to God's. This pleases the Father, which is what it means to worship the Father in spirit and truth. Begin memorizing and meditating on the first line of Psalm 119:81 – 88, so that you can pray it throughout the day.

March 13

Read and pray Psalm 73, Proverbs 16:13 – 19, Luke 11:29 – 54, 1 Thessalonians 2, Psalm 119:81 – 88.
2nd Leviticus 15.
3rd Jeremiah 40.
4th 2 Kings 23 – 25.

Worship Wars

The term "worship wars" was coined a few years ago describing different styles of music and settings for God's people as they gathered to worship Him. The disagreement among the people of God over these preferences has caused some a great deal of grief, especially our Father. But in the Bible, the term has a totally different meaning. True worship is a powerful weapon in defeating the enemies of God when it is learned from God, according to His word.

One of the places this is seen is in 2 Chronicles 20:1 – 30, the story of king Jehoshaphat and the war that was won with worship. The first few verses describe the situation as three great nations from the south gathered together to invade and conquer Jerusalem and the nation of Judah. When king Jehoshaphat received the news of the armies and their location, just south of Jerusalem, the Bible says that he was afraid. But the next phrase is telling, *"Then Jehoshaphat was afraid and set his face to seek the LORD, and proclaimed a fast throughout all Judah."* 2 Chronicles 20:3.

The word "set" is instructive. It is the Hebrew word *nathan*, which means to give, to appoint, to place one object before another for the purpose of an exchange. The first place this word is used is in the creation account in Genesis 1:17, *"And God set them in the expanse of the heavens to give light on the earth..."* When God "set" the sun, the moon, and the stars in place it was for the purpose of providing seasons and signs for man. This word *nathan*, is also used in Genesis 1:29 describing the food that God provided for man to eat, *"...Behold, I have given you every plant yielding seed that is on the face of the earth...every tree with seed in its fruit. You shall have them for food."* The point is this: *nathan* puts one thing before another for a particular purpose.

When Jehoshaphat *nathan* his face to seek the LORD, he was setting himself and giving himself completely to God for the purpose of seeking the Lord. For Jehoshaphat, the threat of being invaded and destroyed was a call to worship; it was an invitation from God to show Himself mighty on behalf of those who trusted in Him. Jehoshaphat was afraid, but his fear guided him in the right direction rather than driving him away in the wrong direction. King David wrote, *"When I am afraid, I put my trust in you. In God, whose word I praise, in God I trust; I shall not be afraid. What can flesh do to me?"* Psalm 56:3 – 4.

Jehoshaphat must have learned this worship song by reading and worshiping with the song that David wrote. In that song, David repeats that confession twice for emphasis (56:3 – 4, 10 – 11). It is the theme of Psalm 56. And king Jehoshaphat knew what to do because he had learned to worship from God's word before he found himself in the threatening situation of that moment. The question is, have you?

Learning to set your face to seek the Father is done each day as you present yourself before God, giving Him all of your attention to worship Him. Some call this "the quiet time," others call it "being in the secret place," and still others "the morning watch." Whatever you call it, make sure you do it, and make sure all of you is there when you do. Your mind will wander if you are not prepared to keep it "set" before the Lord.

One of the ways you can keep your mind focused is by reading the psalm for the day and the Bible reading out loud, with your mouth; maybe not too loud; others may still be asleep. But by engaging your body in the activity of worship, especially your voice, something actually happens in the atmosphere around you; it gets filled with praise. Like humidity, you can saturate the space around you with the truth of God, from the word of God, for the glory of God. As you do, you may want to be prepared for lightning to strike!

Today, try speaking your prayer from Psalm 119:81 – 88 out loud. Practice before closing your time with the Lord, and then throughout the day, say it and watch God do it.

March 14

Read and pray Psalm 74, Proverbs 16:20 – 27, Luke 12:1 – 21, 1 Thessalonians 3, Psalm 119:81 – 88.
2nd Leviticus 16.
3rd Jeremiah 41.
4th 1 Chronicles 1 – 2.

A Clear Confession with a Vague Request

The story of king Jehoshaphat teaches on many levels. One of the main lessons is on prayer. The situation for his prayer is found in 2 Chronicles 20:1 – 30. Three great armies were advancing to Jerusalem from the south. Jehoshaphat set his face to seek the LORD, which is how he began his prayer. His prayer teaches one of the ways of God in prayer.

Jehoshaphat's prayer begins with the covenant name of God, LORD. In the Old Testament, you will find many names of God. The Hebrew name *Elohim*, is one of the most frequent names of God. It is translated "God." The shortened form of this name is *El*, which means Creator God. Many Hebrew names end with this shortened form to indicate a relationship with God, such as "Daniel, Ezekiel, Bezalel, Samuel, Mishael, Michael, and Gabriel." When *Elohim* is used it refers to God as the Creator God.

When God appeared to Moses in the burning bush passage (Exodus 3), Moses asked God for His name so he could tell the Israelites in Egypt who it was that was sending him to free them. God spoke to Moses His name *Yahweh*, which is God's covenant name. Only Israel knew God in a covenant relationship. It was His personal name for the nation of Israel. In English Bibles the covenant name *Yahweh* is written in all capital letters as "LORD." The shortened form of this name is *Yah*. Many Hebrew names will end in *ah* to also indicate a personal relationship with *Yahweh*; names like "Isaiah, Jeremiah, Jonah, Josiah, Elijah, Zephaniah, and Zechariah," are a few.

As Jehoshaphat began his prayer, he addressed God with His name, LORD, which is a powerful confession of his personal relationship with God. Jesus taught to begin your prayer with *"Our Father, in heaven, hallowed is your name,"* Matthew 6:9. Through faith in Jesus Christ, you have a child/Father relationship with God; the relationship that Jesus has with the Father, He has shared with you. Beginning your prayer with this clear confession is the way to begin every prayer. It is an expression of your faith and confidence in Jesus Christ.

The next line in Jehoshaphat's prayer is also a clear confession, *"You rule over all the kingdoms of the nations. In your hand are power and might, so that none is able to withstand you,"* 2 Chronicles 20:6. This confession declares that God is God over all humanity, and that no nation can stand up against Him.

The next verse, verse seven, makes a clear statement of God's will, according to the word of God, *"Did you not, our God, drive out the inhabitants of this land before your people Israel, and give it forever to the descendants of Abraham your friend?"* Even though this confession is a question, it does not question the will of God. It states the will of God, according to His word. He will go on in his prayer to restate more of God's will for Israel based upon what he had learned from Israel's history with God. This is called praying God's will according to God's word.

Finally, at the end of his prayer, he made a vague request, *"...will you not execute judgment on them? For we are powerless against this great horde that is coming against us. We do not know what to do, but our eyes are on you."* 20:12. Jehoshaphat's prayer teaches an all-important lesson: Know God's will, from God's word, and declare it to God in prayer. Make your confessions clear and don't worry if your requests are vague; God will take care of you.

When you learn this truth you will declare in prayer God's will for your life. You will thank God for sending His Son, Jesus Christ, to be your Savior and Lord. This is God's will for your life. You can pray the plan of God for your life, to grow in wisdom, understanding, and discernment by feeding on and praying God's word. Psalm 119 gives you so many truths to confess concerning the will of God for your life. This is why it is so important to learn these confessions and to declare them out loud to God in prayer.

Today as you pray Psalm 119:81 – 88, notice the confessions of truth that are prayed in that prayer, and pray them as your confessions throughout the day. God loves to hear your prayer filled with His will, from His word. Powerful things will begin to happen when you pray God's will from God's word.

March 15

Read and pray Psalm 75, Proverbs 16:28 – 33, Luke 12:22 – 59, 1 Thessalonians 4, Psalm 119:81 – 88.

2nd Leviticus 17.

3rd Jeremiah 42.

4th 1 Chronicles 3 – 4.

The Battle is the Lord's

God's word gives instructions in becoming a true worshiper. Setting your face to seek the Lord, just as Jehoshaphat did in 2 Chronicles 20, is the first step. Learning what God has done, according to His word, and praying what God has done with clear confessions of truth, is essential in the process of becoming a true worshiper. The next lesson in the story of Jehoshaphat is key; listen to what God will say and then watch Him do it.

The Bible says in 2 Chronicles 20:14 – 15, *"And the Spirit of the LORD came upon Jahaziel, the son of Zechariah, the son of Benaiah… thus says the LORD to you, 'Do not be afraid, nor dismayed at this great horde, for the battle is not yours but God's.'"* Notice the endings on the names of these three Levites, *el, ah, ah*; their names identified them as having a personal relationship with God. The Levites were given the responsibility to teach Israel the word of God. They led them in worship and taught them the ways of God. The Levites were not given any land in the Promised Land; they were given cities to live in that were scattered throughout all the land of Israel so that they lived among the people in order to teach them. God was their inheritance. Jahaziel was about to speak God's word, as well as from his experience of being taken care of by God as a Levite.

The word Jahaziel spoke was very particular, *"Tomorrow go down against them. Behold, they will come up by the ascent of Ziz. You will find them at the end of the valley, east of the wilderness of Jeruel. You will not need to fight in this battle. Stand firm, hold your position, and see the salvation of the LORD on your behalf."* He told them when to go out, where to go out, where to find them, in order to watch God fight for them. The phrase "stand firm" is the Hebrew word *yahtsab*, which means to present before another. It is one of the words for worship, as people would stand before the Lord, presenting themselves before Him as His servants. They were about to engage in a worship war; the kind that pleases the Father.

The phrase "hold your position" is the Hebrew word ***ahmad***, which means to abide, to remain, the position of a servant before his master. The Greek companion of this word is ***menow***, which Jesus used in John 15:1 – 8 describing how His followers would "abide in Him" and bear fruit. Both of these words and phrases, ***yahtsab*** and ***ahmad***, describe the position of a true worshiper. God told His people to worship Him without fear of the approaching threat. And they listened to Him.

But how do you know when God is speaking to you, and how can you know for sure what He is saying to you? First, like Jehoshaphat, always set your face to seek the Lord in a position of worship. Worship is an atmosphere conducive to hearing God. Then, know God's word. Jehoshaphat reviewed God's word as he set his face to seek the Lord. Third, God will send a witness to confirm a particular word. Many times it will be a witness with experience, like Jahaziel, and it will be someone who belongs to Him. But you will recognize the word because it will encourage trust in God, it will be in line with His word, and from someone who belongs to God and walks with Him.

These three lights, worship, the word, and a witness from the word will line up into a laser beam of direction for you. In worship there is an inner witness of the Holy Spirit. In the word of God there is a clear moral witness from God's eternal word. With the witness, there will be a confirmation of the inner witness in line with the eternal word.

Today, set your face to seek the Lord. Present yourself before God as His servant. And stay in His presence, abide in Him, and you will see God fight for you. He loves you. Trust Him today.

March 16

Read and pray Psalm 76, Proverbs 17:1 – 3, Luke 13, 1 Thessalonians 5, Psalm 119:81 – 88.
2nd Leviticus 18.
3rd Jeremiah 43.
4th 1 Chronicles 5 – 6.

Becoming an Amen

When the three great armies came against king Jehoshaphat in 2 Chronicles 20:1 – 30, the king set his face to seek the Lord. He prayed out of his relationship with God and from the activity of God from His word, and worshiped. He gathered all Jerusalem together and they heard a word from Jahaziel, the Levite, who encouraged them to stand before the Lord and to watch God win the battle for them. After Jahaziel spoke God's word, Jehoshaphat fell down before the Lord, while the Levites rose up to praise the Lord. What a scene! Would that we had national leaders who would set their face to seek the Lord, hear a word from God, and fall before Him in humble worship.

The next day, Jehoshaphat addressed the nation, saying in 2 Chronicles 20:20, *"Hear me, Judah and inhabitants of Jerusalem! Believe in the LORD your God, and you will be established; believe his prophets, and you will succeed."* The word "believe" is the Hebrew word *amen*, which means to believe, to be firm, to affirm, to be certain. Our English word "amen" is from this Hebrew word. This word is used three times in this verse. It is translated "believe...be established...believe," but it is the same word; *amen*.

This is one of the ways of God. When you believe, you become an *amen*, a believer. In that way, you do not have faith, you become faith; faithful. This new identity is an affirmation of what God has said. His word changes you from the inside out, but not until you receive it from the outside in. The first word that Jehoshaphat spoke was the word "Hear," which is the Hebrew word *shamah*. This is one of the main words in the Old Testament for Israel. The word *shemah*, means to receive a word from God, which then leads to obedience. For Israel, hearing was believing.

When Jesus was asked which commandment was the greatest, in Matthew 22:36 – 38, He quoted Deuteronomy 6:4 – 5, *"Hear, O Israel: The LORD our God, the LORD is one. You shall love the LORD your God with all your heart and with all your soul and with all your might."*

This was and still is known as the ***Shemah***. Paul referred to this in Romans 10:17 when he said, ***"So faith comes by hearing, and hearing by the word of Christ."*** God's word produces faith in the heart of the one who receives it, and carries in it the fruit of obedience. Obedience is the work of God, from His own word in you, with you, through you, as you, before the Father and the watching world around you.

You will become what you receive and believe. If you listen to and follow your physical appetites, you will become addicted and enslaved to them. But you are not your appetites. You are not defined by your feelings, either. Feelings can deceive you. You have physical appetites and feelings; you cannot deny nor suppress them. But you have something greater to guide, define, and empower your life; you have received the word of God. You are a blood-washed, born again, Spirit possessed, child of the Most High God! You are an AMEN to what God has said, because first He says it, then, He does it; in you, with you, through you, as you, before the Father and the watching world around you.

Today, hear the word from God as you read the word of God. Pray for His word to find the good soil of your heart, and to be planted deep, AMEN. Ask the Father to water His word with the Holy Spirit, by the reign of the Spirit, in order for Christ Jesus to be glorified in and with and through you, and you will become an ***amen*** of Him. This pleases the Father. You will become a true worshiper, one who worships the Father in spirit and truth.

March 17

Read and pray Psalm 77, Proverbs 17:4 – 8, Luke 14, 2 Thessalonians 1, Psalm 119:81 – 88.
2nd Leviticus 19.
3rd Jeremiah 44.
4th 1 Chronicles 7 – 8.

The Song That Destroys the Enemy

In 2 Chronicles 20:1 – 30 you find the story of how God saved Jerusalem from three great armies that had gathered together to invade and conquer Judah. Upon hearing this news, king Jehoshaphat set his face to worship the Lord. God spoke through Jahaziel, one of the Levites, and assured the king and the people that He would fight for them. They received God's word and became the *amen* of it. The next part of the story, 2 Chronicles 20:21 – 23, is thrilling.

Jehoshaphat appointed the priests to dress in their holy attire, to go before the army, and to sing one song to the Lord, *"Give thanks to the LORD, for his steadfast love endures forever."* This song is found in several psalms, but is primarily in Psalm 107 and 136. Both of these songs tell the stories of great trials and threats and how God stepped in to save and to deliver His people. They celebrate the greatness and goodness of God on behalf of His covenant people. Placing this priestly choir in front of the army was reminiscent of what Joshua did when he and the people encircled Jericho for seven days (Joshua 6:1 – 7).

Gratitude is the foundation of worship because it celebrates the greatness and goodness and love of God. Likewise, ingratitude is the foundation of sin and is an expression of suppressing the truth of God's revelation of Himself. Paul states it clearly in Romans 1:18 – 23, that *"...what can be known about God is plain to them, because God has shown it to them...his invisible attributes, namely his eternal power and divine nature...but they did not honor him as God or give thanks to him..."* But Jehoshaphat responded to God's revelation with gratitude and praise.

When the choir and the army left Jerusalem, following the particular word from God through Jahaziel, they were still several miles from the three invading armies. But 2 Chronicles 20:22 says that God *"...set an ambush against the men of Ammon, Moab, and Mount Seir..."* The word "ambush" is the Hebrew word *ahrab*, which means to wait for the purpose of destroying someone or something. God was waiting for the invading armies. It says that God *"...routed them."* The word "routed" is the Hebrew word ***nagap***, and is used in the Old Testament to describe a death-blow. It literally means to strike, but has the meaning of death as the result of the blow. As God's people, led by gratitude and praise, marched toward the enemy, God caused the invading armies to turn on each other and they literally killed each other without a single one surviving.

The author was telling this story to his sons, ages five and three at the time, when the oldest, Ben, asked, "Daddy, if they all turned on each other, killing each other, how did the last guy die?" Dan, his brother, always watching Ben, looked at me and also nodded, wanting to know the answer. I said, "It doesn't say in the Bible, but I guess the last guy had been wounded so badly during the confusion, that he must have bled to death." Both boys are now doctors and I have often wondered if this story may have encouraged them to pursue the medical profession. Not sure, but today they are both dedicated Christian physicians.

When Jehoshaphat with the choir and the army arrived on the scene, it took them three days to gather up the spoil and on the fourth day they had a great celebration and named the place the Valley of Beracah, which means the valley of blessing. God had blessed them with a victory and with the spoils of war while they were blessing Him with gratitude and praise. The point is clear: Listen to what God has said in His word and is saying to you through His messengers. The revelation will be of Himself. You will learn from it, which will result in gratitude and praise for Him. And the enemies of God will be routed, which will result in great victory and blessings. This is the kind of worship war that pleases the Father.

March 18

Read and pray Psalm 78, Proverbs 17:9 – 13, Luke 15, 2 Thessalonians 2, Psalm 119:81 – 88.
2ⁿᵈ Leviticus 20.
3ʳᵈ Jeremiah 45.
4ᵗʰ 1 Chronicles 9 – 10.

Lessons For Revival From King Hezekiah

The life of king Hezekiah teaches lessons for revival. According to 2 Chronicles 29:1, Hezekiah began to rule as king when he was twenty-one, and he reigned twenty-nine years. The people of God enjoyed a twenty-nine year revival during his lifetime. One of the most powerful prophets of the Old Testament, Isaiah, prophesied during this long revival. For the next seven days you will learn seven lessons for revival from the life of king Hezekiah, found in 2 Chronicles 29 – 32.

The Bible says that the first thing the Hezekiah did was to open the doors of the Temple, *"In the first year of his reign, in the first month, he opened the doors of the house of the LORD and repaired them."* 29:3. The word "opened" is the Hebrew word *patah*, which means to open, to loosen bonds, to set free. It is used most often in the Old Testament to describe opening the mouth, ears, and to unfetter the feet, and hands. The word "repaired" is the Hebrew word *kazak*, which means to make strong. In other words, Hezekiah opened the doors of the Temple and then propped them open to stay opened. He opened up and set in motion the real strength of Israel; true worship.

It also says that Hezekiah summons the Levites together and commissioned them saying, *"Hear me, Levites! Now consecrate yourselves, and consecrate the house of the LORD, the God of your fathers, and carry out the filth from the Holy Place. For our fathers have been unfaithful and have done what was evil in the sight of the LORD our God."* 29:5 – 6. Imagine the boldness of this rookie king, only twenty-one years old, giving such a strong command his first day in office. The word "consecrate" is the Hebrew word *qadash*, which means to hallow, to make holy, to be holy. It is used three times in verse five, twice as "consecrate" and once as "Holy." God is holy. He reveals Himself in His word as holy. This is the first request in the prayer that Jesus taught His disciples, *"Father, hallowed be thy name,"* Luke 11:2. It is what God reveals about Himself in His word.

According to 2 Kings 18, Hezekiah followed after king David in keeping God's commandments. King David was the worship king of Israel. David's heart had two beats; worship and war. He united the nation of Israel into a worshiping nation with Jerusalem as the hub of that worship. David defeated the enemies of Israel and never lost a battle (except with himself. See 2 Samuel 11). Hezekiah followed David's example, which is why he began his reign by reestablishing true worship, based upon God's holiness, according to God's word.

Revival begins where true worship is opened and kept open. Those who have studied the revivals of the past all agree that repentant prayer always precedes revival. Repentant prayer is result of God opening up a sinner's ear to hear His word, the sinner's eyes to His holiness, and then the sinner's mouth to confess and clean out the filth of sin. Revival is strengthened by revived leaders, like Hezekiah, calling the people of God to follow and keep the word of God. When God opens the ears of His people to hear His word, He reveals His holiness, His power, His love, and there is an invitation to repent, to turn back to Him. This is known as true worship. Revival follows true worship.

Some would say that revival leads to worship. Revival does not produce worship; worship produces revival, because true worship is the result of the revelation of God, of Himself, from His word. When God's people respond to His revelation of Himself, their eyes are opened to the attributes and true nature of God by their ears having been opened by God to His word. As they respond with repentant prayer, gratitude, and praise, revival results. God will not revive the flesh; He gives life to the spirit in the Spirit of holiness.[6] God gives the gift of revival through true worship. This is one of the ways of God; He gives through, and He gives revival through true worship.

If ever asked, "What comes first, revival or worship?" know that the answer is worship. In fact, no matter what the question is, the answer is always true worship.

March 19

Read and pray Psalm 79, Proverbs 17:14 – 22, Luke 16, 2 Thessalonians 3, Psalm 119:89 – 96.
2nd Leviticus 21.
3rd Jeremiah 46.
4th 1 Chronicles 11 – 12.

Revival House Cleaning

The first thing that young king Hezekiah did when he began to reign was to open up the Temple for worship and to reinstall the Levites to their duties of standing before the Lord and ministering to the people of God, according to His word. Hezekiah told the priests to consecrate themselves and the house of the Lord. In 2 Chronicles 29:16 you find the account of the cleansing of the Temple by the priests, *"The priests went into the inner part of the house of the LORD to cleanse it, and they brought out all the uncleanness that they found in the temple of the LORD..."*

The word "cleanse" is the Hebrew word *taher*, which means to purify, to be clean in a moral sense. It was used extensively in the Old Testament to describe anything in relationship with God; people, food for God's people, items in the Temple, and gold, all were described with the word *taher*.

The Temple in Hezekiah's day had been defiled with idols and idolatry from previous kings. It had also been abandoned. Hezekiah told the priests to start in the *inner part*, which was where the Holy of Holies was located. They were told to carry out all of the things that were unclean. These items were the detestable items associated with Baal worship. God had forbidden any association of His people with the pagan worship of the Canaanites. They worshiped creation rather than the Creator.

The second lesson to learn about revival is that cleansing must start in the *inner part* of your life; your heart and mind. The things of the world, the flesh, and the devil accumulate over time. These things creep in when true worship is neglected. They defile the mind. When your thoughts are unclean, your will (choices) is deceived, and your feelings get in motion to support and carry out the corrupted desires of your will with your body. Your body has memory and quickly programs these choices into learned behavior. The New Testament calls these learned behaviors strongholds.

But when the light of the revelation of God appears, true worship results and these idols are seen for the detestable and vile things that they are. Getting rid of them is the new choice, informed by the Holy Spirit in you. The Bible calls this choice, repentance; changing your mind about what had been tolerated and acceptable. Your body will object because it gets quickly comfortable with the routine of sinning. But it will submit to new thoughts, which are based upon the truth of God's word, and will also learn and remember them just as it did with sinning.

When John the Baptist appeared on the scene, he began preaching the same message that Hezekiah had instructed the priests in his day. John preached a baptism of repentance; a cleansing experience of getting rid of the detestable things in the *inner part* of life. When Jesus came into Jerusalem for the last week of His life before His crucifixion, He also cleansed the Temple and immediately began healing and teaching there (Matthew 21:12 – 16).

The same cleansing takes place each time you go before the Lord in your personal worship time. The light of God's word will uncover those things that do not please Him. As you carry out the filth, taking it to the cross, you experience revival house cleaning. This pleases the Father and is vital in your walk with Christ. When the house is cleansed, the Lord moves about freely with healing and sound doctrine.

Today as you spend time in God's presence, ask Him to reveal the things that He wants removed. As you take them to the cross, ask God to fill you will His healing power and learn of Him. Take a verse from Psalm 119:89 – 96 with you and rejoice with it during the day.

157

March 20

Read and pray Psalm 80, Proverbs 17:23 – 28, Luke 17, 1 Timothy 1, Psalm 119:89 – 96.
2nd Leviticus 22.
3rd Jeremiah 47,
4th 1 Chronicles 13 – 14.

Revival and the Cross of Christ

King Hezekiah began his reign as king of Judah with revival. The word "revival" means to live again. The life of Israel revolved around worshiping God. The kings before Hezekiah had abandoned the worship of God. They substituted the worship of the gods of other nations. Israel lost her identity and life in the process. But Hezekiah led the nation to return to her true identity. And worship, according to God's word, was who they were. So Hezekiah began by reestablishing true worship, according to God's word.

After opening the doors of the Temple and giving the charge to the Levites to consecrate the Temple by carrying out the filth, Hezekiah commanded them to sacrifice seven bulls, rams, lambs, and male goats for a sin offering, 2 Chronicles 29:20. The sacrificial system was the central aspect of Israel's worship. God's instructions concerning sacrifice were an expression of God's grace and mercy. The sacrifice was a substitute for the worshiper in order to pay the penalty for sins committed by the worshiper. The innocent animal died in the place of the sinner. Sacrifice revealed Israel's sin against a holy God as well as God's love by providing a way to remain in relationship with Him. The seven-fold sacrifice initiated by Hezekiah was according to God's word and was presented in the place of the nation of Israel for their sin of abandoning God.

In 2 Chronicles 29:24 an important word is used to describe the purpose of the sacrificial system in Israel. *"Then the goats for the sin offering were brought to the king and the assembly, and they laid their hands on them, and the priests slaughtered them and made a sin offering with their blood on the altar, to make atonement for all Israel."* The word "atonement" is the Hebrew word *kippur*, which means to cover, to conceal, to purge, to reconcile, to ransom. It is a major word in the Old Testament describing the purpose for sacrifice.

The blood of the sacrifice would cover the sins of the people, which would restore the relationship with God that had been severed by sin. This was the first act done in the cleansed Temple to restore true worship to God by the nation. Hezekiah was leading the nation back to their true identity, back to true worship in relationship with God. Sacrifice was the cornerstone. It was the first expression of worship because it recognized the holiness of God and the separation of the people caused by sin. It also celebrated God's provision, according to His word, for restoring the relationship. This was an expression of God's grace and love.

The next element of worship that Hezekiah gave instructions for was for the music of king David to be played while the whole burnt offering for Israel was being given up to God. In 2 Chronicles 29:25 – 30, a beautiful picture is seen of the Levites playing the instruments that king David had made for the sole purpose of worshiping the Lord with the words he had written for the Lord, while the smoke of the burnt offering was rising to the Lord. This was a picture of Israel at her best, in true worship, according to the word of the Lord. The spiritual significance of that moment in the life of the nation is hard for us to imagine. But for Israel, it was the very heart of her identity and life with God, according to His word.

That scene from king Hezekiah's day pointed forward to the new covenant of God, not for a single nation, but for each individual person of the world; for you. The sacrifice was not an innocent animal, but the holy Son of God, the Lord Jesus Christ. He died your death for you that you might live His life in Him. The Father made this possible by raising His Son from the dead. Praising God as a result of this revelation with words of praise from God in His word is an even more beautiful picture than the one in Hezekiah's day. The spiritual significance of your daily time with God, in His word, while praying to Him with words of praise from Him in the Psalms is far-reaching. And the Father is pleased by it.

Keep one of the lines of praise from your psalm for the day in your heart today, and give the sacrifice of thanks and praise to God for the cross and your eternal relationship with the Father. This is your true identity in Christ. AMEN.

March 21

Read and pray Psalm 81, Proverbs 18:1 – 3, Luke 18, 1 Timothy 2, Psalm 119:89 – 96.
2nd Leviticus 23.
3rd Jeremiah 48.
4th 1 Chronicles 15 – 16.

Revival Gathers and Separates

During the first month of the first year of the reign of king Hezekiah, a revival began in Judah that lasted for twenty-nine years. There are several things that Hezekiah led the nation to do during the first year of the revival that set the momentum for it to last as long as it did. One of the most powerful things Hezekiah did was to reinstitute the Passover, and he invited Israel (ten tribes in the north) to come. Not only had Israel and Judah been divided for over 300 years, but they had also been enemies and had experienced several wars against each other.

The Passover celebrated Israel's deliverance by God, out of slavery in Egypt and into possession of the Promised Land. God brought them out in order to take them in. Israel's twelve tribes became a nation, God's nation, as a result. God gave instructions to keep the Passover in order to remember their birth as a nation, their identity in relationship with Him, and of God's faithfulness to His promise to Abraham, Isaac, and Jacob. The sacrifice of the Passover lamb was the first sacrifice God gave to Israel and it did not require a priest; it was a family sacrifice led by the father of the house.

But following the death of Solomon, Israel's third king, the nation split; ten tribes in the north and two in the south. The northern tribes called themselves Israel while the two tribes of the south took the name Judah. They had not celebrated the Passover as one nation for centuries, and in 2 Chronicles 30 you see the impossible take place; Israel had the Passover as a nation just like they did when they came out of Egypt.

Hezekiah invited the ten tribes in the north according to 2 Chronicles 30:6 – 12. Many rejected the offer and even mocked Hezekiah for even considering such a crazy idea. But others came. In fact, 2 Chronicles 30:13 describes the scene, *"And many people came together in Jerusalem…a very great assembly."*

Revival is the result of God's people laying aside their differences and coming together in unity and in worship around the mighty deeds of Christ. But the only way to gather together is to separate from something else. The ones that gathered had to separate themselves from those who were mocking, from centuries of division and war, and from their heritage of their places of worship in the northern part of the Holy Land. Revival unites and it also divides.

Hezekiah knew God's word and God's heart. He knew that remembering the way God delivered Israel from bondage, which was according to His word to Abraham, Isaac, and Jacob, was to celebrate God's faithfulness. Celebrating God's faithfulness to His people included the ten tribes in the north. They could not be left out even though they had sinned by going away and by forming their own version of God's word and worship. Hezekiah knew of God's mercy and steadfast love and forgiveness, and that inviting them back would be an expression of God's grace and loving-kindness. Hezekiah was willing to be divided from his own prejudice in order to unite with God's people in worship. This is what revival looks like. The opposite is what we are all too familiar with in the church today.

Some of the ones that came from the north had not followed the rules of cleansing when they arrived in Jerusalem for the Passover. Rather than excluding them over the cleansing details, it says in 2 Chronicles 30:18 – 19, *"For a majority of the people, many of them from Ephraim, Manasseh, Issachar, and Zebulun, had not cleansed themselves, yet they ate the Passover otherwise prescribed. For Hezekiah had prayed for them, saying, 'May the good LORD pardon everyone who sets his heart to seek God, the LORD, the God of his fathers, even though not according to the sanctuary rules of cleanness."* The lesson is clear: We must put aside our petty "sanctuary rules" in order to gather together as the people of God around the cross of Christ and His table, the Lord's Supper.

There was a strong moving of God's Spirit and revival that swept across the United States during the 60's and early 70's.[7] It was called the Jesus Movement. It reached many young people. Some had already gotten involved in the drug culture and sexual revolution of that time. But they were saved, delivered, and changed in the fires of revival. Their hearts and minds were transformed but their outward appearance remained.

They began singing of their new faith with their guitars and drums. They went to the churches in their long hair, granny glasses, bell bottom pants, and music, but so many of the churches would not let them in; too many "sanctuary rules." As a result, they went underground and scattered into the culture, but they never lost the fire of revival that God had birthed them in. Today, they are scattered all over the world, still on fire for Jesus. What would happen if all of the "Jesus freaks" from the Jesus Movement were to come together like the nation of Israel did in Hezekiah's day? How about a twenty-nine year revival? Anyone interested? Pray for it, today.

March 22

Read and pray Psalm 82, Proverbs 18:4 – 8, Luke 19:1 – 27, 1 Timothy 3, Psalm 119:89 – 96.
2nd Leviticus 24.
3rd Jeremiah 49.
4th 1 Chronicles 17 – 18.

Revival Organization

When some hear the word "organization" they recoil as if it were a bad word. Organization sounds boring, limiting, and even dead. But the human body is organized, something for which you can be thankful. And there is even more organization in spiritual life. According to Webster's Dictionary, the word "organize" means to have a systematic coordination of parts forming an integral element of a whole. Words like *organ, organic, organism,* are all built upon this word.[8] It is a word that describes life, especially revival life.

One of the things that Hezekiah did during the twenty-nine year revival, according to 2 Chronicles 31:2, was to organize the Levites into their divisions for service, ***"And Hezekiah appointed the divisions of the priests and of the Levites, division by division, each according to his service, the priests and the Levites, for burnt offerings and peace offerings, to minister in the gates of the camp of the LORD and to give thanks and praise."*** King David was the first to do this, and Hezekiah was following his example for revival.

King David organized the Levites into divisions, according to 1 Chronicles 23 – 26, to lead Israel to ***"...make offerings before the LORD and minister to him and pronounce blessings in his name forever."*** 1 Chronicles 23:13. They were ***"...to stand every morning, thanking and praising the LORD, and likewise at evening,"*** 23:30. He also arranged the Levites to sing his songs of praise with instruments he had made (23:5), and stationed them as gatekeepers and on the walls surrounding Jerusalem (26:1 – 19).

David surrounded and guarded the city with songs of praise and thanksgiving, declaring the greatness of God's name and power. The people of Jerusalem were literally surrounded by praise. Anyone approaching the city knew immediately whose city it was; it was the LORD's! Hezekiah followed this same arrangement. He had the record of David's administration as well as the songs he wrote (the Psalms).

You do the same thing as you regularly, daily, and systematically begin your day with one of the Psalms and readings from the Bible. It is a discipline, which requires organization and administration. You set the thermostat of your life and day with praise, thanksgiving, and blessing by organizing your life and day around God's word. Neglected, your life becomes a thermometer of problems and stresses of the world. But resting your heart and mind at the start of each day on the goodness and majesty of the Father brings focus with an eternal perspective, and literally changes the environment around you. As people come near you, they can sense that you are different and, like Jerusalem during the days of David and Hezekiah, that you belong to the Lord.

Taking one of the verses from the Psalm for the day, and/or one of the verses from the readings or Psalm 119, keeps the gates of your heart, the eye-gate and the ear-gate, guarded and well armed. The sacrifice of praise from your lips is offered up continually throughout the day. This is what revival looks like and sounds like. Hezekiah learned it from David's life, according to God's word, and so can you. Stay faithful in the organization of revival.

March 23

Read and pray Psalm 83, Proverbs 18:9 – 14, Luke 19:28 – 48, 1 Timothy 4, Psalm 119:89 – 96.

2nd Leviticus 25.

3rd Jeremiah 50.

4th 1 Chronicles 19 – 20.

There is Sacrifice in Revival

Within a few months of the revival in Hezekiah's day, people began to tithe according to God's word, *"And he commanded the people who lived in Jerusalem to give the portion due to the priests and the Levites, that they might give themselves to the Law of the LORD. As soon as the command was spread abroad, the people of Israel gave in abundance the firstfruits of grain, wine, oil, honey, and of the all the produce of the field. And they brought in abundantly the tithe of everything."* 2 Chronicles 31:4 – 5.

When the pastor announces a sermon on tithing, some people yawn and think, "Oh brother, not again; all he talks about is money, money, money. I guess we are behind in the budget." But not in revival. When God's Spirit begins moving, almost immediately, people will give; not reluctantly, but willingly; not stingily, but abundantly. It was so in Hezekiah's day. May it be so in our day.

The word "tithe" means tenth. God told His people to give Him a tenth of what He blessed them with each year. It was a sacrifice of gratitude for all that God had blessed them with. It was to be enjoyed in His presence, in worship of His goodness and generosity (Deuteronomy 14:22 – 29). The purpose of giving the tithe was to teach Israel to fear the LORD. Tithing is an essential element in learning true worship. It is not given because God needs it to operate His Kingdom; no. God needs nothing. He is sufficient all in Himself. It is given in order for you to learn of Him, to worship Him in spirit and truth.

Tithing is a sacrifice. When you begin to experience the sacrifice of tithing, you begin to learn of the sacrificial nature of God. God gives and gives and gives because He loves, loves, loves. As you give, you learn to love Him by learning of Him. This is what it means to worship the Father, to learn of His love and to know Him more and more. *"For God so loved the world, that he gave his only Son, that whoever believes in him should not perish but have eternal life."* John 3:16.

In Hezekiah's day the people gave so much that they had to pile the produce up in heaps, *"And the people of Israel and Judah who lived in the cities of Judah also brought in the tithe of cattle and sheep, and the tithe of the dedicated things that had been dedicated to the LORD their God, and laid them in heaps."* 2 Chronicles 31:6. It goes on to say in the next few verses that for five months the people continued to bring in the tithe and continued to create these great heaps.

In Hebrew, the word "heaps" is the word *aremah*, and means to pile up. But the unusual thing about this word in these verses is that it is repeated twice each time it is used; as in *aremah aremah*. When the Hebrew language emphasizes something it will repeat the word twice. But this is rare. Only on a few occasions do you find this, and you find it here. You get the picture that the tithe was piled up, piles upon piles, heaps upon heaps; in other words, abundantly. It goes on to say that they gave so much that they had to open up new storerooms for all that the people were bringing.

Revival brings about heaps upon heaps of obedience to God's word, willingly and abundantly. Today, as you ask the Father to teach you to worship Him in spirit and truth, be prepared to learn to fear Him and learn of His sacrificial love by giving to Him a tenth of all He has blessed you with; willingly, abundantly, worshipfully, faithfully, and most of all lovingly.

March 24

Read and pray Psalm 84, Proverbs 18:15 – 19, Luke 20, 1 Timothy 5, Psalm 119:89 – 96.
2nd Leviticus 26.
3rd Jeremiah 51.
4th 1 Chronicles 21 – 22.

The Opposition in Revival

As the revival in Hezekiah's day continued, it was not long until the opposition rose up. In revival there will be opposition. In 2 Chronicles 32:1 – 8, you find the account of the opposition and what Hezekiah did about it. *"After these things and these acts of faithfulness, Sennacherib king of Assyria came and invaded Judah..."* As you begin to learn to worship the Father in spirit and truth and experience personal revival, get ready for the world, the flesh, and the devil to come against you. Learn from Hezekiah how to prepare.

The first thing Hezekiah did was to provide a constant water supply into the city of Jerusalem. Hezekiah's tunnel is still there today. Bringing water into the city and stopping up the other water sources outside the walls limited the water for the enemy and gave the city a constant supply.

In revival you stay filled with the Holy Spirit, the water of life, and give no foothold to the devil (Ephesians 4:27). Sometimes the flesh will take over during a season of revival and will quench the Spirit. In Ephesians 6:16 you find that the shield of faith will quench the flaming arrows of the evil one. Learning which fire to quench is essential anytime, but especially in revival. Having the water of life, the Holy Spirit, keeps the fire of the Spirit burning and quenches the flaming arrows of the devil.

The next thing you see Hezekiah doing to prepare for Sennacherib is that he built up and strengthened the wall around Jerusalem, *"He set to work resolutely and built up all the wall that was broken down and raised towers upon it, and outside it be built another wall, and he strengthened the Millo in the city of David."* 2 Chronicles 32:5. The *Millo* was an old fortification that David built in his day to protect the city. By the time of Hezekiah, Jerusalem had grown beyond its original size during the days of David, but *the city of David* was still there and was in need of being strengthened.

When revival comes and God begins to do a new thing, it is important not to lose sight of how God first began to move in your heart. *"Jesus Christ is the same yesterday and today and forever."* Hebrews 13:8. The

Lord does not change, nor does the enemy and his schemes. The fortifications of accountability, of discipline, of faithfulness to God's word, to prayer, the fellowship of believers, and of missions have not changed. But in times of revival they can easily be neglected if not guarded. Make sure you *strengthen the Millo* in revival. Hezekiah did.

Another thing that Hezekiah did in preparation for attack was that *"... he made weapons and shields in abundance. And he set combat commanders over the people..."* 2 Chronicles 32:5 – 6. In 2 Corinthians 10:3 – 6 you learn that *"...the weapons of our warfare are not of the flesh but have divine power to destroy strongholds. We destroy arguments and every lofty opinion raised against the knowledge of God, and take every thought captive to obey Christ, being ready to punish every disobedience, when your obedience is complete."* The word "destroy" is the Greek word *kataluo*, which means to demolish completely. Keeping God's word in your mind by meditating on memory verses is a powerful weapon against the attacks of the world, the flesh, and the devil. It will completely demolish the lies you have believed from the enemy.

Hezekiah also encouraged God's people by saying, *"Be strong and courageous. Do not be afraid or dismayed before the king of Assyria and all the horde that is with him, for there are more with us than with him. With him is the arm of the flesh, but with us is the LORD our God, to help us and to fight our battles."* 2 Chronicles 32:7 – 8. The phrases that Hezekiah used are almost word-for-word from Joshua's day. No doubt he knew those words as well as the people. Prepare for the opposition by being and staying encouraged in God's word and the promises that He has given to you of His presence with you. Pray His promises and yours.

Learn the lessons of revival from God's word and practice them. Most of all, keep you eyes on Jesus, *"...the Lion of the Tribe of Judah, the Root of David, for He has conquered!"* Revelation 5:5. AMEN.

March 25

Read and pray Psalm 85, Proverbs 18:20 – 24, Luke 21, 1 Timothy 6, Psalm 119:89 – 96.
2ⁿᵈ Leviticus 27.
3ʳᵈ Jeremiah 52.
4ᵗʰ 1 Chronicles 23 – 24.

Worshiping the Father With Wise Choices

The book of Proverbs is a companion to the book of Psalms. It is a collection of wise statements for practical and godly choices in life. Your will is central in the direction of your life. As you make a decision, your body carries it out, and immediately learns from that choice. The body is a quick learner with a tremendous memory. Once you learn to ride a bicycle, you never forget it. The same is true of learning to drive. Your body can carry out the choices you learned long ago without even thinking about it. But it all begins with your will.

Your will is a trinity of mind, will, and emotion. Your thoughts inform your will while your emotions move it into action through your body. Those who study the soul (psychologists; from the Greek word *psooche*, which means the essence of life in terms of thinking, willing, and feeling, and the Greek word *logos*, which means a collection of words with a single meaning; hence, the study of the mind, will, and emotions) focus on the thoughts, the choices, and the feelings of individuals who are seeking to change behavior. You cannot separate these three; the mind, the will, and the emotions. They are a trinity.

God's word informs with spiritual truth for the purpose of transformation. From the new heart of a believer, the Holy Spirit speaks in perfect communion with you, the new you in Christ. The truth from that communion is then revealed to your intuition, which informs your conscience with a word of knowledge, which bears witness of the truth to your mind.[9]

This is the process of God working in you, with you, through you, as you, before the Father and the watching world around you. In Philippians 2:12 – 13, the apostle Paul said, *"...work out your own salvation with fear and trembling, for it is God who works in you, both to will and to work for his good pleasure."* God's will and activity originates in your heart and moves through you, redeeming you from the inside out.

The book of Proverbs majors on truth for your will; wise choices, which are the will of God for you. One of the choices addressed in

Proverbs has to do with choosing the influences in your life. You are surrounded by invitations everyday. These advertisements all have this in common; they invite you to the offer of a lifetime. They appeal to an appetite of some kind in your life with the promise to satisfy. How can you know which one to pursue? God's word, especially in Proverbs, answers that question. This is why it is important for you to read a portion of Proverbs everyday along with your Psalm for the day.

The book of Proverbs is the Father speaking to you, His child, of wise choices to make each day by the wisdom He imparts from His word. Listen to your heavenly Father as He says, *"My son, if you receive my words and treasure up my commandments with you, making your ear attentive to wisdom and inclining your heart to understanding... then you will understand the fear of the LORD...for the LORD gives wisdom..."* Proverbs 2:1 – 6. In this chapter, the writer of Proverbs goes on to say that wisdom from God's word will deliver you from two very strong, deceptive, and destructive influences in life; anger and lust.

Anger is described as a man of perverted speech, 2:12 – 15, whose way is evil, which leads to dark and devious paths. The Hebrew word used in verse twelve for "evil" is the word *rah*, which is violent wickedness, *"...delivering you from the way of evil, from men of perverted speech...who rejoice in doing evil...who are devious in their ways."* The word "devious" is the Hebrew word *looz*, which means to turn away. It describes someone who has turned away from God's word and the direction He leads.

But notice, it all begins with **perverted speech**, with a word. The word "perverted" is the Hebrew word *tahpookah*, which has the meaning of a violent upheaval, as in a volcanic eruption. The picture is of a man who has lost his temper and feels a rush of power as a result. Beware of the intoxication and addiction of anger. Jesus said it is inseparably connected to murder (Matthew 5:21 – 26). Tomorrow, the second powerful influence of lust.

But today, know that God's word provides a choice and direction vastly different than the perverted speech of anger; the wisdom of God from the word of God. His word will draw you away from and heal you from the destructive curses of angry people who spew hatred from a wounded soul. His word will become in you a fountain of living water, springing up to eternal life. AMEN.

March 26

Read and pray Psalm 86, Proverbs 19:1 – 5, Luke 22:1 – 38, 2 Timothy 1, Psalm 119:97 – 104.
2nd Numbers 1.
3rd Lamentations 1.
4th 1 Chronicles 25 – 26.

The Seductive Influence of Unbridled Lust

Yesterday you learned of the influence of God's word for informing and shaping wise choices and the outcome of those choices, which is worship in your daily life. You also learned from Proverbs 2 that you are constantly bombarded and surrounded by ungodly opportunities and messages in the world. One of those advertisements is to respond to situations with anger, Proverbs 2:12. The perverted speech of anger is an invitation to power and to manipulate with intimidation and fear. The problem is the outcome, which is destructive violence and death, none of which are from God.

Another destructive influence that Proverbs warns against is the seductive power of unbridled sexual lust, Proverbs 2:16 – 19. This is described as the adulteress who lures men away from God by her seduction and with lies that deceive sexual appetites, *"So you will be delivered from the forbidden woman, from the adulteress with her smooth words, who forsakes the covenant of her God; for her house sinks down to death, and her paths to the departed, none who go to her come back, nor do they regain the paths of life."* Never underestimate the power of sexual lust.

When the book of Proverbs speaks of the angry man and the adulteress woman it is not warning against particular men or women, but rather the seductive and influential power and destruction of life without God and the life-giving influence of His word. The phrase *"...who forsakes the covenant of her God..."* is key in understanding what happens when a person receives identity from their appetites rather than from their relationship with God.

God created you with many desires, appetites, and lusts. The word "lust" is not a bad word. It sounds bad, but the word itself simply identifies an earnest desire. In Luke 22:15, Jesus said, *"I have earnestly desired to eat this Passover meal with you before I suffer."* The Greek word for "earnestly desired" is *epithumia*. The English word "thermometer" comes from *thumia*, which means to boil. The word *epithumia*

171

means to deeply long for something, to desire something with a passion. It is translated in other passages with the word "lust," but in Luke 22:15 it described the deep longing, the lust, that Jesus had when He instituted the Lord's Supper with His disciples. The word is not necessarily bad.

Lust is not a bad thing until the thing longed for leads you away from, and outside the boundaries of, God's word. When it does, idolatry is the result, because at that point the person is deceived into seeing their identity in the desire rather than in relationship with God. You are not your desires. You have desires (no brainer), but you are more than your appetites. You are a child of God through faith in Jesus Christ, with passions that glorify the Father when placed under His authority, not your authority.

The first Psalm describes the blessed man as the one *"...who walks not in the counsel of the wicked, nor stands in the way of sinners, nor sits in the seat of scoffers; but his delight is in the law of the LORD, and on his law he meditates day and night."* The progress is subtle and yet very real in first choosing to follow appetites rather than God's word, then to embrace the desire as your identity, followed by a lifestyle of activities seeking to satisfy the lust. Of course, the lust is never satisfied, which underlines the lie and deception of it, until placed under the authority of God's word.

Likewise, when you follow the direction and calling of God's word, choosing to trust the truth and the direction of it, and begin to see and embrace your identity in relationship with God through faith in Christ, followed by the activities and lifestyle of a child of God, your passions find their deepest longing and you are satisfied in Christ. John Piper says it this way; "God is most glorified in me when I am most satisfied in Him."[10] Today as you pray and read God's word, experience Him in it and you will find rest and peace for the deepest longings of your soul. AMEN.

March 27

Read and pray Psalm 87, Proverbs 9:6 – 10, Luke 22:39 – 71, 2 Timothy 2, Psalm 119:97 – 104.
2nd Numbers 2.
3rd Lamentations 2.
4th 1 Chronicles 27 – 28.

When Honey Turns to Wormwood

The book of Proverbs continually holds up two choices; the word of the world and the word of God. Everything starts with a word. Creation started with a word (Genesis 1:3). The ministry of Jesus began with a word, *"Repent,"* (Matthew 4:17). Lazarus came out of the grave with a word, *"Lazarus, come forth,"* (John 11:43). The last word of Jesus from the cross was an announcement of the perfection of salvation, *"It is finished!"* (John 19:30) Believers will be caught up together with the word, a shout of victory like a trumpet blast (1 Thessalonians 4:16).

Likewise, temptation begins with a word, *"My son, be attentive to my wisdom; incline your ear to my understanding, that you may keep discretion, and your lips may guard knowledge. For the lips of a forbidden woman drip honey, and her speech is smoother than oil, but in the end she is bitter as wormwood, sharp as a two-edged sword."* Proverbs 5:1 – 4. You are continually faced with which word you will believe and follow. Both have set outcomes, predetermined outcomes. Once you begin following, you cannot change the outcome; they are already determined, predetermined by God. You can change direction, either for better or for bitter, but you cannot change the outcomes. Choosing wisely is the message of Proverbs.

There is a story in Greek mythology that illustrates the two choices. It is found in two epic stories, Homer's Odyssey and Jason and the Argonauts.[11] In the Odyssey, Ulysses and his men sail around the Aegean Sea from one adventure to another. They had heard about the seductive songs of the Sirens. As sailors would pass by the island of the Sirens, they would hear the most beautiful, seductive, inviting songs, which sounded like the honey and oil of the adulteress in the fifth chapter of Proverbs. They would follow its irresistible allure, only to be destroyed on the rocks.

Ulysses knew of the danger. His plan was to have his men fill their ears with bee's wax so they could not hear the seduction. But Ulysses wanted to hear their sensual songs, so he had himself tied fast to the main mast of the ship. He instructed his men that no matter what he did, he was not to be untied. As they passed by the island, the songs nearly drove Ulysses mad with lust, but his men had their ears stuffed with wax and could not hear his angry commands nor the Sirens deceptive invitation.

Jason, who also knew of the legend of the Sirens, had a different method of escape. He brought Orpheus with him on the voyage. Orpheus was known for his beautiful songs and music. They said that no other on earth who could sing and play like Orpheus. His songs had healing powers according to the myth. Jason was betting that the beauty of the songs of Orpheus would drown out the deceptive and destructive songs of the Sirens.

As Jason and his crew drew near the islands of the Sirens, before the first notes of their seduction began, Orpheus was already playing his songs of peaceful beauty. As the sailors enjoyed the music of their beloved Orpheus, they did not even notice the allure of the Sirens, and escaped while singing with Orpheus and enjoying his music.

The lesson is clear: God's word has an eternal beauty and grace that is not of this world. The sweetness of God's word, with the oil of the Holy Spirit, makes the rotting slop of the world, the flesh, and the devil go unnoticed. Religion will seek to stuff your ears with bee's wax or tie you up with restrictive rules. Neither will last very long. According to Colossians 2:23, the rules of religion *"...are of no value in stopping the indulgences of the flesh."* Something greater is offered in a personal relationship with God, through faith in His Son, Jesus Christ. With your eyes on Jesus, and your ears tuned to His word, you will sail past temptation and not even notice it's deceptive lie, allowing God to satisfy your desires as you enjoy His presence and feast on His word, forever.

March 28

Read and pray Psalm 88, Proverbs 19: 11 – 16, Luke 23:1 – 43, 2 Timothy 3, Psalm 119:97 – 104.

2ⁿᵈ Numbers 3.

3ʳᵈ Lamentations 3.

4ᵗʰ 1 Chronicles 29.

Pleasing the Father in Spirit and Truth

The theme of this book is pleasing the Father in spirit and truth. The word "pleasing" is the Hebrew word *ratson*, which means having God's favor, something that is pleasing, desirable, and being accepted. It is used in describing someone who has followed God's instructions for worship; they were "accepted" by God. But it is stronger than that; they "please" the Father and give Him great joy and glory. The word *ratson* is key in learning to worship the Father in spirit and truth.

The book of Proverbs majors on the wisdom and truth of God's word and the importance of your words. Many of the proverbs address the power of your speech. Whole chapters in Proverbs are devoted to this subject. The sharp contrast between lying lips and lips that speak the truth are seen throughout the Proverbs. And when you speak the truth, it pleases the Father, *"Lying lips are an abomination to the LORD, but those who act faithfully are his delight."* Proverbs 12:22. The word "delight" in that verse is the Hebrew word *ratson*.

The word "abomination" is the Hebrew word *toebah*, which means to detest, to abhor, to loathe, to turn away. It is used of unclean things in the Old Testament. It is the opposite of *ratson*. An interesting study is to identify everything that is an abomination and abhorrent to God. One is seen above; lying lips.

There are different kinds of lies. One kind is when something false is spoken, intentionally. The author asked this question to a group of children at a children's camp setting, "Why does a person tell a lie?" One little boy spoke up and said, "To stay out of trouble." We all know the logic of that lie. And then, one little girl said, "To make people feel better." We have probably all been guilty of that type of false encouragement.

Saying something that is not true is lying. This was the sin of the Pharisees and religious leaders in Jesus' day. He called them hypocrites because they had the right words but the wrong heart. They were play actors with a mask of righteousness, but a heart of deceit. Then there is the lie of saying something, but not doing it. The word spoken is true, but the action is false. Jesus also spoke to the crowds about this kind of lying by the Pharisees when He said, *"...so do and observe whatever they tell you, but not the works they do. For they preach, but do not practice."* Matthew 23:3. You may have heard the saying, "Practice what you preach." And again, we have all known the deception of the talk without the walk.

This type of lying is what Proverbs 12:22 is addressing, the kind that speaks but does not do as compared to the one who speaks and then faithfully acts, which is like God. First God says it, then, God does it. And that is why God loves this in you because it reminds Him of Himself. God says it, then, He does it, every time, because God is faithful. What He says, He does. God acts faithfully, and so, when you do, it pleases Him.

This begs the question: So how can I act faithfully? The answer comes with a question: Act faithfully to what word, yours or God's? A person can act faithfully to his own word and always be doing the wrong thing, always be doing things that are contrary to God's word. These are the one who are faithful in sinning; they do it every time. But being faithful to God's word is a different kind of faithfulness. God speaks, you hear and believe, and then God acts in you, with you, through you, as you, before Himself and the watching world around you. And He will do that every time you believe that what He says, He will do.

When you receive the word of God each day in your time with God, His Spirit begins His work in you and with you. And, *"...he who began a good work in you will bring it to completion at the day of Jesus Christ."* Philippians 1:6. Trust that God is doing it, but know that He will not do it without you.

One of my earliest memories as a child was watching my father, Dick Stahl, mow our back yard with one of those old turning-blade mowers. No motor, just a turning blade powered by the two wheels. As I watched from the back porch, it looked like so much fun. Suddenly he stopped and motioned me to join him. I jumped off the porch and ran as fast as I could, reached up and took hold of the handles and started mowing with my dad. As the cut grass flew up on my legs it felt so cool. We were mowing the grass. I felt like such a big boy, so good. And daddy was enjoying it too.

So who was mowing? Me? You better believe I was. I had the cut grass on my legs to prove it. Was he? Oh yeah he was. He was doing all the pushing and I was having all the fun. But it was also work for me. Its not easy holding on to those big handles so far above your head. But I didn't mind, didn't even notice. I was mowing and was with the one I loved so much while doing with him what only he could do.

This is what your Father desires. He wants you to see and hear His invitation to join Him in what He is doing.[12] As you do, it pleases Him. He is the one doing the work, but not without you. He gets the glory because only God can do what pleases Him. But you get the joy of being with Him and sharing in the love He has for you, His child. This is what it means to worship the Father in spirit and truth. And it pleases Him when you do.

March 29

Read and pray Psalm 89, Proverbs 19:17 – 22, Luke 23:44 – 56, 2 Timothy 4, Psalm 119:97 – 104.
2nd Numbers 4.
3rd Lamentations 4.
4th 2 Chronicles 1 – 2.

"Lord, Teach Us To Pray"

Psalm 119 is the longest chapter in the Bible with 176 verses. It is divided up into twenty-two sections, each section being eight verses long. Each section corresponds to a consecutive letter in the Hebrew alphabet. In the Hebrew Bible, the first word in each verse of a particular section begins with the letter of the alphabet for that section. For example, the first letter in the Hebrew alphabet is the letter *aleph*. The first word in each of the first eight verses of Psalm 119 begins with the letter *aleph*. The second letter is *beth,* with the first word of the next eight verses all beginning with the letter *beth.*

Another characteristic of this psalm is that it is a prayer, the longest prayer in the Bible. This prayer has one theme, the importance and necessity of God's word in the life of a believer. This makes this prayer unique, especially in teaching someone to pray. One of the reasons you are encouraged to pray a different section of this psalm each week is so that God's word will teach you and shape you in learning to pray.

For several weeks you have been praying a different section of this Psalm each week in order to learn to pray from God's word. As you continue this practice, you will be learning to worship the Father in spirit and truth, God's truth, from His word.

The first three verses of Psalm 119 are an introduction. These verses are not speaking directly to God, but rather are speaking about God. *"Blessed are those whose way is blameless, who walk in the law of the LORD! Blessed are those who keep his testimonies, who seek him with their whole heart, who also do no wrong, but walk in his ways!* The introduction is an invitation for those who desire to learn to pray from God's word and to allow God's word to shape their prayers. The invitation is a direction in life, a way to live and pray. It is not a performance. It is after God and according to His word.

The next few verses, 4 – 6, combine a confession with a request and a vow. The confession, *"You have commanded your precepts to be kept diligently."* is a confession of God's will. Most of this prayer is confession of the truth. The next verse is a request, based upon this confession, *"Oh that my ways may be steadfast in keeping your statutes!"* Can you see how that request is based upon that confession? The word "diligently" and the word "steadfast" are synonyms. They echo each other.

The first vow, or promise, is found in the next verse, *"Then I shall not be put to shame having my eyes fixed on all your commandments."* You will learn to make vows in your prayers from this prayer. Some are hesitant to make promises to God, although He is not hesitant to make promises to you. A relationship of trust is based upon promises, or vows, as in wedding vows. Don't be afraid to make vows to God, just make sure they are based upon His word.

The next two verses bring this first section to a close. You find two more vows along with a request. *"I will praise you with an upright heart, when I learn your righteous rules. I will keep your precepts; do not utterly forsake me."* Notice that praise and learning go hand-in-hand. You will find this pattern throughout this psalm. Also notice how the third vow, *"I will keep your precepts,"* reflects the first confession, *"You have commanded your precepts to be kept diligently."* Allow the confession of truth from God's word to shape your vows to God. In doing so, your vows will be according to God's word. The final request is a confession of total dependence upon God for the vows you have made. When your vows are from God's word, He will be with you to keep His word, if you will ask Him.

As you pray God's word today, you will be learning to worship Him in spirit and truth, His truth. Allowing God's word to shape your prayers is to allow Him to teach you to worship Him according to His word. This pleases the Father and is what it means to worship Him in spirit and truth.

March 30

Read and pray Psalm 90, Proverbs 19:23 – 29, Luke 24:1 – 35, Titus 1 – 2, Psalm 119:97 – 104.

2nd Numbers 5.

3rd Lamentations 5.

4th 2 Chronicles 3 – 4.

Praying For Purity

The second section of Psalm 119 corresponds to the second letter of the Hebrew alphabet, the letter *beth.* In most Bibles you can see these letter titles over each eight-verse section. In the second section, 119:9 – 16, the theme of purity is prayed. The prayer begins with a question for God, *"How can a young man keep his way pure?"* The word "pure" is the Hebrew word *zakah*, which means to be clean, perfectly clear, shining. It is used in other places in the Old Testament along with the word "righteous" for the understanding of being clean and right in God's sight. It is good to ask questions when you pray, especially when those questions address your personal relationship with God and His glory.

The answer to the question is heard in the next line, *"By guarding it according to you word."* The word "guarding" is one of the key words in this prayer and in the Old Testament. It is the Hebrew word *shamar*, which means to keep, to hold fast to, to recognize the great value of something in order to treasure it. This word is first used in Genesis 2:15 when God placed Adam in the Garden of Eden with the instructions to tend it and to keep it. God's word is to be seen in light of what He entrusted to Adam when He gave him the garden. The value and fruit-fulness of God's word is the theme of Psalm 119. As you pray it more and more, you will see the value of it more and more.

The next verse, verse ten, makes a bold statement with a simple request, *"With my whole heart I seek you; let me not wander from your commandments."* The bold confession at first seems a little extreme until you see it as a vision statement, a goal to keep in mind and to regularly confess. The request is a confession of total dependence upon God in order to reach the goal. Only God can make it happen. And it is His will that you arrive at that goal. This prayer will reveal to you God's will for your life and instruct you how to pray for God's will to be done on earth as it is in heaven.

The next verse is one that many have put to memory because it under-lines the blessing of Scripture memorization and meditation. *"I have*

stored up your word in my heart, that I might not sin against you."
The word "stored up" is the Hebrew word *tsawfan,* which means to hide
something valuable, to treasure something by keeping it safe. This is
the word used to describe what the mother of Moses did when she "hid"
Moses for three months before "hiding" him in the ark she had made
(Exodus 2:2 – 3). It is a verb in 119:11 describing the action of memorization and meditation. Your heart is the safe place, the secret place that
Jesus talked about in Matthew 6:6 when He instructed His followers to
go to that place when praying to the Father. The outcome is obvious. Sin
will not be produced from God's word when it is treasured and hidden
in the heart. This does not mean that you will become sinless, but it will
enable you to sin less and less!

The next verse is a confession of praise, *"Blessed are you, O LORD,"*
with a simple request, *"teach me you statutes."* One of the things you
will learn as you learn to pray from God's word is that praise and learning
are inseparable. This verse is a companion to 119:7, *"I will praise you
with an upright heart, when I learn your righteous rules."* You will
find this combination in several other verses in this psalm.

This section ends with another three-fold vow, *"I will meditate on
your precepts and fix my eyes on your ways. I will delight in your statutes. I will not forget your word."* Think of the vows you make to God
as veiled requests. Without the power and life of God's word, you will
not be able to keep a single promise. But by His presence in your life, and
the power of His word at work in your life, His faithfulness will. God is
faithful. His desire is to be your life through His Son, Jesus Christ. As
He is, your life pleases the Father. This is what it means to worship the
Father in spirit and truth.

March 31

Read and pray Psalm 91, Proverbs 20:1 – 4, Luke 24:36 – 53, Titus 3, Psalm 119:97 – 104.

2nd Numbers 6.

3rd Ezekiel 1 – 2.

4th 2 Chronicles 5 – 6.

Abundant Life Is Growing Life

The third section of Psalm 119 is entitled *gimel*, the third letter in the Hebrew alphabet. The theme of these eight verses is seen in the first verse, 119:17, *"Deal bountifully with your servant, that I may live and keep your word."* This request unfolds over the next seven verses. The word "deal bountifully" is the first word in verse seventeen and is the Hebrew word *gamal*. This word is rich in meaning. It is used to describe being rewarded, bearing fruit, a child being raised up and maturing from breast milk to solid food.

This request describes the spiritual growth that God desires for you to have, but He wants you to want it first, which is a sign of it. One of the ways of God is that He wants you to ask Him for what He wants to give you. Jesus taught this in the Sermon on the Mount when He said, *"… your Father knows what you need before you ask him."* Matthew 6:8.

Another thing to notice with this request is that it has a purpose clause attached to it, *"…that I may live and keep your word."* Some will call this a result clause. It is a request with a result. God loves these kinds of requests because they are not just asking for things He wants to give, but things that will accomplish His will. This is like the little boy who asked his father for $20, so that he could go to the store to buy a Mother's Day gift. What father would deny that request?

Another way to pray this verse is to pray, "Lord, according to Your word, there is only one way for me to live and keep you word, and that is if You grant me spiritual growth and fruitfulness. And so, grant me spiritual growth and fruitfulness, so that I can live and keep Your word!"

The next request is an echo of the first, *"Open my eyes that I may behold wondrous things out of your law."* As God gives you spiritual growth, your eyes are opened to more and more of His eternal truth. His word becomes more and more amazing. The word "law" is the Hebrew word *torah*, which means instructions. God's word reveals His instructions for living in such a way that you learn to love Him with all your heart, soul, mind, and strength, and your neighbor as yourself. Jesus said this was the first and greatest commandment and the second was like it. He said that all of the Law and the Prophets rests upon these two. The next two verses are a confession of the need for the eye-opening request, *"I am a sojourner on the earth, hide not your commandments from me. My soul is consumed with longing for your just decrees at all times."*

The next three verses introduces an important understanding in spiritual growth; the opposition to it. As you learn to pray from God's word, you will learn how to identify the enemies of God and how to pray against them. In these verses, the opposition is identified as those who are insolent, accursed, who wander away from God's word; the scornful, those full of contempt; and the powerful who take advantage of God's people. These words and others like them will come up again and again in this psalm.

These enemies fall into one of three categories, the world, the flesh, and the devil. They are not people; they are powers, spiritual powers bent on stealing, killing, and destroying everything that God has done and loves, which include you. Prayer is a mighty weapon that defeats them, if you learn how to wield it.

This section ends with a beautiful statement describing the wonderful result of asking for more light, *"Your testimonies are my delight, they are my counselors."* The word "delight" is a delightful word. It is the Hebrew word *shahshooah*, which means pleasing, delightful, pleasurable. This is everything that God's word is to Himself. He delights in His own word and will. Imagine how different it would have been if Adam and Eve would have seen the pleasure and delightfulness of the counsel from God's word rather than turning to a tree for goodness, pleasure, and wisdom.

God loves it when you ask Him for spiritual growth and fruitfulness with an ever-increasing eye-opening joy in His word. It pleases Him, which is what it means to worship the Father in spirit and truth.

April 1

Repeat same readings from March 31.

Praying Through Difficulties With Wisdom

The fourth section of this great prayer is entitled *daleth*, Psalm 119:25 – 32. The first line is telling, *"My soul clings to the dust..."* A modern expression of this could be, "I am really feeling down-in-the-dumps!" Everyone goes through times of discouragement, doubts, and even crushing depression. Feelings are powerful and can mislead and distort everything. They are not reliable for decision-making, but they are very real.

The rest of verse twenty-five is instructive, *"...give me life according to your word!"* This is a direct request and is similar to the prayer that Jesus prayed in the Garden of Gethsemane, *"...not my will, but yours be done."* Luke 22:42. When you pray "according to Your word," you are submitting yourself to God's will and timing for the answer, rather than dictating to Him how and when He should "give you life." The New Testament equivalent of this is praying in the Name of Jesus.

The next verse, 119:26, gives guidance as you pray through difficulties, *"When I told of my ways, you answered me; teach me your statutes."* The psalmist remembers a past experience of difficulty and the answer God gave, and then asks for instruction from God's word. The word "statutes" is the Hebrew word, *khok*, and has the meaning of engraving into stone. It is also used to describe a tattoo, an engraving under the skin. It communicates permanence rather than something that can be erased. The stability and permanence of God's word will hold you and carry you through difficulties, especially when emotions are pushing you around.

The third request is found in the next verse, *"Make me understand the way of your precepts, and I will meditate on your wondrous works."* The word "understanding" is the Hebrew word *bayin,* which means to cut and separate. It is translated in the Old Testament with words like understanding, discernment, and wisdom. It has to do with being able to distinguish between good and evil so that you can make the right choice.

This is a powerful prayer request because in praying it, you are asking God to shape and mold your thoughts in such a way as to cut and separate the difference between good and evil, right and wrong, in order to make the wisest choice. The vow that follows is similar to a request with a result attached to it. Meditating on God's wondrous works will shape your thoughts to see clearly the difference between good and evil. God is good and He only does what is good.

The next line, *"My soul melts for sorrow, strengthen me according to your word."* This is a companion to the opening line and emphasizes the on-going struggle a person has with their emotions trying to call the shots. But God's word gives strength, if you will ask Him for it. God's word informs and transforms at the same time so that wise decisions can be made.

A fourth request is seen in the next verse, *"Put false ways far from me and graciously teach me your law!"* The request for learning is probably not high up on your prayer list, but it is in this prayer. It is the number one request in Psalm 119. As you allow God's word to shape your prayers, this request will become more and more important and valuable to you.

This section ends with a flurry of confessions and a powerful vow. The three-fold confession *"I have chosen the way of faithfulness; I have set your rules before me. I cling to your testimonies..."* are all declarations of the will informed and transformed by God's word, not the emotions. These are statements of determination not to stay in the dumps but to rise up and get through them. God does not take you around, over, or under difficulties; He takes you through them with the strength and instruction from His word.

The last line is a vow; *"I will run in the way of your commandments, when you enlarge my heart."* This is a powerful vow of faith and very different from the way this section began. Praying God's word will move you from *my soul clings to the dust*, to *I cling to your testimonies...I will run in the way of your commandments*, if you are willing to allow God's word to shape your prayers. As you do, you will be learning to worship the Father in spirit and truth.

April 2

Read and pray Psalm 92, Proverbs 20:5 – 10, Acts 1, Philemon, Psalm 119:105 – 112.
2nd Numbers 7.
3rd Ezekiel 3 – 4.
4th 2 Chronicles 7 – 8.

Developing An Appetite For God's Word

The fifth section of Psalm 119 is full of requests; eight in all. It also gives one of the most complete lists of words for God's word. In these eight verses, 119:33 – 40, there are eight different words used for God's word, each one with a particular meaning describing the beauty and blessing of God's word.

In the first verse you find the word "statutes," *khok,* which you have already learned to mean engraved. This emphasizes the permanence of God's word. Then in verse thirty-four you find the word *torah*, which you have already learned as the instructions of God. The next verse talks about the "commandments" of God. This is the Hebrew word *mitzvah*, and has built into it the idea of a relationship with responsibility. It is used in the Old Testament to describe the relationship of a father with his son (1 Samuel 17:20), a farmer with his workers (Ruth 2:9), a king with his servants (2 Samuel 21:14), and God with His people (Deuteronomy 5:33).

The fourth word is "testimonies," which is the Hebrew word *aydooth*, from the root word for "witness." It was a legal word describing a person who repeated an event as true. God's testimonies are His words, which are true. He bears witness of Himself. The word "testimony" points to what is true, reliable, and real. You can trust the testimonies of God. His word is reality.

The fifth word in this section for God's word is the word "ways." On the surface this may not seem to fit, and yet the ways of God are only known from the words of God. All of the words of God point in a direction, and lead to a relationship with God. Jesus Christ is the full revelation of God. He called Himself, *"...the way, the truth, and the life."* John 14:6. The Hebrew word for "way" is *derek*, which is from a root word meaning "foot." The concept is the path that your feet make when walking in a particular direction, which becomes a foot trail that others will follow. The "way" is a word describing the path that God has laid in His word that leads to a personal relationship with Him.

The sixth word in this section for God's word is the word "promise." It is the Hebrew word *emrah*, which literally means a spoken word. When God speaks, it is a promise because, first He says it, then He does it, but not until He first says it. What God says, He always does, because God is faithful. This word, *emrah*, emphasizes God's faithfulness to His own word. He is able to do what He says, which means that you can trust Him.

The seventh word is the Hebrew word *mishpawt*, which is translated "rules." This word is built upon the word "ruler" and has the concept of the edict of a sovereign king. The word of a sovereign king is the government. The rules of God communicate His sovereignty and control over everything. He established the universe by His righteous decrees and He rules by His own word. This word gives assurance that God is the ultimate Ruler of everything. He rules with righteous judgments. You can trust Him.

The eighth word in this section of requests, 119:33 – 40, is the Hebrew word *pikqood*, "precepts." This Hebrew word has the meaning of overseeing, ordering or numbering. The Greek equivalent of this word is *arithmein,* from which we get our English word "arithmetic." The understanding of "precepts" is that God's word has order, arrangement, and oversight. His precepts put life in its proper perspective and order. God superintends life according to His word. Following His precepts adds up and equates to a life well ordered.

Take time to review Psalm 119:33 – 40 and adopt one of the requests as your prayer request for the day with your new understanding of the Hebrew words. As you do, you will be praying God's word and discovering the rich flavor that is only found in Him. This is what it means to worship the Father in spirit and truth.

April 3

Read and pray Psalm 93, Proverbs 20:11 – 16, Acts 2, Hebrews 1, Psalm 119:105 – 112.
2nd Numbers 8.
3rd Ezekiel 5 – 6.
4th 2 Chronicles 9 – 10.

Praying the Promises of God and Your Promises Too

The sixth section of Psalm 119 is about promises; praying the promises of God, and your promises, too, 119:41 – 48. The first line teaches the important truth of praying the promises of God, *"Let your steadfast love come to me, O LORD, your salvation according to your promise."* One of the first lessons to acquire when learning to pray is to ask God for what He has promised. This lesson is clearly seen in Psalm 2 when the Son, the King, tells of the decree of the Father in verse seven, *"The LORD said to me, 'You are my Son; today I have begotten you. Ask of me, and I will make the nations your heritage, and the ends of the earth your possession...'"* The Father told the Son to ask Him for what He had promised. So must we.

The word "steadfast love" is the Hebrew word *hesed*, which describes faithfulness to the covenant relationship between God and His people Israel. It is covenantal love. It is love that chooses and remains faithful to that choice. This is God's love. It is conditional; conditioned by the response of the one God loves. The only way to respond to God's love is to receive Him at His word, by believing Him. As you do, you will respond with a promise in the same way a man and a woman do at their wedding. A covenant marriage is based upon *steadfast love*, where faithfulness to the vows is the strength of the union. So it is, only more so, with God and the relationship He desires to have with you.

The prayer for what God has promised has a result, verse forty-two, *"...then I shall have an answer for him who taunts me, for I trust in your word."* The word "taunt" is the Hebrew word *charaph*, which means to defy, to blaspheme, to reproach, to condemn, and also means betrothed. Satan is all the above, including betrothed. He comes with a lie in order to wed and enslave and reproduce sin in a person's life. But praying the promises of God answers his lie with the truth worth waiting for.

The next request is answered with the asking, *"And take not the word of truth utterly out of my mouth, for my hope is in your rules."* In asking, you receive. Jesus promised this when He said, *"Ask, and it will be given to you..."* Luke 11:9. When you pray God's word, the word of truth is in your mouth. The word of faith and hope is your request. This is not asking for what you want, but rather it is asking for what God has promised, and then waiting in faith for God's timing to give it.

The rest of this section is full of vows, *"I will keep your law...I will walk in a wide place...I will also speak of your testimonies before kings...I shall not be put to shame...I will lift up my hands toward your commandments...I will meditate on your statutes."* Why would a person be hesitant to make a promise to God? The answer: "Because I might not be able to keep it." But if God has given you the promise in His word, then He will do it. His word carries in it the obedience He looks for, if you are willing to trust Him to do it in you, with you, through you, as you, before Him and the watching world around you.

Knowing and praying God's promises is what it means to learn to pray. But you also must make promises to God and pray your promises. Make sure you shape your vows from God's word, according to His promises. In a covenant relationship, faith is the strength of the relationship, faith in the promise that began the relationship. Your promise to God grows out of the faith from His word. *"Faith comes by hearing, and hearing by the word of Christ."* Romans 10:17. *"He who calls you is faithful; He will surely do it."* 1 Thessalonians 5:24. When you pray the promises of God, it pleases Him. This is what it means to worship the Father in spirit and truth.

April 4

Read and pray Psalm 94, Proverbs 20:17 – 23, Acts 3, Hebrews 2, Psalm 119:105 – 112.
2nd Numbers 9.
3rd Ezekiel 7 – 8.
4th 2 Chronicles 11 – 12.

Remembering God's Word

The seventh section of Psalm 119 is entitled *zayin*, the seventh letter in the Hebrew alphabet. The theme of this section and prayer is remembering. The first word in the first line is the Hebrew word, *zekar*, which means to remember, to recall, to recite, to meditate, to record. It has action built into it similar to the Hebrew word *shemah*, which means to hear and obey. The Hebrew name *Zechariah* is from the word *zekar*. This is one of the most important words in the Old Testament for God's covenant people.

All of the feasts of Israel were given to the nation so that they would not forget the mighty deeds of God and their covenant with Him. The feasts were celebrations to help them to remember and to recite the blessings and curses of the covenant; to help them remain faithful to God. Remembering brought the past into the present in order to move into the future in relationship with God.

When the word "remember" is applied to God, as it is in the first line of this section, 119:49 – 56, it is similar to praying the promises of God. God does not forget, especially His own word. When you, like the psalmist, pray, *"Remember your word to your servant, in which you have made me hope,"* it is a reminder to you of what God has said to you. As you pray God's word, you record God's word in your memory. This is the key to Scripture memorization and meditation, praying your memory verses.

The blessings of this are listed in the rest of this section. You are strengthened to keep moving forward through difficulties, *"This is my comfort in my affliction, that your promise gives me life."* The word "comfort" is the Hebrew word *nawkham*, which literally means to breath deeply. It means to be consoled, to be strengthened in a time of great distress. God's word comforts by reminding you of His presence with you and His plans for you.

The third line in this section talks about the lie of the world, the flesh, and the devil to mislead and to misguide God's people. The struggle you have is not with flesh and blood, not with people, but with spiritual powers of wickedness and evil identified by the phrase, the world, the flesh, and the devil. This phrase is found in Ephesians 2:1, *"And you were dead in the trespasses and sins in which you once walked, following the course of this world, following the prince of the power of the air, the spirit that is now at work in the sons of disobedience; among whom we all once lived in the passions of our flesh, carrying out the desires of the body and the mind, and were by nature children of wrath."* But God's word cuts through the lie and shines brightly with the truth.

Singing God's word is mentioned in 119:54, *"Your statutes have been my songs in the house of my sojourning."* Singing is one of the ways you remember and learn. You probably learned the alphabet with a song. Many have learned the books of the Bible with a song. Scripture songs are musical prayers. God gave us music for this purpose. He loves it when we sing His word in prayer to Him. And you learn the truth of God's word more and more, His word becomes more and more interwoven into the fabric of your life. Next time you are faced with temptation, sing your way through it with a Scripture song.

Today, pray your memory verse for the day. It you don't have one, memorize one from this section on remembering, and then pray it throughout the day.

April 5

Read and pray Psalm 95, Proverbs 20:24 – 30, Acts 4, Hebrews 3, Psalm 119:105 – 112.
2nd Numbers 10.
3rd Ezekiel 9 – 10.
4th 2 Chronicles 13 – 14.

Praise is a Learning Experience

The eighth section of Psalm 119 is entitled *heth*, 119:57 – 64. The first line reads, *"The LORD is my portion; I promise to keep your words."* The Hebrew word *helek*, is the first word in the first line and is translated as "portion." It is used in the Old Testament to describe a portion or distribution of land, of food, of an inheritance, a reward, and of sharing fellowship with a particular group of people. In this verse it seems to encompass all of the above to indicate praise. Anytime you see the phrase, *the LORD is...*, God's word is revealing something of the nature or character of God. This is for you to know Him and praise Him. As you read the rest of this section you can see that it emphasizes the activity of praise.

The second line is a request based upon the promise of God as well as His gracious character, *"I entreat your favor with all my heart; be gracious to me according to your promise."* The word "favor" is the Hebrew word *paneem*, which is always plural and is built upon the root word for face. It means to turn to a person in order to be face-to-face with them. It is plural because of the many facial features that make a person recognizable to another. This is the heart of praise; to seek the face of God in order to know Him more and more rather than seeking His hand in order for Him to give more and more.

The third and fourth line reflects upon the role of repentance in praise, *"When I think on my ways, I turn my feet to your testimonies; I hasten and do not delay to keep your commandments."* The word "turn" is the Hebrew word *shoob*, which means to repent, to turn away from sin and to turn in obedience to God's word. When you consider how much time is spent in considering your plans, your health, your feelings, your looks, your reputation, and what you should do about all of that, you too will repent and turn to Someone more interesting, more powerful, more loving, more holy, more of everything good and perfect and pleasurable and kind, namely God the Father, God the Son, and God the Holy Spirit as revealed in His eternal word.

The fifth line reminds you of the opposition you face, especially when you turn seeking the face of God, *"Though the cords of the wicked ensnare me, I do not forget your law."* The weapons of the world, the flesh, and the devil are lies that trap, hinder, enslave, and cause God's people to stumble. The psalmist recognizes these snares and the reality of being caught, but also of being set free by the deliverance of reflecting upon the instructions of God's word. God's instructions are preventative as well as redemptive in setting the captive free.

The last three lines list the different settings for praise. The first is when you are all alone, at midnight. The second is when you are in the company of God's people. The third is when you surrounded by God's creation. In each case, God's word is essential in obeying, encouraging, and instructing in praise. Praise and instruction from God's word are inseparable because God's word reveals His character and nature. The only way to know God is for His Spirit to reveal the eternal and perfect truth of God for you to know. You don't know about God in that moment, you know of Him in a personal and intimate relationship of faith and trust. Praise is the result of knowing Him more and more.

Today, throughout the day, complete the sentence prayer, "O Lord, you are…," with the request, "…teach me Your commandments." As you do, you will be allowing God's word to shape your praise with His desire to teach you in that setting. This is what it means to worship the Father in spirit and truth.

April 6

Read and pray Psalm 96, Proverbs 21:1 – 5, Acts 5, Hebrews 4, Psalm 119:105 – 112.
2ⁿᵈ Numbers 11.
3ʳᵈ Ezekiel 11 – 12.
4ᵗʰ 2 Chronicles 15 – 16.

Learning the Hard Way is Still Learning

The ninth section of Psalm 119 is entitled *teth*, the ninth letter in the Hebrew alphabet. This section of prayer, 119:65 – 72, teaches the important lesson of praying the experiences of what you are learning, even when you learn the hard way.

The first line confesses the truth of the goodness of God, and for that reason is an expression of praise, *"You have dealt well with your servant, O LORD, according to your word."* The phrase, "dealt well," is made up of two Hebrew words, *asah*, which means to make or to accomplish, and *tob*, which means good. Both of these words are very common, used hundreds of times in the Old Testament. Both of these words are used in almost every verse in Genesis 1 – 2, the two chapters on creation, describing God's creative activity of making and forming everything and seeing the goodness of Himself in His creation.

Following the expression of praise comes a request for learning. These two are always found following each other. *"Teach me good judgment and knowledge, for I believe in your commandments."* The word "judgment," is the Hebrew word *taham*, which is from a root word for taste. It developed into the meaning of discernment from the understanding of distinguishing different flavors by tasting. It means learning by experience.

The second word, "knowledge," echoes this word. It is the Hebrew word *dahath*, from a family of words based upon the Hebrew word *yadah*, used of the knowledge of God. Like *taham, dahath* is knowledge that can only come from a personal and intimate relationship with God. Together, these words *taham* and *dahath* point to a learning experience with God, of God, according to the word of God.

The next five lines describe how God uses painful situations in life to teach eternal truth. *"Before I was afflicted, I went astray, but now I keep your word...It is good for me that I was afflicted, that I might learn your statutes."* The word "afflicted," is the Hebrew word, *naham*, which means to be humbled by a painful and distressing experience.

Trauma is one of the teachers of God. No one asks for difficulties and distress, and no one is immune to them, but very few recognize the blessings that result from them if a person is willing to turn to God's word and be taught by God in the midst of them. The main lesson God teaches through difficulty is a total dependency upon Him and the nourishing strength from His word.

Also notice the present tense of *"It is good for me...,"* and the past tense of *"...that I was afflicted..."* For believers, suffering is temporary and blessings are now and are eternal. For unbelievers, it is the opposite; blessings are temporary and suffering is eternal. The other thing to notice is the option, even for the believer, of learning, *"...that I might learn your statutes."* Learning is not automatic. It is chosen. It is not easy, but it is simple, if you will turn to the Lord and ask for it.

The last line is a beautiful confession of the value of God's word to a believer, *"The law of your mouth is better to me than thousands of gold and silver pieces."* One afternoon, the author was riding in his truck with his nine-year-old granddaughter. He reviewed this verse, Psalm 119:72 with her and said, "Emma, do you know what this verse means?" Emma turned and said, "I think I do. But tell me." I said, "It means that if a pile of gold was before me, along side of a Bible, I would choose the Bible rather than the gold. What about you?" Emma kept looking straight ahead and said, "I would choose the gold, and then go out and buy Bibles for the people who do not have one!" AMEN.

You can learn from the Bible, you can learn from your mistakes, you can learn from others (even from a nine-year-old), if you believe that God is good, all the time, and that all the time, His desire is for you to know Him more and more, through good things, as well as through difficult things; *"God is at work in all things, working them together for good, for those who love Him, for those who are called according to His purpose."* Romans 8:28.

195

April 7

Read and pray Psalm 97, Proverbs 21:6 – 11, Acts 6, Hebrews 5, Psalm 119:105 – 112.
2nd Numbers 12.
3rd Ezekiel 13 – 14.
4th 2 Chronicles 17 – 18.

The Fellowship of True Worship

The tenth letter in the Hebrew alphabet is *yodh*. In this section of prayer, 119:73 – 80, the psalmist prays for fellowship with other worshipers. The first two lines set the theme of this prayer, *"Your hands have made and fashioned me; give me understanding that I may learn your commandments. Those who fear you shall see me and rejoice, because I have hoped in your word."* This prayer begins with a confession of creation and identity. God made and fashioned the first man from dust and the first woman from his rib bone. He made and fashioned you in the same way in your mother's womb. You belong to God, who created you. When you were saved, you were born from above, made and fashioned by the Father with the righteousness of His Son, Jesus Christ.

Once God created Adam and Eve, He continued His creative work in their lives with His word. The same is true for you. God's word continues what He has begun in you. This is the reason for the request, *"... give me understanding that I may learn your commandments."* God's word requires God's understanding and wisdom to learn, know, and grow. Just as food gives your body nourishment and growth, so God's word, with the gift of His wisdom, gives your spirit and soul nourishment and growth. You are His creation; body, soul, and spirit, created for fellowship with Him and others like yourself.

The confession of *"Those who fear you shall see me and rejoice, because I have hoped in your word,"* identifies you with other worshipers who also see God as their Creator and Sustainer, according to His word. There is joy in fellowship with God and with His people, when worship is according to His word. The phrase *those who fear you* is repeated in verse seventy-nine, *"Let those who fear you turn to me, that they may know your testimonies."* The phrase *those who fear you* is an expression of worship. The word "fear" is the Hebrew word *yahrey*, which means to be afraid, to be reverent, to have great awe and respect. When used in the context of worship it describes a person who recognizes the supreme power and authority of God and is humbled before Him.

When this phrase is linked with words describing God's word, as in 119:74, 79, it provides a full definition of what it means to worship the Father in spirit and truth. God reveals the knowledge of Himself through His word. His Spirit and His word are inseparable; the two are one. Knowing Him in spirit and truth describes fellowship with His Spirit, according to His word. This is true worship. And true worship gathers true worshipers together in fellowship with one another as each one is in fellowship with God.

This prayer also teaches that there is discipline and correction in this kind of fellowship and true worship. The third line is a confession of what the psalmist has discovered, *"I know, O LORD, that your rules are righteous, and that in faithfulness you have afflicted me."* The request that follows is also a confession of what the psalmist has learned, *"Let your steadfast love comfort me according to your promise to your servant. Let your mercy come to me, that I may live; for your law is my delight."* This request has been shaped by God's love, faithfulness, and word. Worship, learning, and God's word are a trinity that are one and cannot be separated.

The fellowship of true worshipers pleases the Father because He sees the image of His own Son, Jesus Christ, in their midst. God sees the fruit of His word in the obedience of their lives as they gather together to worship and to learn of Him. This pleases God. This is what it means to worship the Father in spirit and truth.

April 8

Read and pray Psalm 98, Proverbs 21:12 – 17, Acts 7:1 – 29, Hebrews 6, Psalm 119:105 – 112.
2nd Numbers 13.
3rd Ezekiel 15 – 16.
4th 2 Chronicles 19 – 20.

Worship When Your Wood is Wet

You may have heard the old expression, "If that does not light your fire, then your wood is too wet!" Actually, that expression describes a soul so dry, it cannot get excited about anything. It is a common condition. For some, it is an on-going state. The eleventh section of Psalm 119 addresses this condition. The eleventh letter in the Hebrew alphabet is *kaph*, and the prayer is found in 119:81 – 88.

The first three lines describe the condition with a simple request, *"My soul longs for your salvation; I hope in your word. My eyes long for your promise; I ask, 'When will you comfort me?' For I have become like a wineskin in the smoke, yet I have not forgotten your statutes."* The simple request is echoed in 119:84, *"How long must your servant endure? When will you judge those who persecute me?"* The questions "when...how long?" are asked often in prayers, especially when your wood is wet.

Delays in God's timing are only from our perspective, not from God's. We are limited within time constraints, which equates to delays. But God works according to the counsel of His own will, for His own purpose, according to His own word, and in a particular order, His timing. During those times of delay, your soul can feel like it is drying up, like everything is soaked in worship-quenching anxiety and fear. This is very real, more often for some than for others. So, how do you pray when you can't pray? This section will guide you through those times.

The phrase "longs for" in the first line is the Hebrew word *kalah*. This is a root word with several variations of meaning. The basic meaning is to hold back, or to delay. It also has the meaning of something that has come to completion in a positive sense, and something that has been totally depleted or consumed in a negative sense. For the psalmist who is described as *a wineskin in the smoke*, this word is understood with a combination of all three; a delay, a completion, and a total depletion.

In the sense of delay, it describes waiting for an answer from God. The question, "when...how long?" points to this meaning of the word.

In the understanding of completion, it points to God's salvation, God's promise, and faith that God has provided fully all that is needed in order to overcome. The psalmist believes in what God has promised and the fullness of the answer. The depletion is understood as descriptive of the condition. This is a prayer that you pray when you feel like you are at the end of your rope; all options are depleted; all you have is God's promise, and your feeling of total exhaustion.

The Apostle Paul knew that condition and heard the Lord say to him in 2 Corinthians 12:9, *"My grace is sufficient for you, for my power is made perfect in weakness."* His confession was *"...I am content with weaknesses, insults, hardships, persecutions, and calamities. For when I am weak, then I am strong."* 2 Corinthians 12:10.

Praying through those times of longing, delays, and exhaustion is done with a total dependency and focus upon God's word. You will not have words at a time like that. All your words will have been dried up in the fire, like the *wineskin in the smoke.* But God has words for you to pray in 119:81 – 88. And you can pray them with confidence that the Father hears and answers. He gives words for your confession. He gives words for your longings. He gives words that are sure and steadfast. His words give life.

As you regularly pray through Psalm 119, you may not feel totally depleted when you come to the *kaph* section, but you will know someone who is and can intercede for them with this powerful prayer. God loves this prayer because He loves hearing His own word, from His own child, and will work out His own will in His own good time. Thank Him for it, today. As you do, you will be worshiping the Father in spirit and truth, even if your wood is wet.

April 9

Read and pray Psalm 99, Proverbs 21:18 – 24, Acts 7:30 – 60, Hebrews 7, Psalm 119:113 – 120.
2nd Numbers 14.
3rd Ezekiel 17 – 18.
4th 2 Chronicles 21 – 22.

Confessing Eternal Truth With One Eternal Request

The twelfth letter in the Hebrew alphabet is *lamed.* This prayer is found in Psalm 119:89 – 96. Immediately you hear eternity in this prayer, *"Forever, O LORD, your word is firmly fixed in the heavens. Your faithfulness endures to all generations; you have established the earth, and it stands fast. By your appointment they stand this day, for all things are your servants."* God is eternal. God's word is eternal. Your prayers are eternal when you pray God's eternal word. This prayer reminds you and teaches you to pray with eternity in mind.

The confessions of this prayer go all the way back to creation. They also remember times of difficulty when God's eternal word gave strength needed to stand under great pressure, *"If your law had not been my delight, I would have perished in my affliction...the wicked lie in wait to destroy me, but I consider your testimonies."* 119:93, 95. Many prayers are full of temporary requests and then are over. Prayer lists are notorious for this. Some will occasionally remember to give thanks for answered prayer. But Psalm 119 teaches to pray with confessions of truth, talking to God about what His word has revealed. This section reminds and teaches this important truth; God loves to hear His eternal word prayed from His child.

The one big request in this prayer is found in verse ninety-four, *"I am yours; save me, for I have sought your precepts."* The request is introduced with a confession; an eternal confession, *I am yours.* This echoes the first few lines about creation. The psalmist identifies with creation as belonging to God. Then the simple request; *save me.* The Hebrew word for "save" is *yeshua,* which means to rescue, to deliver, to save. It is a verb in this sentence, but it also used as a noun in the Old Testament; it is the name Joshua. In the New Testament it is the name Jesus. When king David and the Old Testament believers prayed this prayer, they had no idea how far their prayer was reaching into the future and into eternity, but it was. They were praying for Jesus Christ to come as the Savior of the whole world. Praying God's word gives prayer an eternal reach, which pleases the Father.

The last line of this section is a powerful declaration of God's eternal word, *"I have seen a limit to all perfection, but your commandment is exceedingly broad."* The word "limit" is the Hebrew word *qets*, which means border or the end of property. The confession declares that the vast expanse of a single commandment from God is greater than everything that is beautiful and perfect in God's creation. By a single word, the universe came into being. When you learn to pray God's word and allow His eternal word to shape your prayers, your prayers will take on an eternal reach and beauty in God's eyes. This is what it means to worship the Father in spirit and truth.

April 10

Read and pray Psalm 100, Proverbs 21:25 – 31, Acts 8, Hebrews 8, Psalm 119:113 – 120.
2rd Numbers 15.
3rd Ezekiel 19 – 20.
4th 2 Chronicles 23 – 24.

Praying With Wisdom From the Word

The thirteenth section of Psalm 119 is about wisdom. This section, 119:97 – 104, is entitled *mem*, the thirteenth letter of the Hebrew alphabet. One of the first things you notice is that there is not a single request in this prayer. This prayer is one confession of truth after another. This is the first indication of wisdom, which this prayer prays. The first line reveals the secret of wisdom, *"Oh how I love your law! It is my meditation all the day."* The rest of this prayer unfolds the truth of that confession by describing the result of that confession, which is wisdom.

The next three lines highlight three powerful words for wisdom in the Hebrew language, which results from loving and meditating on God's word. *"Your commandment makes me wiser than my enemies, for it is ever with me."* The word "wiser" is the Hebrew word *hokmah*, which has the meaning of a special skill or ability that God gives in His word. This word is used in Exodus 28:3 to describe men whom God filled with His Spirit and skill to construct the Tabernacle. It is used extensively in Proverbs. Here it describes the wisdom and skill to overcome opposition by a single commandment. The New Testament declares this truth in this way, *"...and take the sword of the Spirit, which is the word of God."* Ephesians 6:17.

The next word for wisdom is in the next line, *"I have more understanding than all my teachers, for your testimonies are my meditation."* The Hebrew word for "understanding" is *sakal*, which means wise behavior, good success, to prosper. It points to the application of wisdom from God. This word is used in Isaiah 52:13 and Jeremiah 23:5 to describe the Messiah in the way He would suffer, and the way He would reign; with *sakal.* It is also the word that God used when He commanded Joshua to meditate on His word, in Joshua 1:8, and promised him that he would have good success, *sakal*, as a result. This declaration does not minimize good teachers, it points to the fact that all of the earthly teachers combined fall short of the wisdom God gives in His word.

The third word for wisdom is found in the next line, 119:100, *"I understand more than the elders, for I keep your precepts."* The word "understand" in that verse is the Hebrew word *bayin*, which means discernment. It is from a root word meaning to cut and separate. It is the ability to see the clear difference between good and evil in order to choose the good and to reject the evil, apart from an experience. It is wisdom before an experience. Have you ever heard the expression, "learn from your mistakes?" This word, *bayin*, is learning before a mistake. This powerful confession declares that obedience to God's word teaches *bayin*. The elders can speak from experience, but *bayin* is wisdom before an experience. This word is used again in the last line, *"Through your precepts I get understanding, therefore I hate every false way."* The sense of seeing clearly the difference between good and evil is a gift from God; it is *bayin,* and it only comes from God's word.

The next two lines, 119:101 – 102, declares how God's word guards and keeps you focused, *"I hold back my feet from every evil way, in order to keep your word. I do not turn aside from your rules, for you have taught me."* This is a statement of preventative repentance, recognizing the tendency toward sin and how God's word will keep you on track in the word.

The last confession in this section is telling, *"How sweet are your words to my taste, sweeter than honey to my mouth."* Your spirit has senses just like your body has senses. Your spirit can taste, according to this verse. When Eve saw that the fruit of the tree of the knowledge of good and evil was good for food, it must have looked sweet. This verse declares that there is nothing sweeter than the taste of God's word, which gives wisdom.

Today, try praying without making any requests. Declare what God has said and you have personally experienced as true. This pleases the Father. Pleasing God is what it means to worship Him in spirit and truth.

April 11

Read and pray Psalm 101, Proverbs 22:1 – 5, Acts 9, Hebrews 9, Psalm 119:113 – 120.
2nd Numbers 16.
3rd Ezekiel 21 – 22.
4th 2 Chronicles 25 – 26.

Praying God's Word Every Step of the Way

The fourteenth letter in the Hebrew alphabet is the Hebrew letter *nun*. This prayer, 119:105 – 112, highlights the light God's word gives for every step of the journey of life. In every situation, God's word gives direction and outcome. The first line of this section is often memorized for that reason; *"Your word is a lamp to my feet, and a light to my path."* This verse speaks to the present situation and to a future outcome; the next step to take, the direction of that step, and the destination of that direction.

The next line is a present tense confession of a vow with future tense implications; *"I have sworn an oath and confirmed it, to keep your righteous rules."* A vow is a promise made in the present, with an outcome for the future. The word "confirmed" is the Hebrew word *koom*. It literally means to rise up and begin something. In this context it means that the vow has been made and the action of it has begun. This is a present tense confession, with a future outcome, that has already begun. The way to keep God's word is to promise you will and then to rise up and begin doing it. When you leave the *koom* out, nothing happens. A promise with no action is a cloud with no rain.

The next few lines underscore the fact that once you make a vow and rise up and begin to do it, you will have a fight on your hands from the world, the flesh, and the devil; *"I am severely afflicted; give me life, O LORD, according to your word!"* But God's word gives strength for the fight. His word is a mighty weapon for the battle. God's word will keep you moving forward in the conflict, and is victorious. God does not promise an easy life, He promises a victorious life. God is with you and He has already won.

The next line is another reminder of the connection between praise and learning, *"Accept my freewill offering of praise, O LORD, and teach me your rules."* You will find this connection in several other places in Psalm 119. But in this context, the instructions for the victory spoken of in the previous verse are revealed; praise. This freewill offering is one that has been prepared from instructions in God's word before the opposition rose up. It is exercised in battle from the training given in God's word before the conflict. Some will pray in times of affliction, "O Lord, I know that this trial is to teach me something. Help me to learn the lesson." Wrong prayer. You learn before the battle, not in it. A test is not for learning. A test reveals what you have, or haven't learned. Difficulty does not build character; it reveals it. God will teach you of Himself, from His word, so that you will be prepared with praise when the opposition comes in like a flood. You will overcome by having your eyes on Jesus and by declaring His praise.

This prayer section ends as it began, *"Your testimonies are my heritage forever, for they are the joy of my heart. I incline my heart to perform your statutes forever, to the end."* The word "heritage" is the Hebrew word *nachal,* which means an inheritance you already possess. In the Old Testament it was used to describe land with growing potential that a person would already possess and begin planting. Once again, the theme of a present condition with a future outcome is seen. In Christ, God has given us eternal life by giving us His Holy Spirit as the guarantee. This is what Peter calls *the living hope* we have by the resurrection of Jesus Christ and through faith in Him, 1 Peter 1:3. We have both a present possession and a future promise.

Today, thank the Lord for the lamp of a new heart that He gave to you when you were born from above through faith in Jesus Christ, and for the light of His word that shines from your new heart for every step of the way into eternity with Him. In the light of His word, every step is an act of worship in spirit and truth.

April 12

Read and pray Psalm 102, Proverbs 22:6 – 11, Acts 10:1 – 23, Hebrews 10, Psalm 119:113 – 120.
2nd Numbers 17.
3rd Ezekiel 23 – 24.
4th 2 Chronicles 27 – 28.

Learning To Pray Against Evil

When you begin learning to pray, you must learn how and why to pray against evil. Some only pray for things, or for people, or for certain outcomes. But the Bible, especially the book of Psalms, teaches how and why to pray against evil in the world. The fifteenth section in Psalm 119 is entitled *samekh*, 119:113 – 120. The theme of this prayer section is how and why to pray against evil.

The first line identifies evil with the word "double-minded," *"I hate the double-minded, but I love your law."* The Hebrew word for "double-minded" is *seep*, which means half-hearted, divided, confused. This word is from a root word describing a whirlwind or a storm. In James 1:6 – 8, the Bible describes praying without faith with this same idea, *"...but let him ask in faith, with no doubting, for the one who doubts is like a wave of the sea that is driven and tossed by the wind. For that person must not suppose that he will receive anything from the Lord; he is a double-minded man, unstable in all his ways."*

The confession of the first line is a subtle warning of how quickly doubts and unbelief can creep into the mind of a believer. The first thing to learn in praying against evil in the world is to pray against it in your own life. Recognize any *seep* in your thoughts. Confess your whole-hearted devotion to God's word. The next line will guide you in that confession; *"You are my hiding place and my shield; I hope in your word."*

The word "hiding place" is the Hebrew word *sayther*, which means a secret place. This is the word that is used in Psalm 91:1, *"He who dwells in the secret place of the Most High, shall abide in the shadow of the Almighty."* It is used throughout the Psalms to describe the place of personally meeting with God. It is sometimes translated with the word "shelter," as in a place to protect you from the wind and waves of a storm.

This is what Jesus had in mind with His teaching on prayer when He said, *"But when you pray, go into your secret place and shut the door and pray to your Father who is in secret."* Matthew 6:6. In that secret place, the Father will shine the light of His word on any doubts and unite your thoughts with His to drive out the darkness of doubt in your mind.

The next line is unique in Psalm 119 because it is the only line outside of the introduction (119:1 – 3) that is not addressed directly to God, *"Depart from me, you evil-doers, that I may keep the commandments of my God."* The word "evil-doer" is the Hebrew word *ra-ah*, which means wicked and evil with the understanding of evil activity. It is a root word that developed into the understanding of something broken. It is often used in the Old Testament as something that is placed before a person's eyes, as in a decision to make between good and evil. It was certainly placed before Adam and Eve's eyes in the garden, which did not have a good outcome. But here the confession is given for a different outcome. Jesus learned this confession as He prayed in the wilderness, *"Be gone, Satan..."* Matthew 4:10, and again in Matthew 16:23, *"Get behind me, Satan! You are a hindrance to me. For you are not setting your mind on the things of God, but on the things of man."*

The last three lines of this prayer give further description of evil, *"You spurn all who go astray from your statutes, for their cunning is in vain."* The word "spurn" is the Hebrew word *salah*, which means to reject and to cast away. It also has the meaning of weightlessness and no value. This is what the hand wrote on the wall in Daniel 5:24 – 28, *"You have been weighed in the balance and found wanting..."* King Belshazzar in Daniel's day had no fear or regard for God or the things of God. The message from the hand, as Daniel interpreted it, did not faze this wicked king.

The last line brings this to light, *"My flesh trembles for fear of you, and I am afraid of your judgments."* This does not mean that you are to be afraid of God, rather that you recognize the outcome of those who do not value the weight of God's glory and His eternal word. Learn to pray against evil as you learn to worship the Father in spirit and truth. Faith gives your life an eternal weight of glory.

April 13

Read and pray Psalm 103, Proverbs 22:12 – 16, Acts 10:24 – 48, Hebrews 11:1 – 19, Psalm 119:113 – 120.
2ⁿᵈ Numbers 18.
3ʳᵈ Ezekiel 25 – 26.
4ᵗʰ 2 Chronicles 29 – 30.

A Servant's Prayer

The sixteenth letter in the Hebrew alphabet is the letter **ayin**. All of the first words in Psalm 119:121 – 128 begin with this letter. The theme of this section of prayer focuses upon being a servant of God. The first two lines set the theme; *"I have done what is just and right; do not leave me to my oppressors. Give your servant a pledge of good; let not the insolent oppress me."* The servant confesses having done what is just and right. Both of these words are used to describe the nature of God, **mispat**, and **sedeq**. The first word is sometimes translated as one of the words of God, "just decrees." It has the meaning of a just ordinance. The second word has the meaning of being straight, righteous, aligned with God. Both of these together are attributes of God. The servant's activities are reflections of the Lord. This is the confession of a servant.

The phrase *"...do not leave me to my oppressors,"* refers to the environment the servant has been serving in. It is among the enemies of God. The word "leave" is the Hebrew word **nuah** and has the understanding of being left to dwell in a place, to rest. The servant is asking God not to keep him among the opposition. The second line echoes this request asking for a down payment of good. God is good. The Hebrew word **tob** is used to describe an attribute of God. He is good; all the time.

This is similar to the line in the model prayer, *"...and lead us not into temptation..."* Matthew 6:13. A servant does not want to be away from the Master. If the situation requires it, the servant asks for something of the Master's to remind him of the Master, and will guarantee His ownership of him. The Hebrew word "servant" is **ehbed**, and describes ownership. It also is used to describe a slave that had been set free from his owner and had chosen to stay in servitude because of his love for the master. He was then called a bond slave (Exodus 21:2). The Apostle Paul referred to himself as a bond slave of Jesus Christ. This is the confession and prayer of a servant.

The fourth line in the servant's prayer is a double request, *"Deal with your servant according to your steadfast love, and teach me your statutes.*" The first request asks for something that has already been established. The relationship of the servant with the Master is based upon covenant love, steadfast love. The Hebrew word is *hesed.* Some might say that to ask for something that has already been given is an expression of unbelief. But this prayer teaches differently. The second request is an echo that gives meaning to the first. It's not that the servant does not believe there is a covenant relationship with the Master, but rather that he wants to learn more and more of it. It is a confession that he has not yet fully realized the depth of *hesed*, of the steadfast love of the Master, but he wants to. This is the prayer of a servant.

The closing lines of the servant's prayer ask for a deeper understanding of God in His word, *"I am your servant; give me understanding, that I may know your testimonies,"* as well as a confession of the great value and wealth of God's word, *"Therefore I love your commandments more than gold, above fine gold. Therefore I consider all your precepts to be right; I hate every false way."* This is the request and confessions of a servant.

Today, pray as the servant that you are. Confess your desire to be near your Master and not left in a hostile environment. Ask for what God has already given as a confession that you do not yet fully understand the great love of the Father in the Son, but that you want to. Confess the growing value and worth that God's word has to you as you see more and more of the Father in His word. This is what it means to worship the Father in spirit and truth.

April 14

Read and pray Psalm 104, Proverbs 22:17 – 23, Acts 11, Hebrews 11:20 – 40, Psalm 119:113 – 120.
2nd Numbers 19.
3rd Ezekiel 27 – 28.
4th 2 Chronicles 31 – 32.

The Beauty and Strength of God's Word

The Hebrew letter *pe* is the title of the next section of Psalm 119:129 – 136. The theme of this prayer section is the beauty and strength of God's word. The confessions and requests of this section all relate to this theme. It begins with a powerful confession; *"Your testimonies are wonderful; therefore my soul keeps them. The unfolding of your words gives light; it imparts understanding to the simple."* The Hebrew word translated "wonderful" is *pele*. It has the meaning of astonishment beyond understanding. It describes something so marvelous, it is hard, if not impossible, to imagine.

This word is used throughout the Old Testament in describing the works of God and the name of the Lord. In Psalm 77:14 this word describes the work of God; *"You are the God who works wonders; you have made known your might among the people."* And in Isaiah 9:6; *"For to us a child is born...and his name shall be called Wonderful Counselor..."* The amazing thing to note is that the works of God and the names of God are beyond understanding in wonder and amazement. God reveals them so that you might know them and Him through them.

The word "unfolding" is the Hebrew word *paytak*, which means to open a door or to open the mouth. It is also used to describe the opening of a cave. In this context it refers to the way God reveals the wonderful truth of His word for those who lack wisdom and understanding. In James 1:5 this truth is revealed with these words, *"If any of you lacks wisdom, let him ask God, who gives generously to all without reproach, and it will be given him."*

It is also given in the words of Jesus when He said, *"And I tell you, ask, and it will be given to you; seek, and you shall find; knock, and it will be opened."* When you are deep in a cave, groping for light, the mouth of the cave from inside the cave is a beautiful sight. So it is with the light of God's word; it imparts *bayin*, understanding and discernment, to those who ask and depend upon it.

Another request in this prayer is found in 119:133, *"Keep steady my steps according to your promise, and let no iniquity get dominion over me."* The word "keep steady" is the Hebrew word *koon*, which means to establish with preparation. It is the solid foundation of proactive preparation. This is the activity of God's word in your life. He gives you what you need before you need it. He prepares you for the trial before it arrives. But God will not do this without you. Ask Him for what you need before you need it. You can because He has promised, and He will do it.

The thing that is requested the most in Psalm 119 is to learn from God. You find it again in 119:135, *"Make your face shine upon your servant, and teach me your statutes."* There are twelve different words for learning in Hebrew, but the most common is the one used here. It is the Hebrew word *lamed*. It describes a particular way of learning. The root of this word is the word for a yoke, which points to its meaning. The training for a young ox entailed yoking it to an older, more experienced ox, with a training yoke. Yoked together, the younger one would learn from the older one, as they would plow together. The older ox would steady the younger one and keep it on track.

The prayer request *"...teach me your statutes,"* uses this word. When you pray this, you are asking God to bind His word to your life, to steady your steps, to guide you, and to keep you from wandering. Your desire is to learn from Him and of Him. Jesus said in Matthew 11:29 -30, *"Take my yoke upon you, and learn from me, for I am gentle and lowly in heart, and you will find rest for your souls. For my yoke is easy, and my burden is light."*

Today, ask the Lord Jesus for His yoke to be upon you. Ask to learn from Him of the Father's love and joy. Ask for the light of His word to become brighter and brighter until you are led completely free from the bondage of sin and walk in the full light of His glorious face. This is what it means to worship the Father in spirit and truth.

April 15

Read and pray Psalm 105, Proverbs 22:24 – 29, Acts 12, Hebrews 12, Psalm 119:113 – 120.

2nd Numbers 20.

3rd Ezekiel 29 – 30.

4th 2 Chronicles 33 – 34.

Righteous Words From Our Righteous Father

The eighteenth letter in the Hebrew alphabet is *tsadhe*. The theme of this section, 119:137 – 144, is righteousness. This word is used several times in these verses. The Hebrew word for "righteousness" is *tsadeek*. This is a root word with the meaning of being straight. It developed into the meaning of an ethical and moral standard of the nature, word, and will of God. The first line declares this truth, *"Righteous are you, O LORD, and right are your rules."* This is a confession of praise, which is the direct revelation of God's word. Declarations of praise are grounded and grow out of God's word because God's word reveals God's character.

The next line gives more definition to this word *tsadeek; "You have appointed your testimonies in righteousness and in all faithfulness."* The word "appointed" is the Hebrew word *tsavah*, with the meaning of commanded or commissioned. This word is used in Psalm 33:9 concerning creation, *"For he spoke, and it came to be; he commanded, and it stood firm."* It is understood that the one who commands and/or commissions is the one who is in authority. This gives the word *tsadeek* the understanding that God judges and rules according to His righteousness. His righteousness is the standard by which He reigns and judges.

The last word in the line above is the word "faithfulness," which is the Hebrew word *emoon*. The root of this word means firmness, foundational truth, certainty, and assurance. The Hebrew word *amen*, is from this family of words. The Hebrew understanding of faith is the fruit of this word in the sense of the certainty that what God has said, He will do. The assurance of this is the foundation of life, because it puts you right with God.

The writer of Hebrews was steeped in this understanding when he wrote, *"Now faith is the substance of things hoped for, the evidence of things not seen,"* Hebrews 11:1. The Greek word translated "substance" is *hoopostace*, from two words, to stand under; in other words, a foundation, an assurance, a certainty from God's word. Faith gives substance to your life because it rests upon the solid and eternal truth of God's word,

God's will, and God's character. God is righteous because God is faithful. God is faithful because God is righteous. AMEN.

There is only one request in this prayer section and it is found in the last line; *"Your testimonies are righteous forever; give me understanding that I may live."* The word "understanding" is the Hebrew word *bayin*, which has been discussed. It means to cut and to discern the difference between good and evil. It is a gift only God can give. Understanding and discernment do not come from study or from experience, and certainly not from a tree (Genesis 2:16 – 17). It is given as a gift from God, which He gives from His eternal word, through faith in His word.

As you learn to pray from God's word, you will be praying His words, allowing them to shape your thoughts and your prayers. As God's child, you are learning to talk, in the same way a child learns to talk, by listening to the Father's words. As God hears His words, His accent, His character, coming from your lips, because you trust Him, it pleases Him, so much.

Today, confess the character of God in prayer, according to His word. Start with *tsadeek*, righteous. Ask for the gift of *bayin*, discernment, so that from God's word you can clearly see what is the good and righteous will of God. Thank God for His goodness, His faithfulness, and His righteousness fully revealed in the Lord Jesus Christ. The Father loves hearing His righteous word coming from your heart concerning His character, and the Son of His love. This is what it means to worship the Father in spirit and truth.

April 16

Read and pray Psalm 106, Proverbs 23:1 – 5, Acts 13:1 – 12, Hebrews 13, Psalm 119:121 – 128.
2nd Numbers 21.
3rd Ezekiel 31 – 32.
4th 2 Chronicles 35 – 36.

Crying Out For God

The nineteenth letter in the Hebrew alphabet is **qoph**. The main thought of 119:145 – 152 addresses situations when you simply cry out to God. There are times in life when your requests do not come in simple sentences, but rather in tears, in anguish, and in loud cries. This section of Psalm 119 gives meaning to prayer in those situations.

The first line sets the stage, *"With my whole heart I cry; answer me, O LORD! I will keep your statutes."* The word "cry" is the Hebrew word **qara**, with the meaning of a loud cry, proclamation, or announcement. At the heart of every cried prayer is a deep desire for an answer from God. This is the prayer of one who has experienced a season of silence from God. Everyone has or will have a season of silence. It is in those times that you cry out for God with your whole heart. Faith in the darkness cries out for God in the same way a child cries out in the dark for the parents to come.

The second line is a confession of faith, *"I call to you; save me."* The confession of truth and faith is seen in the fact that you do not call to anyone else, only for God because only God can save. The word "save" is the Hebrew word **yeshua,** the Hebrew name of Jesus. His name means to save. In New Testament, in Acts 2:21 and in Romans 10:13, Joel 2:32 is quoted, *"For everyone who calls on the name of the LORD shall be saved."* This is the promise of God to those who cry out for Him.

There is a particular purpose attached to the cry for salvation, *"I call to you; save me, that I may observe your statutes."* The word "observe" is the Hebrew word **shamar**, which means to keep. It is first used in Genesis 2:15 when God placed Adam in the Garden of Eden and commanded him to tend the garden and to keep it. This word has the meaning of watching, of seeing the great value of something, of treasuring, and guarding. Jesus said, *"For where your treasure is, there your heart will be also."* Matthew 6:21. The purpose of being saved is that you will keep, guard, and treasure God's word. The flip side of this is until you are saved, you will not keep God's word. Indeed, you cannot.

In keeping God's word you will begin to see the supreme value of His word in your life. Jesus said, *"Man shall not live by bread alone, but by every word that proceeds from the mouth of God."* Matthew 4:4. The line in this prayer that describes this condition is, *"Hear my voice according to your steadfast love; O LORD, according to your justice give me life."* Declaring this and asking God for it is what Jesus did. How much more do we need to declare and ask for what God has promised, according to His steadfast love and justice.

There are two lines, 119:150 – 151, which describes another occasion for crying out for God, *"They draw near who persecute me with evil purpose; they are far from your law. But you are near, O LORD, and all your commandments are true."* Those who persecute fall into one or more of these three categories; the world, the flesh, the devil. This trinity of evil is characterized by a denial of God's word and a desire to destroy everything and everyone that is of God. They can be picked up and partnered with by anyone, including you.

When one or more are picked up, that person or group becomes an instrument for unbelief to do its damage and carry out its evil purpose. The evil purpose is to deceive you and to lead you away from God's word. But God is near and all of His commandments are true. Cry out for God when evil draws near, because He is nearer.

When the lights go out and you find yourself in a season of silence, cry out for God, even if you don't have a nice sentence to pray, cry out for God. He has promised to hear and in His timing He will answer, according to the counsel of His will. Crying out for Him is an expression of pure faith because only He can save. And He will. As you cry out for God, you draw near to Him and discover that He has been with you all the time. Even when He is silent, He is with you. He has promised. Crying out for God pleases the Father because His own Son did. Your cry reminds Him of His. This is what it means to worship the Father in spirit and truth.

April 17

Read and pray Psalm 107, Proverbs 23:6 – 12, Acts 13:13 – 52, James 1, Psalm 119:121 – 128.
2nd Numbers 22 – 23.
3rd Ezekiel 33 – 34.
4th Ezra 1 – 2.

Revival is Like Breathing

The twentieth letter in the Hebrew alphabet is *resh*. This prayer section is found in Psalm 119:153 – 160. The theme of this prayer is revival. Revival means to live again. It is the life of God that He gives, and gives, and gives. He does not get you started with His life and then turn you loose to go out on your own. No. His life flows out, which means you need a constant replenishment of His Spirit. Life with God is like breathing, and revival is life with God.

The first line of this prayer describes the outward flow of God's life in a believer; *"Look on my affliction and deliver me, for I do not forget your law."* The word "affliction" is the Hebrew word *ownee*, which means oppression, forced into submission, strong opposition. The life of God goes out from you, like your breath, into a world that is hostile to God. The flesh, which is best described as human ability without God, is violently opposed to anything that God offers, as is the world. The devil hates God and everything that God loves. He has been given the earth, temporarily. As the Holy Spirit lives the life of Christ in you, with you, through you, as you, before the Father and the watching world around you, there is strong opposition to His life. Revival, another breath from God, is needed.

The word "deliver me" is the Hebrew word *chalats*, which has the meaning of something being taken away, removed, rescued. The prayer for deliverance is seen in the reality that being in the world and not allowing the world to seep in requires the supernatural work of God in your life. Jesus said it this way, *"Blessed are you when others revile you and persecute you and utter all kinds of evil against you falsely on my account. Rejoice and be glad, for your reward is great in heaven... Love your enemies and pray for those who persecute you..."* Matthew 5:11 – 12, 44. There is a great temptation to take on the evil of the world as you live God's life in it. You need clean air to breath if you are to remain healthy, and you need God's Spirit and word to breath in if you are to stay revived.

The second line echoes this truth; ***"Plead my cause and redeem me; give me life according to your promise."*** The phrase "plead my cause" is a repetition of the Hebrew word ***reeb***, which means to fight against. In this phrase it is used twice and can best be understood with the request, "fight against what fights against me." This is a powerful truth and one of the ways of God. One of the deceptive tricks of the world, the flesh, and the devil is to draw you away from God causing you to fight in your own power. Resisting that temptation is done with this prayer. God fights for you, but only if you refuse to pick up the weapons of the world.

The phrase "redeem me" is the Hebrew word ***ga-al***, which supports this truth. The ***ga-al***, was the close relative that would pay your debt and provide a new life for you. The example of this person in the Old Testament was Boaz in the story of Ruth. In the New Testament, He is Jesus, our Redeemer.

Each line of this prayer reinforces your need to continually receive the life of God as your life in the hostile environment of the world. With God's life as your life, you will face many temptations and will constantly need the inflow of the Holy Spirit. This is not an option, but it is a willful choice. Ask for it and know from this prayer just what you are asking for.

The last line ties this prayer to the anchor of God's word; ***"The sum of your word is truth, and every one of your righteous rules endures forever."*** Praying for revival is forever connected to God's Spirit, God's Son, and God's word. Jesus said, ***"I am the way, the truth, and the life..."*** John 14:6. Jesus is revival and revival is Jesus. Period. Breathing in His life as your life and breathing out the destructive influences of the world, the flesh, and the devil is revival. This is done in His word. Living His life as yours pleases the Father. This is what it means to worship the Father in spirit and truth.

April 18

Read and pray Psalm 108, Proverbs 23:13 – 18, Acts 14, James 2, Psalm 119:121 – 128.
2ⁿᵈ Numbers 24 – 25.
3ʳᵈ Ezekiel 35 – 36.
4ᵗʰ Ezra 3 – 4.

The Greatness of God's Word

The next-to-the-last letter in the Hebrew alphabet is the letter *shin*. The theme of this prayer section is the greatness of God's word. It is a prayer without a request. Confession of truth is the entirety of this prayer. This is instructive if you are willing to learn to pray from God. Prayer is not primarily getting your requests before God, it is first and foremost getting to know the One who knows what you need before you ask, and becoming more and more like Him as you learn of Him from His word. This begins with praying His word and allowing His word to shape your prayers.

The psalmist compares God's word to several images in this section to show its surpassing wealth and strength. The first image is of being falsely accused by powerful political figures, *"Princes persecute me without cause, but my heart stands in awe of your words."* Psalm 119:161. When you are falsely accused, the first reaction is fear, which expresses itself in a flurry to defend yourself and to prove your innocence. But this prayer trumps that reaction with something more powerful than the fear of trying to prove your innocence, which is to stand in awe of God's words. The false words of powerful men quickly dissolve in light of the truth of God's words.

The phrase "stands in awe" is the Hebrew word *pawkad*, which is a powerful word for worship, for trembling in fear, for a growing fear of God. In most places in the Bible, bowing before the Lord is descriptive of worship and fear of God. But in this word you see the rising aspect of worship, of something welling up within you. This is what Jesus was communicating to the woman of Sychar beside Jacob's well (John 4:14), when He said, *"…The water that I will give him will become in him a spring of water welling up to eternal life."* Rather than the fear of man rising up as a result of a false accusation, the fear of God and truth of His word will rise up within you with bold confidence that God will take care of you. You can trust Him.

The next line, 119:162, declares a great truth, *"I rejoice at your word like one who finds great spoil."* The word "rejoice" is the Hebrew word *soos*, which describes the joy and exhilaration of a party. The word "great spoil" is the Hebrew word *shalal*, which means the spoils of war. This is pictured in the New Testament in the parable that Jesus told in Luke 15:11 – 32, known as the prodigal son. When the son returned home with nothing, the father ran out to meet him and took back what the world, the flesh, and the devil had stolen and threw a party. Everyone in the father's house was rejoicing except the fatted calf and the older son, but the party was on. When the truth of God's word is found, you take back what the enemy has stolen, and find the great joy and wealth in that victory. AMEN.

Another powerful truth is declared in 119:165, *"Great peace have those who love your law; nothing can make them stumble."* The word "peace" is the Hebrew word *shalom*, which means wholeness, soundness, strength, fulfillment, a restored relationship. It was and still is a greeting in Israel, *shalom!* The promise of *shalom* is given to those who love God's instructions, and the blessing of *shalom* is the fact that you will not stumble. The Hebrew word *mikshole*, means to trip and fall, to be offended. God's word will keep you from the sin of an offended spirit. An offended spirit has caused more people to drop out of the fellowship of believers, and from following the Lord, than anything else.

When the Father sees that you see the surpassing wealth and strength of His word by declaring it to Him in prayer, it pleases Him. This is what it means to worship the Father in spirit and truth.

April 19

Read and pray Psalm 109, Proverbs 23:19 – 28, Acts 15, James 3, Psalm 119:121 – 128.
2nd Numbers 26.
3rd Ezekiel 37 – 38.
4th Ezra 5 – 6.

The AMEN of Psalm 119

The last letter in the Hebrew alphabet is *taw.* The theme of the last prayer section is a summary of all of the prayers in this great chapter. You could call it the AMEN of Psalm 119. The first request of this prayer teaches the first request of all prayer, *"Let my cry come before you, O LORD; give me understanding according to your word."* Like the disciple in Luke 11:1 who asked Jesus, *"Lord, teach us to pray..."* this request asks for understanding from God's word so that his prayer will be received by God. This is the prayer request of all prayer requests.

The third line, 119:171, once again links praise with learning, *"My lips will pour forth praise for you teach me your statutes."* The word "praise" in Hebrew is *tehilah,* and is the beautiful Hebrew title of the book of Psalms, *Tehilim;* Praises. It describes being fully satisfied and thankful to declare the supreme value and worth of God. It declares His fame and renown, His greatness and goodness, the rightness of His righteousness and purity of His holiness. It is a big word. The Father loves this word, especially when it is declared as the result of the revelation of Himself to you from His word.

The word "understanding" is the Hebrew word *bayin*, which has been discussed in previous sections. The root of this word means to cut and separate, as in seeing clearly the stark difference between good and evil. Choosing the good over the evil is what it means to have *bayin,* understanding. This comes from God's word, not from a tree (Genesis 2:17), or from any other source.

When the good is seen and chosen for what it is, a gift from God, and the evil is seen for what it is, a lie from the devil, God is glorified for His gracious revelation of truth, wisdom is imparted, and God is praised, Hallelujah! As more and more of God's word reveals more of God, more and more of your choices become His for you, then more and more of your life is transformed into His. As this happens, your life becomes more and more of an offering of praise to God. AMEN.

The last line in this prayer is telling as a confession of weakness, *"I have gone astray like a lost sheep; seek your servant for I do not forget your commandments."* It may seem strange at first that this great prayer, Psalm 119, ends with such a confession and request. But it is one of the most powerful confessions and most enlightened requests. One of the ways of God is that in your weakness, His strength is made perfect (2 Corinthians 12:9). When you are weak, He is strong. This defines prayer, for when you pray, you are turning to God out of your weakness to find Him, your strength. You confess in prayer of your weakness and need of Him with a request that is at the heart of His character and nature, which is to seek after you.

This is what Jesus told the woman of Sychar at Jacob's well that day when He said, in John 4:23, *"But the hour is coming, and is now here, when the true worshipers will worship the Father in spirit and truth, for the Father is seeking such people to worship him."* Prayer is asking God for what He is doing and desires to do. The last line of this great prayer summarizes this all-important truth. It is the AMEN of the prayer.

April 20

Read and pray Psalm 110, Proverbs 23:29 – 35, Acts 16, James 4, Psalm 119:121 – 128.
2nd Numbers 27.
3rd Ezekiel 39 – 40.
4th Ezra 7 – 8.

The Life That Pleases the Father

For the next forty days you will see forty events from the life that pleases the Father, the life of the Lord Jesus Christ. His life was a pleasing aroma to God every day, like the morning and evening sacrifice, like the daily incense burned on the altar before the Holy of Holies.

Jesus Christ glorified the Father fully because He revealed the life of the Father fully. And He gave His life for you in order to give His life to you for Him to live in you, with you, through you, as you, before the Father and the watching world around you, for His glory and your joy.

When Jesus was twelve years old, He stayed behind in Jerusalem at the end of the feast of Passover while His parents started back to Nazareth, thinking that He was with other family or friends. After a day's journey they realized that Jesus had been left in the city and returned to look for Him. Luke gives you the details in Luke 2:41 – 52.

Joseph and Mary found Jesus on the third day (one day journey without Him and one day journey back to Jerusalem), *"…sitting among the teachers, listening to them and asking them questions. And all who heard him were amazed at his understanding and his answers."* Luke 2:46 – 47. There would be another three days, during Passover, in Jerusalem, twenty something years later when the religious leaders, maybe even some that were there when He was twelve, would be questioning Him again, but be blind and deaf to His answers (see Luke 19:28 – 20:44).

The Greek word translated "understanding" in the verse above is *soonesis* and literally means the union of two rivers. In the Greek world it came to mean having an understanding by bringing together and connecting ideas to form a clearer picture of something.

You may remember as a child connecting the dots on a sheet of paper to discover a picture that you could not see before. This is similar to the meaning of this word *soonesis,* and is what the teachers of the Israel were amazed at in Jesus. His answers to their Q&A of God's word joined together to reveal a depth of insight that they had not heard or seen before.

Little did they know that they were sitting with the author of God's word. Jesus was fully connected to the Father and so His mind could see the fullness of His word more and more as He grew.

As Jesus discussed God's word with the teachers, listening to them, asking them questions, and connecting the dots for them, it pleased the Father. Seeing His Son learn from His word and teach the teachers, and hearing Jesus speak His word, joining His words with the Father's words, (like the joining of two rivers), brought the Father joy and pleased Him.

When His parents found Jesus, they too questioned Him, *"Son, why have you treated us so?"* Luke 2:48. This is a question you have probably also asked the Lord. It is asked by many people, especially when they are going through a difficult time such as Mary and Joseph were going through that day. But their question was completely out of context with what Jesus was discussing with the teachers in God's word. It focused upon a problem with anxiety and fear rather than an answer with trust and a desire to grow.

Jesus answered their question with two of His own, *"Why were you looking for me? Did you not know that I must be in my Father's house?"* Jesus took the posture of a teacher and the method of teaching by answering a question with questions so that the student can discover the answer rather than just hear it. This is also called connecting the dots. It is brilliant.

So what does this look like in your life? Good question. Do you focus upon your problems when you search for Jesus, wondering why He hasn't helped you yet, or do you search God's word for Jesus trusting Him to lead you through the difficulty as you listen to Him every step of the way? God's word is a lamp and light for every step, but only for the next step. One of the ways of God is that you cannot skip steps. There are no short cuts or loopholes in growing. This event in the life of Jesus teaches this truth. This story concludes with the clear statement, *"And Jesus increased* (grew) *in wisdom and in stature and in favor with God and man."* Luke 2:52.

Today, take the next step in growing by staying in God's word, questions and all. Keep connecting the dots. Stay in a posture of trust, learning, and growing. Jesus did and it pleased the Father. This is what it means to become a true worshiper, one who worships the Father in spirit and truth.

April 21

Read and pray Psalm 111, Proverbs 24:1 – 6, Acts 17, James 5, Psalm 119:121 – 128.
2nd Numbers 28.
3rd Ezekiel 41 – 42.
4th Ezra 9 – 10.

Obedience Fulfills Righteousness

God's word carries in it the seed of faith, which grows into the fruit of obedience when received into the good soil of your heart. Jesus began His ministry on earth with His baptism by John. Jesus came to John and asked to be baptized by him. He was being obedient to the Father.

Matthew 3:14 says that John asked Him, *"I need to be baptized by you, and do you come to me?"* John called the nation of Israel to a life of repentance, turning from their ways of sin to God as they prepared for the coming of the Messiah. John's baptism was an expression of the desire to be totally prepared for the coming of the Messiah by being totally immersed in God's word.

When Jesus came to John to be baptized, he hesitated because he knew Jesus as someone who did not need to repent. He knew Jesus to be a good man because he and Jesus had grown up together. They were related, probably cousins. They were only a few months apart in age. They had traveled to the feasts in Jerusalem each year together since they were boys, no doubt. John knew that Jesus was a good man, and yet he did not know that Jesus was the Messiah until after His baptism (John 1:31 – 34).

But Jesus would not give John what he asked. He said, *"...Let it be so now, for thus it is fitting for us to fulfill all righteousness."* Matthew 3:15. The word "fitting" is the Greek word *prepo*, which has the meaning of becoming right in terms of moral judgment and decision. Jesus told John that by baptizing Him, John would be obedient to the word that God had spoken to him. It was the right thing to do based upon God's word. This is the definition of obedience.

The Lord was also telling him that He was essential in John's obedience and that together they would *fulfill all righteousness.* This was one of the most radical statements made by Jesus. It is the gospel. In that single statement to John, Jesus said that in Him all righteousness would be complete, without any righteous act left out. But Jesus was also saying that He would not do that without John. The Lord Jesus will save you and *fulfill all righteousness* in you, but not without you. The Greek word *playro* means to be totally full and complete. If you are willing to trust Christ, He will completely fulfill your life with the righteous acts that please the Father. But He will not do it without you.

The Lord Jesus comes to you, just as He did to John. He does not give you what you always want, but He does give you what He wants, which is Himself. In Christ and Him in you and with you, all that is right in God's eyes is complete. This is the gospel and it pleases God because it is the *fulfillment of all righteousness*. This is what it means to worship the Father in spirit and truth.

Today as you pray, thank the Father for giving you His Son, and listen to what God wants to give you in Him. And know that what you ask Him to do, He desires to first do in you, with you, through you, as you, before the Father and the watching world around you.

April 22

Read and pray Psalm 112, Proverbs 24:7 – 12, Acts 18, 1 Peter 1, Psalm 119:121 – 128.
2nd Numbers 29.
3rd Ezekiel 43 – 44.
4th Nehemiah 1 – 2.

Faith Filled For Following Through

Following His baptism, Luke tells us that Jesus was full of the Holy Spirit, Luke 4:1. And being full of the Spirit, Jesus was led by the Spirit through the wilderness for forty days. Jesus fasted during those forty days while being tempted by the devil. He overcame every temptation because He was full of the truth of God's word and His faith, which was full of the Holy Spirit. Jesus was immersed in the word of the Father and the presence of the Holy Spirit as He went through the wilderness with all of its dangers.

Jesus went into the wilderness full of the Holy Spirit, following the Holy Spirit, and came out the other side of it, *"...in the power of the Spirit..."* Luke 4:14. The word "power" is the Greek word *dunamis*. The English word "dynamite" comes from this Greek word. It means to have the ability or power to do something. It was often used to describe the potential within someone to accomplish something great.

In the context of Luke 4:1 – 14 you learn that in the life of Jesus, He was first filled with the Holy Spirit, then He followed the Holy Spirit, and only then was He empowered and given the ability of the Holy Spirit to accomplish the Father's will.

Jesus was full of the Holy Spirit following His choice to be baptized by John and together with him, *"...to fulfill all righteousness."* Matthew 3:15. He had waited upon the Father for the right time to begin His ministry. He had taken the first step in His ministry by being baptized, thus demonstrating how He would save us; by His death, burial, and resurrection (pictured by immersion). All of this filled Jesus with the Holy Spirit because it was according to the word of the Father. God spoke at His baptism, *"You are my beloved Son; with you I am well pleased."* Luke 3:22.

In Christ, your faith is full of the Spirit because His was as He lived on earth. In Christ, the Holy Spirit leads you because the Holy Spirit led Jesus as He lived on earth. In Christ, you will go through, not around or over, times of difficulty, temptation, and trial because He did as He lived on earth. And, in Christ, as you follow the Spirit through the wilderness of this life, you will have His power and ability, the same potential Jesus had when He accomplished His ministry.

But the question is this: Are you willing to wait upon the Father to fill you with His word before stepping out to begin some task for Him? The filling of His word precedes the filling of His Spirit. Faith must be full of His word before being filled with His Spirit and power. The disciples spent three years with Jesus and were filled with His word, and only then the Holy Spirit came. Some just want the power of the Spirit without the filling of God's word, much less to first be obedient and to wait upon the Father. Our ways are not God's. Repent of the idea that you need power first for the ministry without the wilderness and without the fullness and obedience of His word.

Today, be filled with God's word and He will fill you with His Spirit. He will lead you through this wilderness by His presence and His word, and empower you to accomplish His will. This is what it means to worship the Father in spirit and truth.

April 23

Read and pray Psalm 113, Proverbs 24:13 – 18, Acts 19, 1 Peter 2, Psalm 119:129 – 136.
2nd Numbers 30.
3rd Ezekiel 45 – 46.
4th Nehemiah 3 – 4.

The Father is Seeking True Worshipers

As Jesus began His ministry of preaching, teaching, and healing, huge crowds began to follow Him. The gospel of Mark records a typical day in the life of Jesus in chapter one. You see Jesus preaching the gospel of the Kingdom of God in Mark 1:14 – 15, followed by calling His first disciples, 1:16 – 20. He then went and began teaching in the synagogue in Capernaum, 1:21 – 22, followed by casting out a demon in a man in the synagogue, 1:23 – 28. Jesus then went to Simon's house and healed his mother-in-law. He ended the day by healing many others who were sick or demon possessed as they gathered at the home of Simon, 1:29 – 34.

The word spread and the crowds kept gathering throughout the night. When you are sick and you hear of others being healed, you do not wait until morning to get relief. And the Scripture says, *"And rising very early in the morning, while it was still dark, he departed and went out to a desolate place, and there he prayed."* Mark 1:35.

As the people were becoming more and more desperate to find Jesus, He was more and more desperate to find fellowship and strength with the Father in prayer, because He knew that the Father was also seeking His presence and fellowship.

This one verse in Mark, in the context of the events of that long day, teaches a definitive truth from the life of Jesus. It reveals the single priority that guided Jesus regardless of what was happening around Him. Jesus sought to worship the Father in spirit and truth because He knew that the Father was seeking for those who desired His fellowship. And like the one thing a sick person desires, which is healing, Jesus desired one thing, which was the Father's presence.

The Psalms present the wide variety of human experience and situations, and yet they all arrive at the same instruction, which is to seek the presence of the Lord, regardless of the situation. A good example is seen in Psalm 27:4, which says, *"One thing I have asked of the LORD, and that will I seek after: that I may dwell in the house of the LORD all the days of my life, to gaze upon the beauty of the LORD and to inquire in his temple."*

The Hebrew word for "dwell" is **yah-shab**, which is the one thing that the psalmist desires. It means to sit, to stay, to inhabit, to live with, to marry. The word "gaze" is the Hebrew word **chazah**, which means to look intently at something to study it, to learn, and to explore the depth of it. The word "inquire" is the Hebrew word **baqar**, which means to reflect upon what you have been looking at and to desire to see more.

All three of these words describe what Jesus was doing as He rose up early that morning, desiring the presence of His Father. As pleased and happy as all of the people were that Jesus healed the day before, Jesus knew that the Father was more pleased and desired to share His joy and pleasure with His Son. Jesus desired more than anything else to look upon the Father and to think upon His desire, His will.

Today, meditate upon Psalm 27:4, memorizing it and making it your priority in prayer, because this is what it means to become a true worshiper, one who worships the Father in spirit and truth.

April 24

Read and pray Psalm 114, Proverbs 24:19 – 26, Acts 20, 1 Peter 3, Psalm 119:129 – 136.
2ⁿᵈ Numbers 31.
3ʳᵈ Ezekiel 47 – 48.
4ᵗʰ Nehemiah 5 – 6.

Seeking and Seeing and Staying

The gospel of John is different than Matthew, Mark, and Luke. It was the last gospel written and is known as the gospel of rest. The first red lettered words in John 1:38 – 39 are a question, *"Jesus turned and saw them following and said to them, "What are you seeking?" And they said to him, "Rabbi" (which means Teacher), "where are you staying?" He said to them, "Come and you will see." So they came and saw where he was staying, and they stayed with him that day..."*

These verses describe two of the followers of John the baptizer, Andrew and John, and their first conversation with Jesus. They started following Jesus because John had pointed Him out as *"...the Lamb of God who takes away the sin of the world!"* John 1:29. But when Jesus turned to them with the question above, it stopped them in their tracks. It is the question you must answer at some point in your walk with the Lord. What is it you are looking for in Jesus?

Some have wanted Jesus to just help them out with their life. Jesus did not come to help you out with your life; He came to be your life. Others have just wanted some good teaching so that they might have a better life. But Jesus came to give eternal life. And still others just needed healing so that they could have a more comfortable and affordable life. But Jesus did not come to patch up broken lives; He came to bring and offer new life. This question is one that everyone who begins to follow Christ must answer. What are you seeking?

Those first disciples did not know what to answer and may have been puzzled by His question. They answered His question with a question, which became the right answer, one that must have pleased the Lord. They asked, *"...where are you staying?"* The word "staying" is the Greek word, *meno*, and means to remain, to stay, to stand, to abide, to live in one place.

This word is used in the Greek translation of the Old Testament to describe one of the characteristics of God's word, *"The grass withers, the flower fades, but the word of our God will stand forever,"* Isaiah

40:8; and of the righteousness of God, *"...and his righteousness endures forever,"* Psalm 111:3; and of God's steadfast love, *"...for his steadfast love endures forever,"* Psalm 136:1.

The disciples would hear Jesus use this word in the upper room on the night He was betrayed when He taught them saying, *"Abide in me and I in you. As the branch cannot bear fruit by itself, unless it abides in the vine, neither can you, unless you abide in me...whoever abides in me and I in him, he it is that bears much fruit, for apart from me you can do nothing."* John 15:4 – 5.

As Andrew and John responded to the invitation of Jesus to come see and stay, *meno*, with Him, it pleased the Father for this was the very purpose for which the Son of God was sent. Seeking and seeing and staying with Jesus pleases the Father. This is what it means to worship the Father in spirit and truth.

Today, meditate on the words of Jesus, *"What are you seeking?"*

April 25

Read and pray Psalm 115, Proverbs 24:27 – 34, Acts 21, 1 Peter 4, Psalm 119:129 – 136.
2nd Numbers 32.
3rd Daniel 1.
4th Nehemiah 7 – 8.

The Life That Blesses the Father

The gospel of Matthew is arranged around five teachings of Jesus for His disciples. These five "sermons" have been used since the beginning of the church as a catechism for new believers. The message in all five is a revelation of the life of Jesus. Each one describes the life of Christ and what His life looks like in the life of the new believer.

The first of these sermons is the most famous, known as the Sermon on the Mount, Matthew 5 – 7. Some have tried to understand the teaching in these chapters as a new outline for what we are supposed to do, as if Jesus were the new Moses, with a new set of rules to keep. Others see it as a far look into the future of how God's people will one day live in heaven. Both overlook the main message of the sermon, Jesus and His life, which is offered to whoever will follow Him.[13]

When you read these chapters, you will soon discover that what Jesus is describing is His own life, how He thinks, feels, and acts. You will also quickly discover how totally foreign this way of thinking, feeling, and acting is to the way you are, which is the main point of the message.

This message reveals the truth that man needs a new heart, a new life. The problem we have is not our environment, nor is it ignorance, nor is it a lack of opportunity; it is a sinful heart, which is totally dead to the things of God and is the spring of every thought, feeling, and act, regardless of our environment, education, or opportunities. The Sermon on the Mount describes the new life that is offered in Jesus Christ to those who desire to receive from Him the life that pleases the Father, His life for you.

The most difficult part of the Sermon on the Mount is coming to the realization that you do not in any way, shape, or form come close to actually thinking, feeling, or doing the things that Jesus outlines in His message. This also becomes the most blessed, the good news of the message. You can't, but Jesus did! And He offers what He did to you and for you.

As you hear His words and begin to follow Him, He begins to live His life in you, with you, through you, as you, before the Father and the watching world around you. The light of His life begins to shine from within you so that others *"...may see your good works and give glory to your Father who is in heaven."* Matthew 5:16. This pleases God and is what it means to worship the Father in spirit and truth.

Today, ask Jesus Christ to be your life, to live His life in you, with you, through you, as you, before the Father and the watching world around you. Do this because you have come to see that without Christ there is nothing that pleases the Father, and that in Him everything pleases the Father. His life is the life that blesses the Father because it is the Father's life. Meditate on this today.

April 26

Read and pray Psalm 116, Proverbs 25:1 – 5, Acts 22, 1 Peter 5, Psalm 119:129 – 136.
2nd Numbers 33.
3rd Daniel 2.
4th Nehemiah 9 – 10.

Giving All That You Are to Receive All That He Is

Matthew's gospel is arranged around five sermons. At the end of each one you will find the phrase, *"...when Jesus had finished these sayings..."* which all five share (7:28, 11:1, 13:53, 19:1, 26:1). Together, these five sermons cover the full range of life with God on earth through faith in Jesus Christ.

The second sermon is found in Matthew 10:1 – 42. The theme of this chapter is the missionary nature of God's Kingdom; we gather to scatter. This pleases the Father because He sent His Son, Jesus Christ, on the same mission to earth. When you follow Christ, He sends, just as He was sent, because He knows that when you go, it pleases the Father.

In this chapter there are several clear instructions for missionaries, the first of which is sometimes overlooked, *"And he called to him his twelve disciples and gave them..."* 10:1. Sometimes, all that comes after the phrase *gave them* is focused upon, namely, the authority, the instructions, the warnings, and the promises. But the main point is missed. Ambassadors of God's Kingdom only go out after they have been with Jesus and received from Him all that He gives. The Lord first gives Himself, so that everything that follows has Him in it, so that of all that is shared, He is shared first, even if it is a cup of cold water to one of the little ones, Matthew 10:42.

The warnings, 10:16 – 39, are the major part of this sermon, the hard part. But one of the major points in the warning section is the best part of the sermon; regardless of the response or the reaction, God works it together for His purpose of revealing Himself through His Son, Jesus Christ. This leads to knowing Christ more and more (great rewards), which leads to greater and greater glory for the Father and greater and greater joy for you (more rewards).

Another verse that is often quoted in the context of our mission on earth is Romans 8:28, *"And we know that God is working all things together for good for those who love Him, for those who are called according to his purpose."* The key phrase in understanding this verse, as well as the warnings in Matthew 10, is a single word in Greek, the word *soon-ergo*, which literally means, "works together with and through."

The idea is of something going through something else and producing something with something. The first "something" is a Person, the Holy Spirit. The second "something" is a person, you. The third "something" is a Person, Jesus Christ. The fourth something are the events of your life with Christ. Look at the sentence again with this understanding. The idea is of something (the Holy Spirit) going through something else (you) and producing something (Jesus Christ) with something (the events in life).

The Holy Spirit is forming Christ in you, with you, through you, seen and known as you, before the Father and the watching world around you, with everything that happens to you. And He will not do this without you.

Every event that happens to you, He forms Christ in you, whether it is something good or something bad, something easy, or something hard. But only as you give it all to Him, knowing what He will do, which is to form Christ in you. This is the method God has chosen to spread His Kingdom on earth. This is what it means for His will to be done on earth as it is in heaven, to worship the Father in spirit and truth.

Today, give all that you are, to receive all that He is, so that as you go, you go with Him, by Him, for Him, knowing that you are becoming more like Him through every event of the day. He gets the glory and you get the joy. AMEN.

April 27

Read and pray Psalm 117, Proverbs 25:6 – 10, Acts 23, 2 Peter 1, Psalm 119:129 – 136.
2nd Numbers 34.
3rd Daniel 3.
4th Nehemiah 11 – 13.

Spiritual Truth in the Flesh

The third sermon of Jesus in Matthew's gospel is a collection of parables that Jesus told on the nature of the Kingdom of God, Matthew 13:1 – 53. The word "parable" is from the Greek word *para-boley*, which literally means to throw something down along side of something else; to set beside.

A parable is one thing that is thrown down along side another thing in order to understand the first thing. In the parables of Jesus, spiritual truth is set beside some kind of everyday occurrences so that the truth of spiritual truth can be seen and understood. Another word for parable is incarnation, spiritual truth in the flesh.

The parables in Matthew 13 reveal the spiritual truth of God's Kingdom, the new creation, along side of God's present created order. From the parables of Jesus you come to see that God's new creation, His Kingdom, is now here just as much as the old is in which we now live. You do not have to wait for the new; receive it now, turn and follow Christ and walk right in.

The disciples wondered why Jesus taught in such an indirect way, with parables. To them it seemed as if He was trying to veil the truth rather than speaking it clearly. They asked, *"Why do you speak to them in parables?"* 13:10. The answer Jesus gave raised even more questions, *"…the one who has, more will be given, and he will have an abundance, but from the one who does not have, even what he has will be taken away."* Matthew 13:12.

The parable that Jesus told about the seed and the four soils, Matthew 13:3 – 9, answered their question. It is the parable of all parables because it points to the way to understand all of the parables. Parables point to something greater. If you miss the point, all you have is a nice story, which does not bear fruit, but rather at some point is taken away from you.

When Jesus told this parable, the disciples went to Him and asked Him to explain it to them. This is the key to understanding the parables; you must go to Jesus and ask Him, or the spiritual truth will never be seen no matter what everyday occasion it is placed beside. Jesus Christ reveals spiritual truth as you follow Him.

Everyone knows that food comes from plants, which comes from seeds, which are planted in soil. But some soil seems to partner with seeds better than others. The fruit is locked up in the seed, but when planted in good soil, the fruit grows and develops, but only when the seed is received in good soil.

This parable points to the spiritual truth that a new heart, good soil, is needed before God's word will bear the fruit that pleases Him. The new heart is the fruit of the life of Jesus, which died and was planted in the tomb, which the Father raised from the dead to plant in you.

When the seed of the gospel is received, new soil is created, which becomes ideal for Him to grow and develop so that more and more of His fruit can be given to the Father. Every believer has a mixture of the four soils, but as the new soil expands into the other "dead fields," more fruit is produced and given to the Father.

This is called spiritual growth, which pleases God. This is what it means to worship the Father in spirit and truth. Today, receive more of God's word in the good soil of your new heart, and you will become more and more of a parable, an incarnation, of spiritual truth for the Father and the watching world around you.

April 28

Read and pray Psalm 118, Proverbs 25:11 – 16, Acts 24, 2 Peter 2, Psalm 119:129 – 136.
2nd Numbers 35.
3rd Daniel 4.
4th Esther 1 – 2.

Being Forgiven Means Being Forgiving

The fourth sermon of Jesus in Matthew's gospel is found in Matthew 18:1 -19:1. The chapter opens with the disciples asking Jesus this question, *"Who is greatest in the kingdom of heaven?"* Matthew 18:1. The theme of this message answers that question with four attributes of greatness in God's eyes. The Greek word *mega* is the word for "greatest," and means being first in terms of importance, something that is a priority before something else.

It is interesting that the disciples were thinking in terms of a person compared with other persons, while Jesus answered with attributes of a person. His answer teaches of the powerful attributes of the Kingdom, the *mega*-attributes of a follower of Christ.

The first of the first is humility, Matthew 18:2 – 6. Jesus illustrated humility by placing a child in their midst. The word "humbles himself" is the Greek verb *tapinos*, and means to view yourself as a servant to others by seeing the greatness in others. In the Bible days, children were servants. In our day it seems like they have become the masters. But they were first taught to have *mega*-respect for elders. It was the priority teaching a child learned. This stands to reason since this is the only way to become a student, to humble yourself, and in so doing, you are in the right state of mind to learn; seeing greatness in the teacher as well as greatness in the subject to learn.

Jesus links this to the second *mega*-attribute of a disciple, which is to choose your teachers, your elders, wisely, Matthew 18:6 – 11. Jesus teaches this truth with the image of one who would take advantage of a child. The Bible calls them false teachers. They taught others to sin (and still do today). The source of this evil is the world, the flesh, and the devil. False teachers have always been around and are still with us today. And Jesus taught in this passage that your own thoughts, emotions, and bodily desires could become false teachers. This is one of the places where Jesus taught of how your bodily desires can become like control freaks, and must be disciplined to learn their role as servants, not masters.

The third *mega*-attribute in God's Kingdom is the activity of bringing others into it. Jesus taught this attribute with the well-known parable of the lost sheep and the shepherd that goes out to find it. Each of these attributes is seen most clearly in the life of Jesus, especially this one. He came to find you, and to bring you back into a right relationship with the Father. When you do this, you are most like Christ, which pleases the Father, giving Him *mega*-joy, Matthew 18:13.

The fourth *mega*-attribute goes under the heading of being forgiving since you have been forgiven, Matthew 18:15 – 35. This is one of the major teachings of Jesus because He came to provide forgiveness and to inaugurate God's Kingdom on earth as the Kingdom of the Forgiven, whose main activity on earth is to forgive others because they have been forgiven of so much.

The instructions are very clear; when you seek to forgive and reconcile with others, Christ Himself is in your midst to answer your prayers to accomplish this *mega*-activity, Matthew 18:19 – 20. Jesus then gave a stern warning with a parable about a servant who was forgiven a $3 billion debt (10,000 talents = 200,000 years of wages of a laborer), but refused to forgive a $5,000 debt (100 denarii = 100 days salary of a laborer). The consequences of such an action, as Jesus describes, will cause you to shutter, Matthew 18:34 – 35.

Today, meditate on the *mega*-attributes of humility, choosing good teachers, bringing others into the Kingdom, and forgiving others since you have been forgiven so much. As you do, these *mega*-attributes of the life of Jesus, will begin to show up more and more in your life, as your life, which pleases the Father. This is what it means to worship the Father in spirit and truth.

April 29

Read and pray Psalm 119:57 – 64, Proverbs 25:17 – 22, Acts 25, 2 Peter 3, Psalm 119:129 – 136.
2nd Numbers 36.
3rd Daniel 5.
4th Esther 3 – 4.

When Veiled Worship is Unveiled as Worship

Matthew's gospel is arranged around five sermons that have been used over the centuries as solid teaching for new and maturing believers. The fifth sermon is found in Matthew 24 – 25. It is called the Olivet Discourse because Jesus shared it with His disciples from the Mount of Olives, which overlooks Jerusalem from the east.

The occasion for this message was when Jesus and His disciples were walking through the Temple compound,*"...when his disciples came to point out to him the buildings of the temple."* Matthew 24:1. But Jesus said, *"You see all these, do you? Truly, I say to you, there will not be left here one stone upon another that will not be thrown down."* Then they asked Him, *"Tell us, when will these things be, and what will be the sign of your coming and of the end of the age?"*

They actually asked Jesus three questions in one; when will the Temple be destroyed, how will we know when you are coming back, and how will we know when the end has come? The Olivet Discourse answers all three, but not necessarily in the order or in the way that the disciples asked.

One of the things that Jesus teaches about these things is that the destruction of the Temple would happen in their lifetime, which it did, in 70 AD by the Romans. It has never been reconstructed. Another thing that Jesus taught was that false doctrine will abound in the last days before He returns. Jesus said there will be many powerful religious and political leaders promising the answer to man's problems with solutions that will only cause more problems, while the gospel continues to spread without slowing down, Matthew 24:4 – 14.

Jesus said that the gospel will spread in the midst of growing turmoil and tribulation, while false leaders will be growing and proclaiming that "all is well." It will be a day when sound doctrine will be the only truth strong enough to sustain the true worshiper and follower of Christ.

The majority of the teaching of Jesus on the subject of His return and the end of the age is on being ready for it, because they would not know when it was coming, *"But concerning that day and hour no one knows, not even the angels of heaven, nor the Son, but the Father only."* Matthew 24:36 – 25:46 is the longest teaching from Jesus on this question of His return. He said to be ready by being His faithful and wise servants. Jesus told three parables on being wise and faithful servants. In Matthew 24:45 – 51 He compared faithful servants with unfaithful servants. In Matthew 25:1 – 13 He compared wise virgins with foolish virgins in the wedding parable. And in Matthew 25:14 – 30 Jesus told of the faithful servants in the parable of the talents.

Jesus concludes the message with the well-known vision of His return as the Good Shepherd separating the sheep from the goats, the *"...blessed by my Father...and the cursed..."* Matthew 25:31 – 46. This vision is of the end of the age when veiled worship is unveiled as worship. The faithful were worshiping their King through ministry to the least, the last, and the lost, and didn't know it. The unfaithful were more discriminating in their ministries, wanting to be more selective than compassionate, and also not knowing that it was the King who was being culled and overlooked.

The message is clear: when you faithfully share what God has blessed you with, you become a blessing to everyone, especially to Christ your King, and ministry becomes worship that pleases the Father. This is what it means to worship Him in spirit and truth.

April 30

Read and pray Psalm 120, Proverbs 25:23 – 28, Acts 26, 1 John 1, Psalm 119:137 – 144.
2nd Deuteronomy 1.
3rd Daniel 6.
4th Esther 5 – 6.

Miracles Teach Truth

Mark's gospel is known as the gospel of action. Most believe that Mark wrote from Rome under the guidance of Simon Peter around 60 AD. Peter was one of those "ready-fire-aim" kind of people; always in motion with thinking a few steps behind. Many can identify with Peter.

Mark's gospel is also the one to use the word "immediately" more than the others. The Greek word is *you-thoos*, and is used to link one event to another in real time. Mark uses this word twelve times in chapter one alone. This is more than Luke uses it in his entire gospel.

Linking the events of the life of Jesus with this word teaches an important truth; no single event can be understood apart from the others, they all connect to present the whole life of Jesus. Every event is linked, from beginning to end, to reveal the new relationship, the new covenant, that God the Father invites you to in His Son, Jesus Christ. This is significant especially when you study the miracles of Jesus. They do not stand alone, but rather teach, like the parables, of the Kingdom of God now here in Christ, and offered to those who would believe in Him.

As you read an account of a miracle of Jesus you must ask the Lord what it points to that is greater and what truth it teaches about God's Kingdom. In Mark, the link word, *you-thoos*, will help you to learn the greater truth from the single event.

For example, in Mark 1:9 – 13, you will find the account of the baptism of Jesus, linked to the miracle of the heavens being ripped apart, the Spirit descending, and the Father speaking, which is then linked to the miracle of the Spirit driving Jesus out into the wilderness to be tempted by the devil for forty days, from which Jesus miraculously emerged victorious. These events are all connected with the word *you-thoos* in verses 10 and 12.

Together they teach an important truth; through Christ's sacrificial death and miraculous resurrection you receive His Spirit and His word, which empower you to overcome Satan's lies and live victoriously in this wilderness, just as Jesus did His whole life.

Jesus was baptized to demonstrate how He would save us. Being low-ered into the water and then raised up out of the water is a clear picture pointing forward to what would happen to Jesus on the cross. As Jesus went out to John to be baptized, He was embracing the Father's will for His life to give us new life in Himself.

"When he came up out of the water, immediately the heavens were torn apart…" 1:10. The word Mark uses for "torn apart" is the Greek word *skidzo*, and literally means to rip into two pieces. The English word "schism" comes from this Greek word. Mark will use this word again in 15:38 to describe what happened to the Temple curtain, which separated the Holy of Holies from the Holy Place, when Jesus died on the cross; it was *skidzo*, ripped apart into two pieces, from top to bottom. The bar-rier between God and man had been violently opened wide by the Father through the death of His Son.

The next event, linked to the ripping apart of the heavens, is the descent of the Spirit upon Jesus with the Father speaking from His word in Psalm 2:7 and Isaiah 42:1. With the barrier removed, now God's Spirit is with man and God's word is clearly understood, *"You are my beloved son; with you I am well pleased."* Mark 1:11. All that the Father has said in His word is understood in Jesus Christ and the well-pleasing rela-tionship of the Father with the Son. This is what it means to worship the Father in spirit and truth.

May 1

Read and pray Psalm 121, Proverbs 26:1 – 5, Acts 27, 1 John 2, Psalm 119:137 – 144.

2nd Deuteronomy 2.

3rd Daniel 7.

4th Esther 7 – 8.

The Miracle of Overcoming Temptation

The miraculous is sometimes only seen as something spectacular. It is often overlooked for that reason. Anytime God works, it's a miracle. And God works according to and by His word. The first chapter of the Bible reveals this truth. It is the first of the ways of God; His word works. First God says it, then, God does it, every time. God is faithful to His own word, always and forever.

After the baptism of Jesus and the miraculous sign of approval of the Father and the Holy Spirit, it says, *"The Spirit immediately drove him out into the wilderness. And he was in the wilderness forty days, being tempted by Satan."* Mark 1:12 – 13. The word "drove him out" is the Greek word *ek-ballow,* and has the meaning of forceful expulsion. It also has the meaning of being guided by a powerful force.

The Holy Spirit did not violate the will of Jesus in this event, but rather gave powerful guidance with clear direction. Some might use the expression, "he had no other choice except to go." The emphasis is upon the power of the word of God guiding every step of Christ Jesus.

The word "immediately," *you-thoos,* connects this event with the approving word that Jesus saw and heard from the Spirit and the Father in 1:10 – 11. This approving word gave powerful assurance to Jesus as He saw what He had to go through next. There was only one way, God's way, to be the Savior, and the wilderness experience was the only way.

Jesus used the word "must," *dey*, which has the same meaning. He said in Luke 2:49 to His parents when they found Him at the Temple as a boy, *"Did you not know that I must be in my Father's house?"* And again to Nicodemus in John 3:7, *"You must be born again."* And also in John 4:4, *"And he had to pass through Samaria."* (translated "had" there). And in Mark 8:31 following the great revelation of God and confession of Peter, *"And he began to teach them that the Son of Man must suffer many things and be rejected by the elders and the chief priests and the scribes and be killed, and after three days rise again."*

Each of these verses communicates the message of singleness, the one way of God for Jesus and for His followers. Some might view "one way" as narrow-minded and restrictive, but in reality it reveals the only way that pleases the Father, God's way, according to and by His word; the miraculous way.

Jesus emerged from the wilderness victorious over every lie and temptation of Satan because He followed God's word, God's way, which was miraculous. Jesus overcame every temptation according to and by God's guiding, assuring, approving word. This is the work of God, which is done exclusively by His word and pleases Him because He sees Himself in it.

Today, know that you have no other choice but to follow the leading of God's Spirit by God's word. This is the only way to worship the Father in spirit and truth, and it is a miracle when it happens, because God is the only one who can make it happen.

May 2

Read and pray Psalm 122, Proverbs 26:6 – 12, Acts 28, 1 John 3, Psalm 119:137 – 144.
2nd Deuteronomy 3.
3rd Daniel 8.
4th Esther 9 – 10.

What Miracles and Parables Have in Common

Miracles and parables are both instructive for followers of Christ because they both point to something greater and they both lead to repentance. Mark's gospel majors on the activities of Jesus, which were all linked together to reveal God's Messiah, Jesus Christ. The miracles of Jesus were one of the major activities of Jesus in Mark's gospel. For many the miracles were just "magic tricks." And some who heard the parables were just entertained by nice stories. But others saw and heard something more profound.

Herod was one of those who wanted to be entertained by Jesus, *"When Herod saw Jesus, he was very glad, for he had long desired to see him, because he had heard about him, and he was hoping to see some sign done by him."* Luke 23:8. Jesus did not come to entertain us, but to save us from becoming the kind of people that need to be entertained all the time with more and more glitz, smoke, and special effects.

There are churches today that have more special effects than sound doctrine. When the lights go out, special effects also go out, but sound doctrine will keep a light shining in the dark, driving back the darkness from the inside out. Church, keep the Light on in the lives of people by giving them sound doctrine from God's word, and less tricks.

In Matthew 11:20, an instructive statement is made about the purpose of the miraculous, *"Then he (Jesus) began to denounce the cities where most of his mighty works had been done, because they did not repent."* One of the things this verse teaches is that the purpose of a miracle is to lead a person to repentance, to change their mind about something. The cities of Chorazin, Bethsaida, and Capernaum had witnessed many of the miracles of Jesus, but they did not repent. John 12:37, says, *"Though he had done so many signs before them, they still did not believe in him."*

Having faith in Jesus means losing faith in something or someone else. This is the definition of repentance. The people in those cities and the people that John was talking about only saw the activities of Jesus, but never saw or heard Jesus. They only saw and heard what they wanted rather than what they needed. To see and to hear what you need from God's perspective, rather than what you want from your perspective is the definition of humility.

When Jesus healed the leper in Mark 1:40 – 45, He gave him strict instructions of what he needed to do next, *"See that you say nothing to anyone, but go, show yourself to the priest and offer for your cleansing what Moses commanded for a proof to them."* The instructions Jesus gave the healed leper were the biggest part of the miracle, which the healed leper missed, because rather than obey Jesus, he went out and spread the news openly.

Why wouldn't Jesus want everyone to know what He had just done for the man? The answer is because the main experience of the miracle was the worship experience following the miracle, according to God's word, which would include a priest. The leper was still healed, but Jesus wanted to reach a priest with the miracle. It never happened.

When you hear of some miracle, do you say, "Wow!" or do you repent, knowing that miracles are God's gift of repentance for you. When His mighty power is demonstrated it means that He is present, and that He desires to do something even greater with the emphasis upon Him, not me. When that happens, a changed life is the result, not entertainment.

May 3

Read and pray Psalm 123, Proverbs 26:13 – 17, John 1:1 – 28, 1 John 4, Psalm 119:137 – 144.
2nd Deuteronomy 4.
3rd Daniel 9.
4th Job 1 – 2.

The Miracle of Not Needing a Miracle

Mark records a day of teaching in the life of Jesus in chapter four. On that day, Jesus taught about the seed and the soils, the grain of mustard seed that grows to a huge plant where birds find shelter, of the small piece of leaven that influences the whole loaf of bread, and of the partnership of the farmer with God as he plants the seed, which becomes a blade, then a stalk, then bears fruit, as the farmer watches in wonder. Jesus told these parables as He taught the disciples and the crowds of the nature of God's Kingdom on earth.

At the end of the chapter it says, *"On that day, when evening had come, he said to them, 'Let us go across to the other side.' And leaving the crowd, they took him with them, just as he was..."* Mark 4:35 – 36. It goes on the say that when they got out into the lake, a great wind-storm rose and the waves were filling the boat, while Jesus slept on a cushion. How could Jesus sleep when the boat and the disciples were in such danger?

One reason is because Jesus was very tired. This is one of those places where you see the full humanity of Jesus. He had been teaching and healing all day, and He was bone-tired. Another reason is because He was resting in the word and direction the Father had given Him to go to the other side of the lake. Jesus was not worried or afraid of the circumstances around Him for He trusted in the Father's word for the direction and timing for His life.

The disciples, on the other hand, were terrified of the storm and for their lives because the storm was speaking louder and with more power than the word that Jesus spoke, when He said, *"Let us go across to the other side."* Jesus was sound asleep with confidence in the Father's word, while they were wide-awake with fear from the voice of the storm. Later in the gospel it will be the other way around; Jesus will be wide-awake in prayer in the Garden of Gethsemane, while the disciples will all be sound asleep, totally oblivious to what was happening and about to take place.

The disciples woke Jesus up with a question that we too have asked, *"...do you not care that we are perishing?"* How does a person answer a question like that? You can't. The question is flawed by fearful unbelief, and we have all been there and done that. John 3:16 reveals God's love in His Son for us so that we will not perish, and yet from time to time we get into similar situations that begin to dictate doubt, causing us to lose faith in the goodness and provision of God through Jesus Christ.

Jesus rose from His sleep and first rebuked the wind and sea, then the disciples for their unbelief. First He spoke to the wind and sea saying, *"Peace! Be still!"* And then He taught them with two pointed questions, *"Why are you so afraid? Have you still no faith?"* Mark 4:40.

As the lake got still and flat, and the only sound they heard was the water dripping from the sail into the water in the boat, the unnecessary miracle began to take hold of them. They had been with Jesus the whole day and had not received a single word He taught. It had fallen on the hard path of their hearts and the wind and the waves had stolen it away. And yet Jesus still spoke to the storm of the sea, as well as to the wind and waves of their unbelief in order to help them believe and to trust Him, that what God says, He does, every time.

Today, reflect upon the miracle of not needing a miracle; the miracle of hearing God's word and watching Him do it, in you, with you, through you, as you, before the Father and the watching world around you. God loves seeing His word at work in you. It pleases Him. This is what it means to worship the Father in spirit and truth.

May 4

Read and pray Psalm 124, Proverbs 26:18 – 23, John 1:29 – 51, 1 John 5, Psalm 119:137 – 144.
2nd Deuteronomy 5.
3rd Daniel 10.
4th Job 3 – 4.

The Only Destructive Miracle of Jesus

The miracles of Jesus are sometimes viewed as transformational miracles, like when He turned the water into wine (John 2:1 – 12); restorative miracles, like when He restored the health of the woman with the issue of blood (Mark 5:25 – 34); multiplication miracles, like when He multiplied the five loaves and two fish and fed 5,000 (Matthew 14:13 – 21, Mark 6:32 – 44, Luke 9:10 – 17, John 6:1 – 13); and the one destructive miracle, when Jesus cursed the fig tree and killed it because it had leaves but no fruit (Mark 11:12 – 26).

This destructive miracle is seen in the context of Jesus cleansing the Temple, the only violent activity of Jesus. Together, they taught a powerful truth about the necessity of faith.

Jesus rode into Jerusalem on a donkey a few days before Passover with shouts of *"Hosanna! Blessed is he who comes in the name of the Lord!"* This is from Psalm 118, the psalm Israel sang during the feast of Tabernacles, in late September or early October, when they came to believe that the Messiah would come into Jerusalem to conquer and rule the earth. This psalm was central for their understanding of the coming Messiah, as was the feast of Tabernacles. But Jesus came into Jerusalem as King and Messiah at Passover, not Tabernacles. He came early! Hold that thought.

As Jesus came riding into Jerusalem, amid palm branches (Tabernacle materials) and praises, He entered the Temple, looked around, and left. Some may have thought this to be somewhat anticlimactic. The following day, however, as Jesus was on His way back into Jerusalem, it says, *"And seeing in the distance a fig tree in leaf, he went to see if he could find anything on it. When he came to it, he found nothing but leaves, for it was not the season for figs. And he said to it, 'May no one ever eat fruit from you again.' And his disciples heard it."* Mark 11:13 – 14.

Then, as He entered the Temple, came the only violent activity of Jesus, when He drove out the merchants and overturned the tables of the moneychangers. And it says that He was teaching them, saying, *"Is it not written, 'My house shall be called a house of prayer for all the nations'? But you have made it a den of robbers."* 11:17. This did not go over very well with the religious leaders, but the crowds were amazed at His teaching.

The next paragraph explains the two events and how they are connected. *"As they passed by in the morning, they saw the fig tree withered away to its roots. And Peter remembered and said to him, 'Rabbi, look! The fig tree you cursed has withered.' And Jesus answered them, 'Have faith in God.'"* 11:20 – 22. Jesus went on to teach them about speaking to mountains and watching them be thrown into the sea, and asking in prayer with faith and receiving, and forgiving one another, and being forgiven by the Father.

This powerful teaching on faith reveals the heart of the Father in His word concerning the removal of the mountain of sin in our lives, through the word of faith, and seeing God cast it into the sea. It teaches the central element of prayer, which is faith, first hearing what God says, then asking Him for what He wants to give. It teaches God's way of forgiveness, by forgiving for His glory.

These events also teach the arresting truth of what happens in a life without faith in God; it withers and dies, violently and quickly. The Father sent His Son, Jesus, so that you might have faith in Him. And it pleases Him when He finds faith in you, because He can see Himself in your faith. God is faithful and He is looking for faith in our lives. Without faith there will be a sudden and violent end, without an end.

And remember, Jesus may come back early, at a time you are not expecting Him. Be ready by having faith in Christ, today. This is what it means to worship the Father in spirit and truth.

May 5

Read and pray Psalm 125, Proverbs 26:24 – 28, John 2, 2 John, Psalm 119:137 – 144.
2ⁿᵈ Deuteronomy 6.
3ʳᵈ Daniel 11.
4ᵗʰ Job 5 – 6.

Do You Question Faith, or Do You Have Faith With Questions?

Doctor Luke is the only Gentile writer of the New Testament. He wrote the gospel of Luke and the book of Acts. His insights as a Gentile, historian, and physician are unique. Many of the well-known events, parables, and miracles of Jesus are exclusive to Luke.

Luke gives us the details of the birth of John the baptizer and of Jesus. John's parents, Zechariah and Elizabeth, were both descendants of Aaron, the first high priest. According to Luke 1:7, they were both advanced in years and Elizabeth was barren. When it came Zechariah's turn to take the incense, fresh bread, and oil into the Holy Place in the Temple, the angel Gabriel appeared to him there with the announcement that his prayers had been answered and that he and Elizabeth would have a son, Luke 1:8 – 17.

More than that, their son would be the forerunner for the coming Messiah of God, prophesied by Malachi. The news must have overcome Zechariah. He responded to Gabriel by saying, *"How can I know this? For I am an old man, and my wife is well advanced in years."* There was something about his question that was not good. Gabriel rebuked him and disciplined him for what he said by telling him that he would be mute until the word would be fulfilled.

Zechariah came out of the Temple unable to share with anyone what had happened and was mute until Elizabeth gave birth to John, Luke 1:57 – 79. When John was circumcised and named, Zechariah's tongue was loosed, he was filled with the Holy Spirit, and praised God with a powerful hymn celebrating the work of God and coming Messiah. He and Elizabeth must have sung this song often over their son while he was growing up.

Gabriel also visited Mary, according to Luke 1:26 – 38. The news Gabriel told Mary was that she would give birth to the Messiah and name Him Jesus. He would be the long-awaited Savior and promised Son of David. Mary's response was very similar to Zechariah's and yet very different. Mary said, *"How can this be, since I am a virgin?"* This was similar to Zechariah's response in that Mary also asked the question based on her age and condition. Zechariah had also asked how, based upon his and Elizabeth's age and condition.

And yet, Gabriel answered Mary without a rebuke by saying, *"The Holy Spirit will come upon you, and the power of the Highest will over-shadow you; therefore the child to be born will be called holy; the Son of the God..."* Luke 1:35. Mary could not have understood the answer she was given, but she responded by saying, *"Behold the maidservant of the Lord! Let it be to me according to your word"* 1:38. She may not have fully understood, but she did declare what she did know; she was a servant of God and trusted whatever He wanted to do in her life.

When she and Elizabeth later met, Elizabeth clarifies in Luke 1:45 the difference between Mary and Zechariah. Elizabeth said, *"Blessed is she who believed, for there will be a fulfillment of those things which were told her from the Lord."* Mary had faith with her question, while Zechariah just had questions.

Everyone has questions, but not everyone has faith. Having questions is the only way to learn. It is not wrong to question, as long as you have faith. With faith, you are given understanding for the answers, but without faith those questions will keep growing and you will never be able to understand the answer.

Zechariah had to learn this lesson the hard way. Mary learned the right way, the way of trusting, the way of faith. And faith pleases God, even when you have a lot of questions. Having faith with your questions is what it means to worship the Father in spirit and truth.

May 6

Read and pray Psalm 126, Proverbs 27:1 – 4, John 3, 3 John, Psalm 119:137 – 144.
2nd Deuteronomy 7.
3rd Daniel 12.
4th Job 7 – 8.

Full-bloom Repentance

One of the miracles in Luke's gospel, the miraculous catch of fish in Luke 5:1 – 11 and the calling of Simon Peter, teaches an important lesson on repentance. There were three different occasions that Jesus invited Peter to follow Him. The first is recorded in John 1:40 – 42, when Andrew went and found Simon, his brother, and brought him to Christ. The second time is recorded in Matthew 4:18 – 22, and Mark 1:16 – 20, when Jesus found them repairing their nets and told them that He would make them fishers of men. And then the third time in Luke 5.

Some may wonder if this is one event told in three different versions, which could cause some doubt as to which is the more accurate account. But in reality, the calling of Peter to change his plans and direction in life was gradual and over time. We want the events of the Bible to fit neatly into a chronological and systematic order, which would make it much easier to study. But life does not work out that way and it is not the way that God works in your life either. Like Peter, we all have the tendency to go back and forth. And like Peter, Jesus keeps coming after us. He will not leave us alone. We can be thankful for that.

The third calling of Peter in Luke 5 is seen in the context of the miraculous catch of fish for a particular purpose and teaching. Jesus was teaching on the shore but the crowd was pressing in, hungry to hear God's word. He saw two empty boats because, *"...the fishermen had gone out of them and were washing their nets."* Luke 5:2. Jesus got in Simon's and asked him to put out a little from the land so He could keep teaching.

Then Jesus said to Simon, *"Put out into the deep and let down your nets for a catch."* 5:4. Simon's response reveals a full-bloom repentance. He said, *"Master, we have toiled all night and took nothing! But at your word I will let down the nets."* Luke 5:5.

Repentance begins as a response to God's word and His desire for your life. Repentance begins to take shape as you confess your inability to do what God desires for your life, and confidence in God's word for

His desire for your life. After God speaks His desire, and you respond with a lack of faith in your own ability, and faith in His, according to His word, God goes to work, according to His word, and repentance takes another step toward being in full-bloom.

The next few verses describe the work of God in Simon's life. Their nets were let down and drawn in, filled with fish, according to God's word, so much that both boats were almost sinking with the blessing. What happened next is instructive, *"But when Simon Peter saw it, he fell down at Jesus' knees saying, 'Depart from me, for I am a sinful man, O Lord."* Repentance is expressed in light of this miracle as Simon realizes that he is in the presence of God, because only God can do what Simon just saw.

Jesus' response develops the beauty of repentance even more when He said, *"Do not be afraid; from now on you will be catching men."* Luke 5:10. The Lord Jesus would depart from the shore, but not without Simon. He invited Simon to go with Him, again, in a new direction and activity for his life, which Simon obeyed, bringing forth the fruit of repentance.

Now repentance is seen for the beautiful thing that it is; the full-bloom and fruit of a complete change of direction, following Jesus, according to His word. Until full-bloom repentance develops, the fruit of repentance cannot develop, and the miracle is incomplete, for it is only God that can bring about a new direction and activity for your life, and He will not do that without you. And He only does His work according to His word, in you, with you, and through you, for His own glory and pleasure.

Full bloom repentance, which leads to the fruit of repentance, looks good, smells good, and tastes good to God, and this is what it means to worship the Father in spirit and truth.

May 7

Read and pray Psalm 127, Proverbs 27:5 – 9, John 4:1 – 42, Jude, Psalm 119:145 – 152.
2nd Deuteronomy 8.
3rd Hosea 1 – 3.
4th Job 9 – 10.

The Sacrificial and Generous Samaritan

The Good Samaritan is one of the most familiar parables of Jesus, and it is only found in Luke's gospel, (Luke 10:25 – 37). This story reveals the attributes of the Son that the Father is searching for in us. Jesus told this story in a hostile environment. The Good Samaritan story was told to a lawyer who stood up to test Jesus with the question, *"Teacher, what shall I do to inherit eternal life?"* Luke 10:25. It was a test because there were different rabbinic traditions on the answer to that question.

Jesus turned the question to the lawyer, and asked, *"What is written in the Law? How do you read it?"* Jesus could teach from any point in the Law and Prophets concerning Himself because He fulfilled every word of the Law and Prophets. The lawyer answered with the classic summary of the Law and Prophets from Deuteronomy 6:5 and Leviticus 19:18, *"You shall love the LORD your God with all your heart and with all your soul and with all your strength and with all your mind, and your neighbor as yourself."* Jesus confirmed that this was correct.

But the lawyer had an ulterior motive. Now the real trap was in play. Jesus already had the reputation for loving the unlovable and reaching out to those who were outside the covenant of Israel. The lawyer knew that Jesus would be going against His reputation if He excluded in His answer those He had been ministering to. But he also knew that within the classic answer, the definition of "neighbor" meant those whom you were most like and liked the most, and so he asked, *"And who is my neighbor?"* The answer Jesus gave caught him off guard.

We are familiar with the story line. A traveler going down from Jerusalem was robbed and beaten by terrorists; a priest came by but went around; a Levite came by but went around (Leviticus is named for this tribe of priests). The surprising element was the one who stopped and sacrificially gave of himself and his resources to help the man who had been robbed and left for dead; a Samaritan.

The Jews hated the Samaritans on every level. They were viewed as traitors and enemies. But this Samaritan had compassion, which fueled his sacrificial gifts of oil, wine, donkey, and accommodations for the wounded traveler, even though the wounded traveler was Jewish and would view him as an enemy. To understand the surprise element would be to tell this story in our country in 1944 with a German stopping to help a wounded American. Or during the cold war, a Russian bandaging the wounds and paying the hospital bill for an American who had been beaten up and left for dead.

Then came the question for the lawyer to answer in order to find the answer to his question (a common rabbinic teaching method); *"Which of these three, do you think, proved to be a neighbor to the man who fell among the robbers?"* 10:36. The lawyer answered, *"The one who showed him mercy."* And the lawyer had his answer.

Today, meditate on this familiar story to see how the actions of the Samaritan were an act of worship that pleases the Father. How does being compassionate and merciful express the character of God? Look for ways to express the compassion of Christ and the mercy of the Father to people that cross your path today, and know that this is what it means to worship the Father in spirit and truth.

May 8

Read and pray Psalm 128, Proverbs 27:10 – 14, John 4:43 – 54, Revelation 1, Psalm 119:145 – 152.
2nd Deuteronomy 9.
3rd Hosea 4 – 6.
4th Job 11 – 12.

The Lost Sons

One of the most familiar stories that Jesus told is called the parable of the prodigal son. It is found in Luke 15:11 – 32, and is one of three stories that Jesus told in that chapter. The first was about a lost sheep that the shepherd went out to find. The second was about a lost coin that a woman searched for until it was found. The third was about lost sons that the father loved and looked for.

All three were told in the setting of tax collectors and sinners drawing near to Him, while the Pharisees and scribes were grumbling and accusing Him of receiving sinners and eating with them! Imagine that. Jesus spoke to both groups with these three stories, revealing the heart of the Father in all three.

In all three stories there is something or someone who is missing, lost, not where they should be, as well as someone who is searching for them. This reaches back to Genesis 3:9 and the first question that God asked Adam, *"Where are you?"* This was after he and Eve had eaten of the fruit of the tree of the knowledge of good and evil. They had separated themselves from God and from each other as a result of their sin, and were hiding.

In each story, Jesus points out the fact that the shepherd, the woman, and the father made special efforts to restore the one that was missing. The shepherd goes out searching, the woman sweeps and cleans the house looking, and the father searches the horizon desiring the son to come home. He also leaves the party to go out to persuade the older son to come in and celebrate when his brother did return home.

The third story is the longest in the chapter and describes how both sons were lost and how one was restored. We are familiar with the younger son, the one who demanded his share of the inheritance and then wasted it in a distant land in unbridled living. The two words used to describe what happened to him in the far country are *diaskorpedzo*, and *asotzo*, *"...the younger son gathered all he had and took a journey into a far country, and there he diaskopedzo his property in asotzo living."* 15:13.

The first word, ***diasporpidzo,*** means to scatter to the wind without any purpose, to throw away. It is used in the Greek version of the Old Testament to describe how God will judge His enemies, scattering them into hiding. The second word, ***asotzo,*** is used to describe a life without any boundaries, undisciplined, unhealthy and sick. In the Greek world it described drunkenness and sexual immorality of the worst kind and the sicknesses that accompanied those vices.

But the younger son returned to the father and was surprised by the joy of the father having received back his son whom he thought had surely died. The older son did not share the joy of his father. The story concludes with the father leaving the celebration to go out the other lost son who was just as lost as the younger was in the distant land.

In the story, the older son was angry because in his mind he had been working like a slave without any reward, *"...Look, these many years I have served you, and I never disobeyed your command, yet you never gave me a young goat, that I might celebrate with my friends."* Luke 15 :29. His condition was just as sick, ***asodzo***, as the younger son, maybe worse, because he was so close to the father and yet at the same time, so far away.

Today, meditate on these three stories and see the heart of the Father and the joy He has when we can celebrate with Him, having received His joy over what has been restored to Him. This is what it means to worship the Father in spirit and truth.

May 9

Read and pray Psalm 129, Proverbs 27:15 – 21, John 5, Revelation 2, Psalm 119:145 – 152.
2nd Deuteronomy 10.
3rd Hosea 7 – 9.
4th Job 13 – 14.

Praying With More Confidence Than Sense

One emphasis in Luke's gospel is the teaching on prayer. Jesus taught His disciples prayer by His life of prayer, as well as with several parables on prayer. In Luke 11:1 – 13 it says that after He finished praying, one of His disciples asked Him to teach them to pray. This teaches the most important request when praying, *"Lord, teach us to pray…"* Luke 11:1.

Luke gives the shorter version of the model prayer with a declaration of truth, *"Father, hallowed be your name,"* four requests, *"Your kingdom come…give us each day our daily bread, and forgive us our sins…and lead us not into temptation,"* with a confessional vow, *"for we ourselves forgive everyone who is indebted to us…"* Luke 11:2 – 3.

With that simple outline, Jesus taught the spiritual basis of a father/child relationship with God in prayer. He taught to ask for what God desires in prayer. He taught a total dependence upon God for every physical appetite with prayer. Jesus taught to pray for a complete focus and dependence upon God's word in order to get through every temptation and so to never arrive at its destination. He taught to make promises in prayer, to desire to become more and more forgiving, like Jesus.

Then Jesus taught on the nature of prayer with a story about the importance of hospitality, Luke 11:5 – 13. The basis of the story was something of extreme importance in Bible culture, hospitality, which is something that has lost its meaning in our day. We think of hospitality in the context of entertaining guests, but in the Bible days it had to do with strangers and a person's reputation and worth.

Being hospitable was one of the highest expressions of being honorable and recognizing the value of another person. Likewise, to withhold the basis necessities of food and shelter from a person in need was considered the greatest insult, viewing another as an object rather than as a person. Hospitality communicated that a person had value and worth as a person.

With that understanding, Jesus told the story of a man who had a late-night unexpected guest and no food to put before him. It is hard for us to imagine not having any food in the house until you realize in that day people did not have the food storage conveniences that we have today. So he went to a friend, at midnight, asking for bread for his guest. The funny twist to the story is seen when his friend, with many young children, will not get up to help at first, but then sees that if he doesn't, the children will all wake up, so he gives in and gets up because of his friend's persistence to be hospitable for his late-night guest.

The word "persistence" in Greek is, *en-i-day-ah,* and is only used in this one verse, Luke 11:8. It has the interesting meaning of describing someone who lacks any sensitivity to what is proper. In other Greek writings it is used to describe someone who was extremely bold and shameless, someone with so much confidence, they lacked sense.

The meaning within the teaching on prayer is clear: God wants you to pray with the confidence of a child with his father, a child that has more confidence than sense. Jesus wants you to learn to understand prayer in the light of what it means to be hospitable; one Person giving to another to communicate the high value of that person in His eyes. And when you pray with *en-i-day-ah*, you communicate to God that you believe He loves you and that you have more confidence in Him than you have sense, and that He will do the honorable thing, every time, and all the time. This kind of confidence in God pleases Him. This is what it means to worship the Father in spirit and truth.

May 10

Read and pray Psalm 130, Proverbs 27:22 – 27, John 6:1 – 21, Revelation 3, Psalm 119:145 – 152.
2nd Deuteronomy 11.
3rd Hosea 10 – 12.
4th Job 15 – 16.

What To Do When Wrong is Called Right

There are several parables that are unique to Luke's gospel. Three of them teach on prayer; the parable of the persistent host, Luke 11:1 – 13, the parable of the unrighteous judge, Luke 18:1 – 8, and the parable of the praying Pharisee and tax collector, Luke 18:9 – 14. Each one gives instruction and encouragement to pray in spirit and truth.

The parable of the persistent widow tells a story we are all too familiar with; injustice. Jesus told about a widow who was pleading with an unrighteous judge for justice against an accuser in a court of law. She cried, *"Give me justice against my adversary."* Luke 18:3. The word "adversary" is the Greek word *antidikos*, which describes an accuser in a court of law. It is used in 1 Peter 5:8 to describe Satan, our adversary.

In the story, Jesus described the judge as someone *"...who neither feared God nor respected man."* This poor widow was being sued by someone who brought false accusations against her, before a crooked judge. The third strike against her was that the judge ruled in favor of her accuser. He called wrong right. This is an example of something that is happening more and more in our world; wrong is being ruled as right by judges, which is neither right nor just.

But in the story, Jesus said that the widow kept hammering the judge. She demanded justice from an unjust judge and would not let up. The judge said, *"Though I neither fear God nor respect man, yet because this widow keeps bothering me, I will give her justice, so that she will not beat me down by her continual coming."* Luke 18:4 – 5. The phrases "bothering me...beat me down...continual coming," all have the meaning of a fight, a wrestling match, of hard work, and intense exertion of energy. The widow would not give up on how wrong it was to call wrong right. She fought back with all she had, right words. And won.

Then Jesus said, *"Hear what the unjust judge said. And will not God give justice to his elect, who cry to him day and night? Will he delay long over them? I tell you, he will give justice to them speedily."* Luke 18:6 – 8. The parable is not about God's hesitancy with our prayers, it is about our activity in prayer and in the face of injustice. We are to pray, pray, pray, and resist unrighteousness and injustice with righteousness and justice. It is right to pray. It is right to call wrong, wrong. Jesus said that right will wear out wrong and that prayer is always right and is a mighty weapon against unrighteousness and injustice.

The word "speedily" is the Greek word *taxos*, and means a very short period of time, quickly, in a hurry. The encouragement from that word gives strength and confidence that wrong is short-lived and that right will prevail and is eternal. Learn to pray believing that right will always be right and will outlast the wrong.

Today, cry out to God, the Righteous Judge, concerning the things in the world that are wrong but are called right; things like abortion, religious persecution, greed, oppression, injustice, pornography, sexual immorality, and sex slavery. Work diligently against these evils and never underestimate the power and influence of prayer to undermine them and bring them crashing down, one day, soon.

May 11

Read and pray Psalm 131, Proverbs 28:1 – 4, John 6:22 – 71, Revelation 4, Psalm 119:145 – 152.
2nd Deuteronomy 12.
3rd Hosea 13 – 14.
4th Job 17 – 18.

A Very Present Danger in Time of Need

Jesus gave a stern warning in the context of teaching on prayer in Luke 18:9 – 14 with the story of the Pharisee and the tax collector. The teaching comes as an introduction to the story, *"He also told this parable to some who trusted in themselves that they were righteous, and treated others with contempt."* Luke 18:9. The Greek verb for "*…trusted in themselves…*" is *pietho,* which means to depend upon and have complete confidence in something.

The danger in learning to pray and worship in spirit and truth is that you could begin to trust in your knowledge and practice rather than in God. When you begin to trust in what you have learned and do, pride sets in and begins to express itself by condemning others who do not have what you have studied hard to have and do not do what you do. Beware.

In the story that Jesus told, a Pharisee stands and prays, *"God, I thank you that I am not like other men, extortioners, unjust, adulterers, or even like this tax collector. I fast twice a week; I give tithes of all that I get."* Luke 18:11 – 12. The problem with his prayer is seen in the little word "I." His prayer was full of himself. He condemned others by comparing them with himself, then, bragged on himself by highlighting his own religious activities compared to their sinful behavior. Beware.

Jesus continued the story by then describing the tax collector as he simply prayed, *"…God, be merciful to me, a sinner."* Luke 18:13. This prayer is used today in certain orthodox Christian churches as a model prayer. Jesus said that this man went home justified rather than the other because of his humility. His request appealed to the goodness of God rather than his own. In that regard, it was full of God and His attributes rather than his own. Humility is not putting yourself down, it is not thinking about yourself at all, because Someone greater has your full attention.

As you begin to learn to pray, you must beware of the flesh, which loves attention and credit for doing good. Some of the worst flesh is good flesh, educated flesh, religious flesh, that would soon be praying, "Lord, I thank you that I am not like this Pharisee…" Beware.

Today, pray in the light of who God is, according to His word. Rather than feeling good that you have prayed, you will begin to feel good about Him when you pray. *"Give thanks to the LORD; for He is good; His mercy endures forever!"* Psalm 136:1.

May 12

Read and pray Psalm 132, Proverbs 28:5 – 10, John 7:1 – 31, Revelation 5, Psalm 119:145 – 152.
2nd Deuteronomy 13.
3rd Joel 1 – 3.
4th Job 19 – 20.

A Fig Tree Experience

John's gospel is different than Matthew, Mark, and Luke. It was written around 90 AD, which made it the last gospel account written. The other three accounts had been copied and circulated for about 30 years when John wrote his account. Matthew, Mark, and Luke are a more chronological account of the life and ministry of Jesus. John took a different approach.

There are two words in the Greek language for time, one is *chronos*, which we get our English word "chronology" from. It means ordered time. The other word for time in Greek is *kiaros,* which describes a particular kind or quality of time. John presents the *kiaros* of the life of Jesus. He does this by recording seven personal conversations that Jesus had with various individuals, seven signs or miracles with seven I AM statements that point to the kind of Messiah Jesus came to be, and then seven sermons or teachings. In each of these three sets of seven, John reveals the Life of Jesus as the "one-of-a-kind" life; the divine Life of God Himself, in the flesh; the God-Man, Jesus Christ.

The first personal conversation John records Jesus having is with Nathanael in John 1:45 – 51. Nathanael's friend, Philip, had met Jesus and then went and found his friend and said, *"We have found him of whom Moses in the Law and also in the prophets wrote, Jesus of Nazareth, the son of Joseph."* And Nathanael said to him, *"Can anything good come out of Nazareth?"* Philip's response is a classic invitation, *"Come and see."*

Nathanael's view of Nazareth was typical of the day. Nazareth was on the border with Samaria and was suspect for that reason. Nazareth was also on the main highway, called the Way of the Sea, going through Israel from the east down to Egypt. It was on the edge of what is called the Valley of Jezreel, also known as the plain of Megiddo. All of the major caravans traveled this route, which made Nazareth a stopover for Gentile traders. Some might call it a "blue-collar town." It was a long way from the religious center of Jerusalem in more ways than one.

Although Nathanael was from Cana, which was north of Nazareth, he still considered it with contempt, like most Jews of his day.

As Philip and Nathanael came toward Jesus, He said, *"Behold, a true Israelite in whom there is no guile!"* The word "guile" is the Greek word, *dolos*, from a root word, which meant decoy. It came to be associated with someone who was deceptive and false. Nathanael was surprised by this kind greeting and asked how Jesus could possibly know him. The answer Jesus gave caused Nathanael to exclaim the first and most accurate confession of the true identity of Jesus when he said, *"Rabbi, you are the Son of God! You are the King of Israel!"* John 1:49. What did Jesus say that caused Nathanael to be the first to recognize His deity as the Son of God, the King of Israel?

Jesus had simply said, *"Before Philip called you, when you were under the fig tree, I saw you."* Before Philip called Nathanael, he must have been alone with God in a very close and intimate moment, praying for the promised King of Israel, seeking the Lord with all his heart, and receiving the indescribable peace and assurance that God was with him and that his prayer had been heard. The experience must have been similar to the one Jacob had with God in Genesis 28:10 – 22, and may have been what Nathanael was meditating on under the fig tree that day. Jesus did refer to it after Nathanael's confession by identifying Himself as the Mediator between heaven and earth, John 1:51.

This first personal encounter with Jesus sets the stage for the rest of John's gospel and the meaning of the gospel of grace; God is now with you and is for you, and desires for you to know Him in a personal, intimate, and interactive relationship. God has revealed Himself and His will through His Son, Jesus Christ. As you *come and see* Him, He reveals Himself to you, for you to know and love, and gives you a fig tree experience. As you declare to Him what He reveals to you, it pleases the Father. He loves to share Himself with you in fig tree experiences. This is what it means to worship the Father in spirit and truth.

May 13

Read and pray Psalm 133, Proverbs 28:11 – 14, John 7:32 – 52, Revelation 6, Psalm 119:145 – 152.
2nd Deuteronomy 14.
3rd Amos 1 – 2.
4th Job 21 – 22.

Born From Above

One of the most well known conversations Jesus had with an individual is found in the third chapter of John. In this chapter, a Pharisee named Nicodemus came to Jesus at night to learn more about Him. He did not ask any questions at first, he simply began the conversation with Jesus by recognizing Him as a teacher from God and with the miracle-working power of God, *"Rabbi, we know that you are a teacher come from God, for no one can do the signs that you do unless God is with him."* John 3:2.

Jesus answered Nicodemus by getting right to the point of what they needed to talk about. He said, *"Amen, amen, I say to you, unless a person is born from above he cannot see the kingdom of God."* The Greek word, *amen,* comes from the Hebrew word, *amen,* and means, "it is true, it is so." In John's gospel it is sometimes translated as "verily, verily" or "truly, truly."

You say "amen" after you have heard something that you would identify as the truth. Jesus would say it before He would say something (notice as you read John the places that Jesus used this word). Some have wondered why. Jesus said that He only spoke what He heard the Father say. Jesus would hear the Father say something, thus responding with *amen, amen,* then, would speak what He just heard.

The word "above," sometimes translated "again," is the Greek word *anothen*, and is called an adverb of place. It is used in Matthew 27:51 to describe how, upon the death of Jesus, the curtain in the Temple was torn from top (used there) to bottom, identifying the place it was torn from.

Nicodemus had trouble with this and Jesus continued leading him to see that the birth He was speaking of was from above by the Holy Spirit. The first birth was a natural birth, by water, but the second birth would be from above by the Holy Spirit, a spiritual birth. Then Jesus told him as straight as it gets, *"…You must be born from above."* John 3:7. The word "must" is the Greek word, *dey,* and communicates the element of necessity, of no other choice.

For example, Jesus used this word when His parents found Him in the Temple as a twelve-year-old boy when He said, *"Did you not know that I must be in my Father's house?"* Also in Matthew 16:21 as Jesus began to tell His disciples *"...that he must go to Jerusalem and suffer many things..."* And again in John 3:14 in His conversation with Nicodemus, *"As Moses lifted up the serpent in the wilderness, so must the Son of Man be lifted up..."* And again in John 3:30 when John the Baptist said, *"He must increase, but I must decrease."*

It was during this personal conversation with Nicodemus that Jesus said the words that are learned by every believer, *"For God so loved the world, that he gave his only Son, that whoever believes in him should not perish but have eternal life."* John 3:16. The Greek phrase "believes in" is, *pestuo ice,* and literally means to "believe into." It is not an agreement of fact, but rather a direction, a destination, a location, which means that when you believe in Jesus, you follow after Him, you rest in Him, you are found with Him.

Nicodemus learned that night with Jesus that there was only one way into God's Kingdom; to be born from above by the Holy Spirit by the sacrifice of Jesus Christ and through faith in Him. There is no other choice but this one. It is an invitation from God and an individual choice that each person must make. The invitation is also a promise from God of life with Him; eternal life.

When you respond to His invitation by receiving His promise, you are born from above and have faith in Christ. God the Father offers His Son to you because of His eternal love for you, in order to live His Life through you, as you, before Him, and the watching world around you. The Holy Spirit makes it happen, and the Son is glorified by this, which brings the Father great pleasure. And this is what it means to worship the Father in spirit and truth.

May 14

Read and pray Psalm 134, Proverbs 28:15 – 22, John 8:1 – 30, Revelation 7, Psalm 119:153 – 160.
2nd Deuteronomy 15.
3rd Amos 3 – 4.
4th Job 23 – 24.

Living Water

The third personal conversation John records Jesus having is found in the fourth chapter of John. It was with the Samaritan woman by Jacob's well. At noon, by the well, Jesus was waiting for this woman to arrive. Noon is not the time for drawing water. But for this woman it was, so that she could avoid the insults from the other women who would draw water early and late in the day. This woman had been married five times and was living with the sixth man. Sychar was a small town. Some would probably call this woman a home-breaker; an adulterer for sure. No one had personal conversations with her.

But Jesus was waiting for her and asked her for a drink. The woman was surprised that Jesus spoke to her, first because men did not speak directly to women in public, but most of all because He was a Jew, and she was a Samaritan. These two did not associate with each other, although they shared a common heritage with Jacob. They were related, but had no relationship with each other. But Jesus continued His conversation, which focused upon the thirst in her life she had no personal relationships.

Jesus said to this woman, *"If you knew the gift of God, and who it is that is saying to you, 'Give me a drink,' you would have asked him, and he would have given you living water."* John 4:10. Like Nicodemus, she was not getting it. Jesus continued, *"Everyone who drinks of this water will be thirsty again, but whoever drinks of the water that I will give him will never thirst again. The water that I will give him will become in him a spring of water welling up to eternal life."*

At this point in the conversation, the woman asked for this *living water* and Jesus told her to call her husband. She said that she did not have a husband, which Jesus affirmed. He then said that she had been married five times and was not married to the sixth. She quickly changed the subject to something less personal, which was at the heart of her thirst, personal relationships. She had been viewed and treated as an object for so long, she had come to believe it about herself. But Jesus was changing the picture by His personal conversation with her.

This conversation is the occasion for the theme of this book, learning to worship the Father in spirit and truth. This is the most personal, the most intimate, the most important relationship of all, knowing God and His great love for each person He has created through a personal relationship with Jesus Christ. As Jesus revealed to her the desire of the Father to find true worshipers, she discovered that He had found her and she ran into town to share the good news of her personal relationship with Christ. What she was looking for, thirsting for, found her. The seventh Man in her life, the One she had been waiting for, was waiting for her that day by the well.

Conversation and relationship are inseparable. Without conversation there is no relationship. God desires for you to hear the conversation He wants to have with you, each day in His word. Like the woman, if you only knew the gift of God and the One who speaks to you from God's word, you would ask Him for that gift. Learning to worship the Father in spirit and truth is to ask for that gift and to stay with Christ as He moves you closer and closer to it.

Today, ask Him for the gift of knowing Him more and more from His word. Desire to learn of Him more than about Him. In doing so, you will find that you have been found, and will never thirst again. The One you have been waiting for is waiting for you, today.

May 15

Read and pray Psalm 135, Proverbs 28:23 – 28, John 8:31 – 59, Revelation 8, Psalm 119:153 – 160.
2nd Deuteronomy 16.
3rd Amos 5 – 6.
4th Job 25 – 26.

A Cemetery Conversation

The shortest of the seven personal conversations of Jesus in John's gospel was with Martha, at the tomb of her brother, Lazarus, found in John 11. Jesus loved Lazarus and his two sisters, Mary and Martha. He and His disciples had visited their home in Bethany many times. The eleventh chapter begins by saying that Lazarus was ill and that Mary and Martha had sent word to Jesus to come and help them. But Jesus waited two days. The delays of God are mysterious to us, but you can know that God knows what He is doing, and His timing, like everything about Him, is perfect.

Four days after Lazarus died. Jesus made it to Bethany on the fourth day, which seemed to Mary and Martha to be too late. Funerals lasted for at least eight days or longer in the Bible lands. Many of the mourners were actually hired by the family to participate in the funeral and honor the deceased by going back and forth from the tomb to the home with loud wailing and mournful cries. Jesus had not yet arrived in Bethany when Martha heard that He was near, and she went out to meet Him, John 11:17 – 27.

Martha began the conversation with Jesus by saying, *"Lord, if you had been here, my brother would not have died. But even now I know that whatever you ask from God, God will give you."* Martha's faith is all too familiar to us, a conditional faith, conditioned upon her understanding. The condition in this scene was based upon Jesus and His ability to heal, if only He had gotten there in time. But He didn't, and so now all she could hope for was to ask for prayer. The expression, *"But even now,"* is a desperate plea for help from God, now that their brother was gone. Martha was the practical sister, and no doubt, had already seen the difficulty that lay ahead for herself and Mary. They needed prayer and would need God's help in the days to come.

Jesus said to Martha, *"Your brother will rise again."* And again, Martha's faith rested upon her understanding and what she had learned at the synagogue concerning the resurrection of the dead on judgment day. She recited from her catechism, *"I know that he will rise again in the resurrection on the last day."*

What Jesus said next was one of the most powerful statements from His lips when He said, *"I AM the resurrection and the life. Whoever believes in me, though he die, yet shall he live, and everyone who lives and believes in me shall never die. Do you believe this?"* This went way beyond Martha's understanding. Jesus was redirecting her faith from her understanding onto Himself. She took His lead and said, *"Yes, Lord; I believe that you are the Christ, the Son of God, who is coming into the world."* She did not know what was about to happen, and it didn't matter. Her faith was in Christ, and whatever was about to happen, would be right because it would be God's will done by God's Son.

When they got to the tomb, Jesus said, *"Take away the stone."* Martha objected, being the practical one, once again relying on personal knowledge and experience rather than on what Jesus wanted to do. His next statement is sometimes overlooked, but once again, is one of the most powerful and instructive statements to refocus faith in Him. He said, *"Did I not tell you that if you believed you would see the glory of God?"* The Lord Jesus wants you to keep your faith on Him so that you will see the glory of God. This is the outcome of faith. This is the destination. This is the reward. There is nothing greater and anything less would be to miss the whole purpose of Christ's coming.

You know what happened next. Jesus called Lazarus' name and he was raised from the dead, and came out of the tomb still wrapped in grave clothes. Jesus told the mourners to unbind him and to let him go. And the mourners became evangelists as they ran into Jerusalem with the good news.

Today, ask the Lord to show you where your faith has shifted from Him to your understanding about Him. Keep your spiritual eyes and your ears riveted on Jesus by keeping your physical eyes and ears in God's word in order to know Him more and more. This is what it means to worship the Father in spirit and truth.

May 16

Read and pray Psalm 136, Proverbs 29:1 – 4, John 9, Revelation 9, Psalm 119:153 – 160.
2nd Deuteronomy 17.
3rd Amos 7 – 9.
4th Job 27 – 28.

A Conversation With the King

The fifth personal conversation that John records of Jesus is found in chapter eighteen and nineteen; Jesus and Pilate, John 18:28 – 19:22. This is one of the most dramatic scenes in all of human history, preserved for us by the Holy Spirit. It is epic.

The chief priest and the religious leaders turned Jesus over to Pilate for Rome to carry out their plans to kill Him. Pilate knew that it was out of envy that they wanted to get rid of Jesus (Mark 15:10), because He was popular with the crowds and they were not. The relationship between Pilate and the chief priest was tenuous. The chief priest was the religious leader of the nation, while Pilate was the political leader, representing Caesar. Both the chief priest and Pilate barely tolerated each other.

As Jesus stood bound before Pilate, the conversation began with a question from the governor, *"Are you the King of the Jews?"* The religious leaders knew that Pilate would not execute Jesus on the grounds of their charge of blasphemy, so they veiled their fears with the charge that Jesus was trying to become the leader of the people, rather than them, by His popularity. So Pilate jumped to the bottom line, not knowing that he was having a conversation with the King.

Jesus answered Pilate with a question, a teaching technique that Pilate was raised on, *"Do you say this of your own accord, or did others say it to you about me?* Jesus also jumped to the bottom line of insecurity in Pilate, the fear of not being in line with popular opinion, with rocking the boat, the fear of declaring a personal confession with conviction. Rather than face it, Pilate tried to avoid it by putting the focus back on Jesus with more questions, *"Am I a Jew?"* Along with this, a statement and question in an attempt to find insecurity in Jesus, *"Your own nation and chief priests have delivered you over to me. What have you done?"*

Jesus informed Pilate that His Kingdom was not of this world. Pilate responded with a question, *"So you are a king?"* Jesus took his question and turned it into a confession, *"You say that I am a king..."* and then described His purpose, to bear witness to the truth. And for those who desire to know the truth, the truth will be heard and received. Pilate responded with a question that still rings with emptiness for those who refuse to know the truth, *"What is truth?"* As you read the rest of the conversation, you discover that Pilate can only ask questions because he refused to know the Truth, Who was standing before him.

This scene is all too familiar as Pilate represents multitudes, who have asked questions but refused the answer; the truth from God. When you are not getting an answer to your questions, consider that you may be asking the wrong questions. When God reveals the truth, but you are asking the wrong question, He appears to be silent. God is never silent, but He is often ignored and not heard.

Today, allow God's word to shape your questions and listen to the Truth from God's word. Hear Him and your questions will become confessions of the Truth. This pleases the Father, which is what it means to worship Him in spirit and truth.

May 17

Read and pray Psalm 137, Proverbs 29:5 – 10, John 10, Revelation 10, Psalm 119:153 – 160.
2nd Deuteronomy 18.
3rd Obadiah.
4th Job 29 – 30.

A Breakfast Conversation on the Beach

After the resurrection, John records an event that took place on the Sea of Galilee, John 21:1 – 25. Peter told the disciples that he was going fishing, and a group of the disciples went with him. They fished all night and caught nothing. Early that morning, they heard a familiar voice from the shore, *"Children, have you caught anything?"* The word "children" is the Greek word *piedion*. This was a term of endearment that parents called their own children. This was not how you would refer to a boatful of men who had been fishing all night, and had caught nothing. Jesus had other nicknames for His disciples, like *little-faiths,* and *sons of thunder, rocky,* and *twin.* The personal and intimate humor of the Scripture is sometimes overlooked. Calling this tired and unsuccessful group of rough fishermen, *piedion*, was one of those times.

The next thing Jesus said revealed His identity to one of them, *"Cast the net on the right side of the boat, and you will find some."* When they did, it was full of fish. This had happened before (Luke 5:1 – 11), and was the occasion for an experience for Peter with the Lord that changed the direction of his life. Jesus was reminding Peter of that earlier decision with this second miraculous catch of fish. John simply says, *"It's the Lord!"* With that, Peter jumped in the water and swam to shore. When he arrived, he found Jesus sitting by a fire with grilled fish and warm bread waiting for him. Jesus said, *"Come and have breakfast."* As they ate, the conversation began.

"Simon, son of John, do you love me more than these?" Jesus did not use the name He had given Peter, but rather his old name he had before he met Jesus. It was as if Jesus was starting over with Peter. Have you ever wondered what Jesus was referring to when He said *these*? Was He pointing to the fish? Or to the boats? Or to the beautiful hills and Sea of Galilee? Maybe all the above.

Peter answered, *"Yes, Lord; you know that I love you."* The word that Jesus used for "love" was the Greek word *agape*, which is the highest expression of love in the Greek language. It was reserved for describing divine love, a perfect love. Peter answered with a different word for "love," the Greek word *phileo*, which is the highest expression of human love, family love. Peter had learned the hard way that he had some spiritual growing ahead of him and that he was just not there yet. He was humbled by this breakfast conversation.

With each exchange, Jesus gave Peter his new direction and calling, *"Feed my lambs...tend my sheep...feed my sheep...."* The growth of lambs to sheep required feeding, tending, and more feeding. The spiritual growth of a follower of Christ also requires feeding upon the milk of God's word, the nurture of a fellowship of believers, with a continual hunger and feeding upon the meat of God's word. It was a new beginning for Peter. His past failures and denial of Christ were past and forgiven. The Lord was pointing Peter forward with a new vision for his life in God's Kingdom. Jesus ended the conversation with *"Follow me."* As you follow Christ, He will lead you away from the past and into the future, with Him.

Today, meditate, not upon the past, but upon the next step God has before you. Everything about God's Kingdom is forward-looking by following Christ. Through blessings, failures, victories, tragedies, disappointments, and miracles, follow Jesus Christ. He has promised to keep you and see you through it all, with Him. God is for you. Love Him more than *these.*

May 18

Read and pray Psalm 138, Proverbs 29:11 – 14, John 11:1 – 44, Revelation 11, Psalm 119:153 – 160.
2nd Deuteronomy 19.
3rd Jonah 1 – 4.
4th Job 31 – 32.

A Conversation With the Father

The seventh personal conversation that John records of Jesus is found in John 17; the Lord's prayer. This is the longest prayer recorded in the New Testament and was prayed by Jesus on the eve of the greatest challenge He faced, His suffering and death for the sins of the world. It reveals what a life of prayer looks like. It teaches how to pray. It is the Mount Everest of the mountain range of prayer that runs through the whole Bible.

The main theme of this prayer is the theme of the life of Jesus; the glory of God. The first request gives meaning to the whole prayer, *"... glorify your Son that the Son may glorify you..."* This is a prayer request with purpose, with a particular outcome, the glory of the Father. Much of our praying is to get a little help or for the relief from difficulty or pain, with the purpose of our comfort and ease. For Jesus, the glory of the Father was greater than anything else in His life. Jesus came to reveal the glory of the Father. As you read and study this prayer, notice the number of times Jesus refers to God's glory. It is the foundation of His prayer. Everything He says and asks for rests upon His desire for God's glory to be known.

Another thing you will notice is that for the length of this prayer, there are only a few requests. So many have learned to pray by listening to others pray who have not been taught to pray from the Bible. They shoot a barrage of requests at God as if He were an answering machine or some kind of eternal search engine. But the prayer of Jesus, like the prayers of the Bible, do not major on requests, but rather on relationship. This prayer is truly a conversation between the Father and His Son, which is what the Bible teaches prayer is to be. In a conversation, there are statements of revelation, of feelings, of joy, and of questions. Prayer is a conversation with the Father.

Jesus conveys the will of the Father in His prayer, *"I have manifested your name to the people whom you gave me out of the world. Yours they were, and you gave them to me, and they have kept your word. Now they know that everything that you have given me is from you."* John 17:6 – 7. There are no requests in that statement. It is simply a statement of the Father's promise and will. Pray the promises and the will of the Father as revealed in His word.

One of the requests of this prayer is for unity; unity in relationship with the Father in His word, and unity in relationship for the followers of Jesus with Him and with each other. This is not something you hear much in prayers today, but it saturated Jesus' prayer. *"Sanctify them in the truth; your word is truth. As you sent me into the world, so I have sent them into the world. And I sanctify myself, that they also may be sanctified in truth."* The word "sanctified" is the Greek word *hagiadzo*, which means to make holy, like God. It is understood exclusively in light of the Old Testament and the Hebrew word, *quedosh*, which describes God and those who are in right relationship with Him. This is a major request of Jesus in His prayer. Is it a major request of yours? It can be if you will learn to pray with Jesus.

Jesus ends His prayer with a vow, a promise. We are slow to make promises to God based upon our track record of breaking them. But when you make a promise to God based upon His promise revealed to you, relying on His presence in you, and the power of His word for you, it is always proper and highly recommended. A relationship with promises requires faith and faithfulness grows it. God has given you very powerful promises, and so can you, if they are based upon His. *"I made known to them your name, and I will continue to make it known, that the love with which you have loved me may be in them, and I in them."*

Today, allow the prayer of Jesus to shape yours. Ask for God's Son to be glorified in your life, so that the Father's glory may be known. Ask for unity with the Father in His word, and unity within the fellowship of believers in Christ. Surround these requests with the promises that God has made and the truth from His word. Promise the Father that you will... because this is His will. And remember, *"He who calls you is faithful; he will surely do it."* 1 Thessalonians 5:24.

May 19

Read and pray Psalm 139, Proverbs 29:15 – 21, John 11:45 – 57, Revelation 12, Psalm 119:153 – 160.
2ⁿᵈ Deuteronomy 20.
3ʳᵈ Micah 1 – 3.
4ᵗʰ Job 33 – 34.

The Value of a Vow

One of the events that took place two days before Jesus was betrayed was the anointing at Bethany at the house of Simon the leper, Matthew 26:6 – 13. Jesus had told His disciples again that, *"...the Son of Man will be delivered up to be crucified."* And just as before, the disciples were not willing to receive this word from Jesus. We do not know anything about Simon the leper except that he invited Jesus to his home on the eve of Passover. This would be the last meal, according to the Scripture, before the Passover meal that Jesus had with His disciples in the upper room. It was also the occasion for a powerful teaching from the Lord on worship.

During the meal, it says that a woman came up behind Jesus *"... with an alabaster flask of very expensive ointment, and she poured it on his head as he reclined at table."* The container, an alabaster flask, was as valuable as the contents. This item referred to a special gift kept and handed down by relatives as a wedding gift. The content was myrrh, which was used as an embalming ointment. It was given at the wedding as both a symbol of the couple's lifelong commitment to each other, and as the substance that would one day be used for the burial of the spouse. This was an extravagant gesture, and costly to say the least.

Some will say that the woman did not know the full meaning of what she was doing until Jesus gave meaning to it by saying, *"In pouring this ointment on my body, she has done it to prepare me for burial."* Matthew 26:12. But others will say that, unlike the disciples, she did believe what Jesus had been saying about His crucifixion, death, and resurrection, and was expressing her belief with this extravagant act. Either way, Jesus commended her for it, but the disciples were indignant over it.

The word "indignant" is the Greek word, *aganoktais*, which has the meaning of a strong opposition and displeasure against someone or something judged to be wrong. The disciples viewed what she did, and possibly her, as wrong. They wondered why she wasted the expensive item. The word "wasted" is the Greek word, *apolia,* and has the meaning

280

of something being destroyed without purpose. Their reasoning was that it could have been sold and the money given to the poor, which they judged as the right thing to do.

But Jesus corrected them by saying, *"...she has done a beautiful thing to me."* The word "beautiful" is the Greek word *kalos*, which means to be intrinsically good and appealing, which would be the exact opposite of *aganoktais.* He also said that they would always have the opportunity to help the poor, but had missed the opportunity that this woman took. She was expressing the extreme value of the relationship she had with Jesus and in what He was about to do. She may not have understood it fully, but who does. She just knew that He was good and so whatever He was about to do would also be good. She also knew that she had something of extreme value to give to Jesus that communicated His value in her life. The question is, have you?

The psalmist cried out, *"What shall I render to the LORD for all his benefits to me?"* Then he (or she) answers the question, *"I will lift up the cup of salvation and call on the name of the LORD, I will pay my vows to the LORD in the presence of all his people."* Psalm 116:12 – 14. Jesus understood what this woman did as an act of worship, just as Psalm 116 describes.

Today, meditate on what it means to make the promise of *lifting up the cup of salvation and calling on the name of the Lord,* and how valuable a vow is to God. As you do, make this vow to the Lord, and call upon Him to do it, in you, with you, through you, as you, before the Father and the watching world around you. This is a beautiful thing to God. It pleases Him. This is what it means to worship the Father in spirit and truth.

May 20

Read and pray Psalm 140, Proverbs 29:22 – 27, John 12:1 – 19, Revelation 13, Psalm 119:153 – 160.
2nd Deuteronomy 21.
3rd Micah 4 – 5.
4th Job 35 – 36.

Learning to Pray From What You Have Learned

Seeing and hearing Jesus praying in the garden of Gethsemane is one of the most revealing aspects into the humanity of Christ in Scripture. It is found in Matthew 26:36 – 46, Mark 14:32 – 42, and Luke 22:39 – 46. In Mark's account you hear Jesus give instructions to His disciples to, *"Sit here while I pray."* You wonder how many times the disciples had heard the Lord say this to them. At least once when Jesus returned from such a time is the occasion when one of His disciples said, *"Lord, teach us to pray..."* Luke 11:1.

In Gethsemane, Jesus took with Him Peter, James, and John, *"...and began to be greatly distressed and troubled."* The word "greatly distressed" is the Greek word, *ekthambos*, and literally means to be afraid at the sight of something extremely unusual, to be hit with something. It is closely associated with sight. The second word, "troubled," is the Greek word *adaymoneh*, which means to be weighted down with a great heaviness. There are three words for "depression" in Greek, and this one is used to describe the deepest and greatest depression. Jesus could see more clearly than ever, the awful sight of the Cross, and it weighed extremely heavy over Him.

He prayed, *"Abba, Father, all things are possible for you. Remove this cup from me. Yet not what I will, but what you will."* Mark 14:36. Prayer is worship. It is going before God with humble gratitude that He has invited you into His presence. It is calling upon the Lord, who is greatly to be praised. The first words from Jesus in His prayer, with this terrible vision of the Cross pressing in on Him, were words of praise, *"Abba, Father, all things are possible for you."*

Praise is the result of having learned something of God. There is a difference between learning something about God and learning something of God. When you learn something of God, He Himself has revealed it to you and given you wisdom to receive it. This comes before praise and is never separated from it. Calling God, *Abba, Father,* was something God had revealed to His Son. Declaring, *all things are possible for you*, was something Jesus had learned from His Father. The true study of God's word always leads to, and forms praise to God for who He is, what He has done, and promised to do. Learning of Him and by Him, prepares you for the dark time of awful trial and heaviness that comes upon every follower of Christ. It came upon Jesus, and He prayed.

And Jesus asked the Father to change this terrible situation. We can all identify with that request. But what must be learned is the rest of His request, *"Yet not what I will, but what you will."* Jesus is again expressing praise with this agonizing prayer by declaring to God that the Father's desire is greater than the request for changing the situation. The will of God is both the plan and desire of God. It is what pleases the Father. Learning to express your desires, all of your desires, to the Father, and then to submit them to His will because you have learned from Him, of Him, is what it means to worship the Father in spirit and truth.

Today, with each of your prayer requests, know that you can trust the Father's desire for that person or situation, and ask Him for His will to be done. In doing so you will be praising God because you have learned from Him, of His excellent greatness, which is greater than any difficulty or situation you will ever encounter. Jesus did and it pleased the Father.

May 21

Read and pray Psalm 141, Proverbs 30:1 – 4, John 12:20 – 50, Revelation 14, Psalm 119:161 - 168.

2nd Deuteronomy 22.

3rd Micah 6 – 7.

4th Job 37 – 38.

Blinded By the Truth

The high priest and religious leaders hired Judas to betray our Lord. As Jesus and His disciples were in the Garden of Gethsemane, the officers of the Temple came and arrested Jesus, bound Him, and took Him to the high priest's house for questioning. All four gospel accounts give the details of this late-night trial on the eve of the crucifixion and death of Christ. The religious leaders sought testimony against Jesus but could not find agreement on the slanderous charges. They finally found agreement on a statement that Jesus made when He said, *"Destroy this Temple, and I will raise it up in three days."* John 2:19. John said that Jesus was referring to His body, not the Temple that Herod had built. But this was not what they were looking for. They needed a charge deserving the death sentence.

Jesus was silent before His accusers until Caiaphas, the high priest, said, *"Are you the Christ, the Son of the Blessed?"* Mark 14:61. When Jesus heard this question it must have reminded Him of when He asked His disciples this question, *"Who do men say that the Son of Man is?"* They replied, *"Some say John the Baptist, others say Elijah, and others Jeremiah or one of the prophets."* And Jesus said, *"But who do you say that I am?"* This was when Peter exclaimed, *"You are the Christ, the Son of the living God!"* Jesus replied, *"Blessed are you...for flesh and blood has not revealed this to you, but my Father who is in heaven."* Matthew 16:13 – 20.

As Jesus stood before Caiaphas and heard His true identity spoken by the high priest, *The Christ, the Son of the Blessed*, it was as if He was hearing His Father calling His name! Jesus answered, *"I AM, and you will see the Son of Man seated at the right hand of Power, and coming with the clouds of heaven."* Mark 14:62.

In saying this, Jesus was revealing as much about Himself as He had to anyone up until that point. Caiaphas was fully aware of the Name, *I AM*; the Name that God had revealed to Moses in Exodus 3:14. He was also very familiar with the reference from Daniel 7:13 – 14 of the coming of God's King and Kingdom, *"...and behold, with the clouds of heaven there came one like a son of man, and he came to the Ancient of Days and was presented before him. And to him was given dominion and glory and a kingdom, that all peoples, nations, and languages should serve him; his dominion is an everlasting dominion, which shall not pass away, and his kingdom is one that shall not be destroyed."*

In that powerful moment, as Jesus was standing before the high priest and the religious leaders of Israel, He fully disclosed His true identity and eternal purpose. But rather than falling down before Him exclaiming, *Blessed is he who comes in the name of the LORD*, the high priest tore his robes and cried *Blasphemy!* They condemned Jesus to die for revealing the truth from God's Word of His true identity. In their blindness they began hitting Jesus in the face and spitting on Him. They were blinded by the Truth.

When your religious practices becomes more important than your personal relationship with God through faith in His Son, Jesus Christ, the same thing can happen to you. When your eyes are more focused on what you are doing for God rather than upon His word and learning more of God, you too can become blinded by the Truth. God's word is not a "how to" manual for better worship and living. It is the revelation of God, of Himself in Jesus Christ His Son.

Today, as you read and study the Bible, tell the Father of your desire to know Him more and more from His word, in His Son, and by His Spirit. As you do, you will be worshiping the Father in spirit and truth.

May 22

Read and pray Psalm 142, Proverbs 30:5 – 14, John 13, Revelation 15, Psalm 119:161 – 168.
2nd Deuteronomy 23.
3rd Nahum 1 – 3.
4th Job 39 – 42.

Seven Words of Worship From the Cross

For the next seven days you will see and hear what worship through suffering looks and sounds like. Jesus said that He only spoke what He heard the Father saying (John 8:25 – 28), and that He only did what He saw the Father doing (John 5:19). As Jesus hung on the cross, dying for the sins of the world, He spoke words from the Father, which pleased the Father. From these words, you can learn to worship under the most painful circumstances imaginable. Jesus did.

The first words of Jesus from the cross are found in Luke 23:34, *"Father, forgive them, for they know not what they do."* This request of Jesus reaches all the way back to Genesis 3, the occasion of the first sin from which all sin originated. Adam and Eve were created in the perfect image and likeness of God. They were placed in an ideal environment, the Garden of Eden. God gave them a simple command, *"You may surely eat of every tree of the garden, but of the tree of the knowledge of good and evil you shall not eat, for in the day that you eat of it you shall surely die."* Genesis 2:16 – 17.

And yet, when tempted to do what God had commanded them not to do, they believed the lie of the tempter rather than the truth of God's word. They ate of the fruit in order to know more, and became totally blind and deaf to the spiritual reality of what they had done. The lie promised that they would know more, but stole the intimate knowledge of God they had. The tendency to suppress the truth in order to believe the lie was passed down from one generation to the next from the seed of Adam until the Seed of woman said, *"Father, forgive them, for they know not what they do."* Jesus was asking the Father for the very thing the Father promised to give in Genesis 3:15, *"I will put enmity between you (the serpent) and the woman, between your seed and her Seed; he shall bruise your head, and you shall bruise your heel."*

In Psalm 2 there is a conversation between the Father, the Son, and the kings of the earth that teaches this important truth. It begins by describing the vain plot of declaring independence from God, *"The kings of the earth set themselves, and the rulers take counsel together, against the LORD and against his Anointed, saying, 'Let us burst their bonds apart and cast away their cords from us.'"* This plan causes God to laugh at the ignorance and futility of such a thing. Then He speaks to them in His fury, saying, *"As for me, I have set my King on Zion, my holy hill."* The Hebrew word "fury" is *charon*, used over forty times in the Old Testament, exclusively of God, describing His intense displeasure and anger. It is the opposite of pleasing God, of worshiping Him.

The next verse, Psalm 2:7, the Son speaks and quotes the Father's decree, saying, *"I will tell of the decree: The LORD said to me, 'You are my Son; today I have begotten you. Ask of me, and I will make the nations your heritage, and the ends of the earth your possession. You shall break them with the rod of iron and dash them in pieces like a potter's vessel.'"* The Son declares what He has heard the Father say and asks the Father for what He has promised to give. This pleases God the Father, to declare what He has said and to ask what He has promised. And this is what Jesus is doing on the cross, asking the Father for the forgiveness He had promised all through the Old Testament, beginning in Genesis 3:15.

When others persecute you, slander you, and curse you, pray the promises of God for your enemies. As you bless them with the promises of God, you become a blessing to God. This is what it means to worship the Father in spirit and truth, and in suffering.

May 23

Read and pray Psalm 143, Proverbs 30:15 – 20, John 14, Revelation 16, Psalm 119:161 – 168.
2nd Deuteronomy 24.
3rd Habakkuk 1 – 3.
4th Ecclesiastes 1 – 2.

Seeing a Suffering King

Two criminals were executed with Jesus, one on either side of Him. All four gospel writers mention them. Matthew and Mark use the term "robber" to describe their crime. It was a word for an armed robber, or pirate. Their names are not given, but you could call one an unbeliever, and the other a believer. It seems as though both knew something about Jesus because they both spoke about Him. The conversation between these two men and Jesus is found in Luke 23:39 – 43.

The unbeliever cried out to Jesus, *"Are you not the Christ? Save yourself and us!"* The word for "cried out" is the Greek word *blasphemeo*, from which we get our English word "blasphemy." It means abusive speech, cursing, reviling, insulting. The words themselves do not seem so bad, but the tone must have been. The believer rebuked him by saying, *"Do you not fear God, since you are under the same sentence of condemnation? And we indeed justly, for we are receiving the due reward of our deeds; but this man has done nothing wrong."* From this conversation, it seems as though these two may have been partners in crime and knew Jesus in some way. The believer certainly knew that they were receiving the wages of their life of violence and sin.

The next statement from the believer adds to the speculation that they may have known Jesus in a unique way. He said, *"Jesus, remember me when you come into your kingdom."* Of the 920 times the name "Jesus" is used in the New Testament, this is the only time a person calls the Lord by His given name only; *"Jesus."* Some think that this man knew Jesus as a boy, possibly growing up with Him in Nazareth, maybe along with the unbeliever as well. We do not know this from the Bible, but it does seem as though the believer knew Jesus in a familiar way. They may have grown up together, one going one way in life, and the other going God's way, and now both paths joined back together at Calvary. Maybe. One thing is for sure; the believer saw a suffering King beside him with eyes of faith, and made a simple request.

Jesus responded to his faith by saying, *"Truly, I say to you, today you will be with me in Paradise."* The word "truly" is the Greek word *amen*, which comes from the Hebrew word *amen*. Our English word *amen* is also from this Hebrew word, which means, "it is true." Everything that Jesus said was true, and yet at times, He would underline the truth with this expression, *amen.* In this case, Jesus is giving this man strong assurance of an answer to his prayer. The Lord is about to go back into the presence of the Father, but not alone. He is bringing one back with Him to present before the Father, a sinner, forgiven of all his sins.

Some have often said, "If you had been the only person who had ever sinned, Jesus would have come and lived His life, died, and been raised, just for you. He died for each one as if there were only one." This word from the cross proves that statement. What a statement. What a scene. And what a glorious moment it must have been when Jesus and this forgiven believer entered into the presence of the Father that day. As he was welcomed into Paradise that day, he must have said, *"AMEN!"*

May 24

Read and pray Psalm 144, Proverbs 30:21 -28, John 15, Revelation 17, Psalm 119:161 – 168.
2nd Deuteronomy 25.
3rd Zephaniah 1 – 3.
4th Ecclesiastes 3 – 4.

Worshiping the Father By Caring For Those Closest To You

The third statement from Jesus on the cross is directed to His mother and the beloved disciple, John. It is found in John 19:25 – 27. It is impossible to know the depth of suffering that Jesus endured on the cross. The physical suffering of intense pain was mild compared to the emotional, mental, and most of all, the spiritual pain of the sins of the whole world being placed upon Him. In 2 Corinthians 5:21, it states, *"For our sake he made him to be sin who knew no sin, so that in him we might become the righteousness of God."* Jesus not only took our sins upon Himself, He became sin in order that we might become righteous. We will forever probe the mystery and depth of God's love and desire for us to know Him and be with Him forever. And in that moment of indescribable pain, with all of humanity on His heart, Jesus made sure that His mother would be cared for. Amazing love.

The Bible only mentions five of Jesus' followers at the cross, His mother, her sister, the wife of Clopas, Mary Magdalene, and John. His other followers had abandoned Him and were hiding in fear. But His mother and the others mentioned above were there when they crucified the Lord.

John was fearless. He followed Jesus right into the house of the high priest for the late-night trial following the betrayal and arrest (John 18:15 – 24). John was an eyewitness to the things that were said and done during that mock trial. Mary, the mother of Jesus, had no fear of being associated with the Lord. She had witnessed the words and actions of Jesus more than anyone else, being with Him His whole life. Mary had stored up much in her heart to be amazed and to wonder over. It is to these two that Jesus spoke when He said, *"Woman, behold, your son!"* And to John, He said, *"Behold, your mother!"* John 19:26 – 27.

The word "behold" is from the Greek word *oida,* which means to pay close attention, to perceive, to see beneath the surface of something. It is also in the imperative tense of the verb, a command, hence the exclamation mark. In that moment, Jesus transferred the responsibility of caring for His mother to the one He knew would not back down or run from the assignment; John. And it was a big assignment. John was the youngest and he was fearless. At that moment, Jesus was also instructing His mother to the one she could lean on and depend upon to care for her, as a first-born son would do.

Jesus demonstrated in many ways the importance of first caring for those closest to you. He told His disciples to first go to the lost sheep of Israel before going to the Gentiles (Matthew 10:5 – 6). He said they would be His witnesses in Jerusalem, Judea, Samaria, and the ends of the earth (Acts 1:8). Jesus appeared to ignore the Canaanite woman who begged Him to heal her daughter saying to her, *"It is not right to take the children's bread and throw it to the dogs."* To which she said, *"Yes, Lord, yet even the dogs eat the crumbs that fall from their master's table."* With that, Jesus made an exception, and healed her daughter, commending her for her great faith (Matthew 15:21 – 28).

The point is clear: the light that shines the farthest shines the brightest at home. The love of God demonstrated by the suffering and sacrifice of Jesus Christ on the cross, providing forgiveness of sin and a new relationship with the Father for everyone who would believe, also provides for the daily needs of orphans and widows and the oppressed. No one is overlooked by God. Jesus revealed this truth from the cross with these words from John 19:26 – 27. This is God's will and it pleases Him when you see the needs of those closest to you as well as those on the other side of the world. This is what it means to worship the Father in spirit and truth.

May 25

Read and pray Psalm 145, Proverbs 30:29 – 33, John 16, Revelation 18, Psalm 119:161 – 168.
2nd Deuteronomy 26.
3rd Haggai 1 – 2.
4th Ecclesiastes 5 – 6.

Worshiping the Father in Darkness

Matthew and Mark describe the fourth words of Jesus from the cross. Both say that at the ninth hour Jesus cried out with a loud voice, *"Eli, Eli, lema sabachthani?"* which means, *"My God, my God, why have you forsaken me?"* Matthew 27:46, Mark 15:34. The people who were standing near the cross heard Jesus but misunderstood Him, and thought He was calling upon Elijah. People today still disagree over what Jesus meant with these words.

Some will say that Jesus was experiencing the full force and wages of sin; separation from God, something He had never known. Others point out that Jesus was quoting the first line of Psalm 22, which ends with triumphant faith in the promises of God and resurrection. They will say that Jesus was teaching from the cross, giving meaning to what was happening to Him in that moment. There is a clear description in Psalm 22 of the agony of crucifixion with the last ten verses of that psalm describing the victory of faithfulness and the triumph of God's Kingdom over sin and suffering. Both views acknowledge that Jesus was praying in the darkness with the overwhelming feeling of abandonment but with His faith firmly fixed upon the Father.

The Bible states that there was literal darkness for three hours when Jesus made this statement. But the scene was darker than just the absence of sunlight. It was a spiritual darkness that enveloped the land that day, representing the absence of God's presence in the lives of sinful man. Jesus was taking our place that day with the abandoned cry of hopelessness that every person has felt as a result of sin and separation from God. Jesus cried out for us in that moment with the word of God from Psalm 22 of triumphant faith.

You may not have cried out the same words as Jesus, but you have, no doubt, had moments of utter desperation and feelings of loneliness when you cried, *"Oh God, where are You?"* It may have been expressed with a cry, night after night, with your head on the pillow and with tears leaking out the sides of your eyes, when all you could pray was *"Oh*

God, Oh God, Oh my God..." And Jesus has been there and went there to lead you out of there, just like Psalm 22 describes.

It is hard to imagine that this could be called a worship experience, but it was and it is because in that moment of darkness and desperation, God the Father is being held onto with nothing but a single strand of faith. This may be one of the most brilliant moments of worship when there is nothing but faith in God, shining in all of its glory, the glory of God from the truth of His word. He has promised to be with you always. God will not abandon you. It may be your darkest hour, but He is there with you and will see you through it, just like He did for His own Son, the Lord Jesus Christ. Cry out to Him in prayer with faith, just like the psalmist did in Psalm 22, just like Jesus did from the cross.

Take time, sometime today, to reread Psalm 22, and remember when you lived there and how God brought you through it, and rejoice. If you are there now, know that you are not alone. God is with you and He loves you. You are worshiping the Father in spirit and truth in that moment.

May 26

Read and pray Psalm 146, Proverbs 31:1 – 3, John 17, Revelation 19, Psalm 119:161 – 168.
2nd Deuteronomy 27 – 28.
3rd Zechariah 1 – 3.
4th Ecclesiastes 7 – 8.

Through Weakness Power is Perfected

The fifth and sixth words of Jesus from the cross go together. They are found in John 19:28 – 30, *"After this, Jesus, knowing that all was now finished, said (to fulfill the Scriptures), 'I thirst.' A jar of sour wine stood there, so they put a sponge full of the sour wine on a hyssop branch and held it to his mouth. When Jesus had received the sour wine, he said, 'It is finished,' and he bowed his head and gave up his spirit."*

Both of these statements are closely related to the humanity of Jesus as the Son of Man. This was Jesus' favorite term for Himself; Son of Man. It revealed Jesus' identity with humanity as being fully human, just like you. He was also the Son of God, being fully divine, the fullness of the Godhead in the flesh. As God the Son, He came to inaugurate the new humanity in the new creation as the sole remnant from the old creation.

God the Father was looking at God the Son as He fashioned Adam from the dust of the ground to form him in His image and likeness in the same way that Moses was shown the pattern for the Tabernacle from the true Altar and Temple in heaven, which is also Christ Jesus.

As Son of Man, Jesus had all of the thoughts, feelings, choices, bodily functions, and desires as you have, yet without ever violating any of God's commands, and always fulfilling every word from God. He accomplished this in His life on earth in the same way that God the Father had established Adam and Eve to, by faith in His word. Adam and Eve failed in the garden. Jesus succeeded in the wilderness of the Promised Land.

As Jesus hung on the cross, He experienced the devastating effects of physical pain and misery, including dehydration. He had already lost an enormous amount of blood from the flogging, the beatings, and from crucifixion. His body, especially His throat, was parched. To fulfill the Scripture, He had one more message to preach and teach, but was unable to vocalize the message because of His weakened condition and the dryness in His throat. You see the humanity of Jesus in this moment like no other. He said, *"I thirst."*

Some who were standing there heard Him and put a sponge on a hyssop branch with sour wine and put it up to His mouth. With it, Jesus was able to preach His last message, *"It is finished."* It is one word in the Greek, *tetelistai.* This was a word to describe something that had been carried out to completion with nothing left undone. It is sometimes translated "perfected," for that reason. It is also in the perfect passive tense of the verb, which adds emphasis to the completed, or perfected, state. Being passive means that the action is done to the person rather than by the person. In this case, Jesus is pointing to the fact that the Father had fully completed His work in His life. Jesus gave all the credit and glory to the Father for the work of salvation that He had completed in His life, finalized and brought to a glorious completion on the cross.

During the day today, reflect upon this scene and the magnitude of the statement, *tetelistai,* and the powerful declaration of praise it was at that moment. Consider the weakness of Jesus and His need for the smallest bit of sour wine to express His worship of and to the Father. Think on this amazing way of God; in weakness He has perfected power through praise. This is what it means to worship the Father in spirit and truth.

May 27

Read and pray Psalm 147, Proverbs 31:4 – 9, John 18, Revelation 20:1 – 6, Psalm 119:169 – 176.
2nd Deuteronomy 29.
3rd Zechariah 4 – 6.
4th Ecclesiastes 9 – 10.

Now I Lay Me Down To Sleep

The final words of Jesus from the cross were a prayer from Psalm 31:5, *"Father, into your hands I commit my spirit."* Luke 23:46. This was a prayer that parents taught their children to pray at night before going to sleep. It was the equivalent to the prayer you may have learned as a child, "Now I lay me down to sleep. I pray the Lord my soul to keep..." The last words of Jesus were spoken to His Father, in a prayer, placing Himself before the Father and into the Father's keeping. This was an expression of complete faith and trust. It was an act of worship.

The word "commit" in this prayer is the Greek word *paratithemai*, which means to set something before another. It was used to describe food being placed before another for a meal (Mark 6:41). It was also used to describe teaching that was presented and entrusted to someone (2 Timothy 2:2). And it was used in the early church, during the days of persecution, on how to endure persecution and suffering (1 Peter 4:19). All of these uses of this word point to a willful act of sacrifice and worship, which pleases God.

With His last breath, Jesus presented Himself before the Father, just as He did every day of His life, just as His parents did every day at mealtime with food that would be presented to Him to eat. No parent would place anything questionable or harmful before a child to eat. For Jewish parents, mealtime was a teaching time, with instructions from God's word concerning what was clean and unclean to eat. It was a time for reminding the family of the goodness and holiness of God. It was a time of worship, enjoying God's blessings in His presence. This was the last conscious thought of Jesus as He prayed this prayer.

With His last breath, Jesus presented everything He had taught before the Father, trusting that it would not return to Him void. He had learned from Isaiah 55:10 – 11, *"For as the rain and the snow come down from heaven and do not return there but water the earth, making it bring forth and sprout, giving seed to the sower and bread to the eater, so shall my word be that goes out from my mouth; it shall not return to me empty, but it shall accomplish that which I purpose, and shall suc-ceed in the thing for which I sent it."* Jesus presented before the Father every word that had proceeded out of His mouth as an offering, an act of worship, to accomplish the purposes of the Father and for His glory.

With His last breath, Jesus presented all of His suffering and pain to the Father as an offering, a pleasing aroma to God. The bitterness of His betrayal, arrest, flogging, crucifixion, and agony were being presented to the Father. Jesus had taught His followers that they too would suffer in the world. The early church learned from 1 Peter 4:19, *"Therefore let those who suffer according to God's will entrust their souls to a faithful Creator while doing good."* Jesus knew that only God could bring about good from something as evil as the cross, which is why He presented His suffering and pain to the Father.

Today as food is presented before you to eat, present yourself before the Father with the prayer, *"Father, into your hands, I commit my spirit."* Today, as you speak before others, do so with the prayer, *"May the words of my mouth and the meditation of my heart, be acceptable in your sight, O LORD, my Rock and my Redeemer."* Psalm 19:10. If you are in a season of suffering, or have just come through one, or about to enter one, present yourself before a faithful Creator, with full confidence and *"...know that God works all things together for good for those who love Him, for those who are called according to His purpose."* Romans 8:28. And rejoice before His presence as you worship Him, for the Father is seeking those who will worship in spirit and truth.

May 28

Read and pray Psalm 148, Proverbs 31:10 – 17, John 19, Revelation 20:7 –
15, Psalm 119:169 – 176.
2nd Deuteronomy 30 – 31.
3rd Zechariah 7 – 9.
4th Ecclesiastes 11 – 12.

Sunday Morning Worship With the Gardener

Jesus died on the cross in your place and for all who trust in Him
for the forgiveness of sins; for a new relationship with the Father. His
body was taken down from the cross on that Friday, and quickly placed
in a borrowed tomb since the Sabbath was about to begin (sundown on
Friday). John recorded in his gospel that the tomb was in a garden near
the place where they crucified Jesus. Mary Magdalene went to the tomb
early on Sunday, the first day of the week, and found that the huge stone
had been taken away that had covered the entrance to the tomb. John
gives the account in 20:1 – 18.

Mary ran and told the disciples. Peter and John ran back with her to
the tomb to find that it was empty, but *"...they did not understand the
Scripture, that he must rise from the dead."* John 20:9. They went back,
but Mary stayed. As she went inside the empty tomb she saw two angels
sitting where they had laid Jesus. They asked her why she was weeping.
She replied that someone had taken away her Lord and she did not know
where His body had gone.

Suddenly, Jesus was behind her and said, *"Woman, why are you
weeping? Whom are you seeking?"* John 20:15. John began his gospel
with a similar question in 1:35 – 38. John the baptizer saw Jesus walking
by and said, *"Behold, the Lamb of God!"* Two of his disciples heard him
and started following Jesus. Jesus turned around and said, *"What are you
seeking?"* The word "seek" is the Greek word, *zeteo*, which means to
search for something that has been lost, to diligently inquire about something of great interest. It is a word used throughout the Bible to describe
the need that every person has to recover what sin has destroyed. This
question, *what are you seeking, whom are you seeking,* is one that each
person must face and answer at some point in their life. For Mary, it was
on a Sunday morning, in a garden, beside an empty tomb.

Mary still did not recognize Jesus. She thought that He was the
gardener. It may have been because she was weeping, or that she was
prevented from recognizing Him similar to the two disciples on the

road to Emmaus (Luke 24:13 – 35). Knowing Jesus is something that must be revealed before He can be known. But when Jesus called her name, *"Mary,"* she knew it was Jesus, and fell at His feet in adoration and worship.

Jesus said to her, *"Do not cling to me, for I have not yet ascended to the Father; but go to my brothers and say to them, 'I am ascending to my Father and your Father, to my God and your God.'"* The word "cling" is the Greek word *hoptoe*, which means to hold fast to something and to not let go. Mary must have had both arms wrapped tightly around the ankles of Jesus.

In essence, Jesus said, "Turn me loose so I can ascend to my Father and to your Father, to my God and to your God." In saying this Jesus was declaring the new covenant of a new relationship with God, His relationship, now made possible and available by His death and resurrection. His death paid the penalty for your sins so that you can have a new relationship with God. His life from the dead gives you His relationship with God; His Father to be your Father and God. Hallelujah!

Have you thought about what you are seeking in life? Have you found the One who satisfies every desire? Do you have the relationship that Jesus provided for you by His life, death, and resurrection? When you do, you, like Mary, will cling to Him and never let go. To find Jesus is to find the Father. To worship Him is to worship the Father, in spirit and truth.

May 29

Read and pray Psalm 149, Proverbs 31:18 – 26, John 20, Revelation 21, Psalm 119:169 – 176.
2nd Deuteronomy 32.
3rd Zechariah 10 – 14.
4th Song of Songs 1 – 4.

An Uplifting Worship Experience

After the resurrection, Jesus appeared to His followers many times over a forty-day period of time. At the end of those forty days, He met with His disciples on a mountain with final instructions before He ascended back to the Father. All four gospel writers describe His final words of encouragement and instruction before His ascension.

In Matthew 28:16 – 20 the disciples are described as a mixed group of believers and doubters; but they were all worshiping Him. This helps you to know that there will be times when you have doubts and even fears, but as long as you willfully choose to worship Christ, He will teach you through and out of your doubts. Jesus encouraged His followers that He had been given all authority in heaven and on earth, even though some doubted. He instructed His followers to make disciples of all people groups, immersing them in the triune presence of the Father, the Son, and the Holy Spirit, and to teach them everything that He had commanded. He assured them that He would never leave them.

In Mark 16:14 – 20 the disciples were told that they would be able to communicate the gospel in every language, that they would walk over and cross every obstacle, and that they would overcome every plot to destroy their lives. Jesus assured them that they would have the power to demonstrate the presence of the Kingdom of God with healing by the laying on their hands. The followers of Christ have been going and crossing over and communicating in more and more languages and healing ever since. And they have overcome every attempt to silence the message and to stop the spread of the gospel. The message is still going out today, with power.

In Luke 24:36 – 53 the witness of the Scripture is emphasized in the message of the gospel, as well as the fact that until the Holy Spirit illuminates the message, it cannot be understood. He also reviewed the essence of the gospel with the essential elements of the death, burial, and resurrection of Christ, from the Scriptures, and the forgiveness of sins from repentant faith made available for all and proclaimed to all people groups. Luke also recalled the instruction from Jesus for them to wait for the promise of the Holy Spirit, which would come from the Father.

John's account of the Great Commission is understood around the little word "sent." Jesus said, *"As the Father has sent me, even so I am sending you."* John 20:21. The Father sent Jesus to reveal His love for the whole world and to provide salvation for all who would believe. Jesus sent His followers to reveal the Father's love in the Son, living in them, and to proclaim the Father's salvation in Christ for all who would believe. It is one mission, from the Father, through the Son, for all who would believe.

Acts (written by Luke) gives the account of the question the disciples had for Jesus moments before He ascended, *"Lord, will you at this time restore the kingdom to Israel?"* Jesus answered them, *"It is not for you to know times or seasons that the Father has fixed by his own authority. But you will receive power when the Holy Spirit has come upon you, and you will be my witnesses in Jerusalem and in all Judea and Samaria, and to the end of the earth."* Acts 1:6 – 8. In saying this, Jesus was teaching them that the power (authority) they would have would be to share the gospel that would transform lives, not to answer theological questions about Israel.

In all of the accounts, at that very moment, Jesus was lifted up and taken into heaven to be seated at the right hand of the Father with all authority in heaven and on earth and under the earth. From His exalted and lifted up position, He carries out God's will on earth as it is in heaven, in and with and through and as His followers, by the Holy Spirit. As you trust Him more and more, He is lifted up more and more, for more and more to see and be drawn to with saving faith. As more and more turn to and trust Christ, the Father is more and more pleased, which is what it means to worship the Father in spirit and truth.

May 30

Read and pray Psalm 150, Proverbs 31:27 – 31, John 21, Revelation 22, Psalm 119:169 – 176.
2nd Deuteronomy 34.
3rd Malachi 1 – 4.
4th Song of Songs 5 – 8.

The Day of Worship To Look Forward To

Jesus told the woman of Sychar, beside Jacob's well, that the Father was looking for true worshipers, those who would worship Him in spirit and truth (John 4:4 – 42). And true worshipers are also looking for something, actually, Someone, who promised to return. The return of Jesus Christ is that event in the life of Jesus that has not yet happened, but will, and soon.

As Jesus was lifted up from the sight of the disciples in Acts 1:9 – 11, the followers of Christ kept staring up into the clouds. The Bible states that two angels said to them, *"Men of Galilee, why do you stand looking into heaven? This Jesus, who was taken up from you into heaven, will come in the same way as you saw him go into heaven."*

Jesus had also told them in John 14:1 – 4, *"Let not your hearts be troubled. Believe in God; believe also in me. In my Father's house are many rooms. If it were not so, would I have told you that I go to prepare a place for you? And if I go and prepare a place for you, I will come again and will take you to myself, that where I am you may be also. And you know the way to where I am going."* And Jesus prayed in John 17:24, *"Father, I desire that they also, whom you have given me, may be with me where I am, to see my glory that you have given me because you loved me before the foundation of the world."* You have the assurance of the return of Jesus for you from the very words of the Lord Himself, as well as from His angels. It is a day of worship to look forward to, and to pray for with great anticipation.

The Bible describes this future event in 1 Thessalonians 4:15 – 17, *"For this we declare to you by a word from the Lord, that we who are alive, who are left until the coming of the Lord, will not precede those who have fallen asleep. For the Lord himself will descend from heaven with a cry of command, with the voice of an archangel, and with the sound of the trumpet of God. And the dead in Christ will rise first. Then we who are alive, who are left, will be caught up together with them in the clouds to meet the Lord in the air, and so we will always be with the Lord."*

This will be the day of worship like no one has ever experienced or could ever imagine. It will be a day of worship that pleases the Father like no other day of worship ever has. It will be a day of worship for true worshipers, for those who worship the Father in spirit and truth. Pray for that day. Look forward to that day. Prepare for that day. As you do, you will be worshiping the Father in spirit and truth. AMEN.

May 31

Read and pray Psalm 1, Proverbs 1:1 – 7, Matthew 1, Romans 1:1 – 17, Genesis 1 – 2, Psalm 119:169 – 176.

You have prayed the Psalms and have finished reading the New Testament. Now it is time to do it again. By now you have developed the habit of beginning your day with the Father, in His word, focused upon His Son, your Savior, Jesus Christ. You are learning more and more of Him from His word and becoming a true worshiper in spirit and truth.

As you begin your second reading, add to it the reading from the Law (2nd reading, Genesis – Deuteronomy), numbering each reading just as you did for the gospels and the letters of the New Testament. Continue praying a section of Psalm 119 each week, and allow God's word to shape your prayer each day. Thank God each day for the revelation of Himself from His word. His desire is for you to know Him as you receive the revelation of Him from His word.

After you complete the second reading (five months from today), begin the reading from the Prophets (Isaiah – Malachi), numbering each reading as you did for the Law. After you complete the third reading, begin the reading from the Writings (Joshua – Job), numbering each reading as you did for the other readings. As you continue this practice, you will be submitting your time with God to being shaped by His word, allowing Him to speak to you of Himself.

Tomorrow, go back to the beginning of the book for the devotional, and now...

May the LORD, the Father, bless you and keep you;

May the LORD, the Son, make His face to shine upon you and be gracious to you;

May the LORD, the Holy Spirit, lift up His countenance upon you and give you peace.

In the Name which is above every name; the Name of the Son of the Living God, the Lord Jesus Christ; AMEN and Hallelujah!

Endnotes

1 Scripture quotations are from The Holy Bible, English Standard Version, copyright 2001 by Crossway Bibles, a publishing ministry of Good News Publishers.

2 New Testament Greek word studies in this book are from The Greek-English Lexicon of the New Testament; Based on Semantic Domains, Second Edition; Editors Johannes P. Louw and Eugene A. Nida, United Bible Societies, NY; 1988. And Theological Dictionary of New Testament by Gerhard Kittel and Gerhard Friedrch, Wm. B. Eermans Publishing Company, Grand Rapids, Michigan. 1964.

3 *The Baptist Hymnal,* (Nashville, Convention Press, 1991), 301.

4 Dallas Willard, *The Spirit of the Disciplines,* (Harper San Francisco, New York, NY, 1988) 153-154.

5 Oswald Chambers, *The Complete Works of Oswald Chambers,* (Discovery House Publishers, Grand Rapids, Michigan, 2000). 1162.

6 Miles J. Stanford, *The Complete Green Letters,* (Grand Rapids, Michigan, Zondervan Publishing House, 1975), 45.

7 Larry Eskridge, *God's Forever Family*, (New York, Oxford Press, 2013).

8 *Webster's Ninth New Collegiate Dictionary,* (Springfield, Massachusetts, Merriam-Webster Inc., Publishers, 1991).

9 Watchman Nee, *The Spiritual Man,* (New York, Christian Fellowship Publishers, Inc. 1968).

10 John Piper, *Desiring* God, (Sisters, Oregon, Multnomah Publishers, 1986).

11 Homer, *The Odyssey.*

12 Richard Blackaby, *Experiencing God,* (Nashville, B&H Publishing Group, 1990).

13 Dallas Willard, *The Divine Conspiracy,* (Harper San Francisco, New York, NY, 1998) 133 – 134.

CPSIA information can be obtained at www.ICGtesting.com
Printed in the USA
BVOW06s0321171115

427058BV00009B/71/P

9 781498 452960